Second Edition

the Classical COMPANION

W9-AZJ-056

by Charles F. Baker III and Rosalie F. Baker

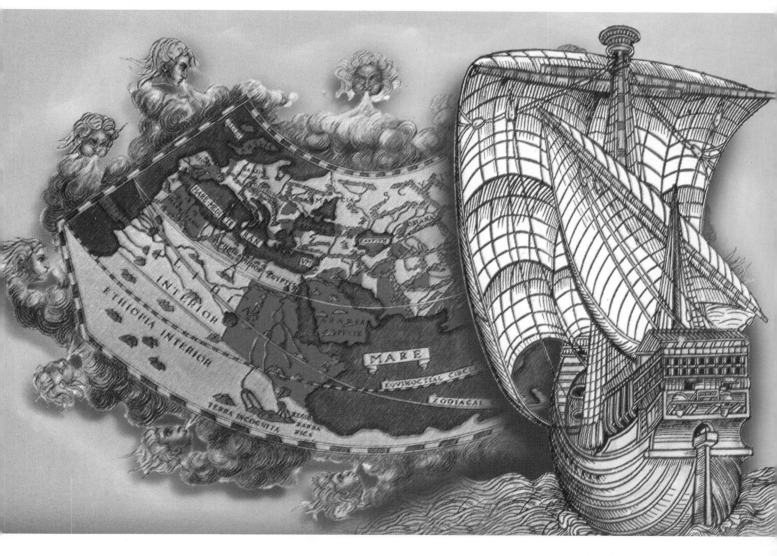

The Indispensable Guide to the Study of Classical Civilization

Complete with Stories, Puzzles, Projects, Classroom Activities, and Original Plays

Cobblestone Publishing Company

For our son, Chip

Those
who neglect
the past are
condemned to
repeat it.

George Santayana,
Madrid-born American philosopher
(A.D. 1863–1952)

Cover: This reproduction of Claudius Ptolemy's map shows the world as the ancient Greek geographer saw it in the A.D. 100s. It is taken from a 1472 edition of the first book to have printed maps.

Inset: The ship is Christopher Columbus' ship, the *Santa Maria*. The design was taken from a woodcut dating to 1493 that is supposed to be after a drawing by Columbus himself. Columbus was very familiar with Ptolemy's map, as its marking were still accepted as accurate. Cartographers (mapmakers), however, were beginning to modify Ptolemy's map as navigators like Columbus brought back more information about the world's waterways and land masses.

Design and Production: Bob Dukette/Sim's Press
Printing and Binding: Transcontinental Press

Printed in Canada.

Cobblestone Publishing Company
30 Grove Street, Suite C
Peterborough, NH 03458

Second Edition

Contents

Foreword

The *Classical Companion* is an invaluable guide to the study of classical Western civilization for upper-elementary and middle school students. Packed with engaging stories, primary sources, plays, classroom activities, projects, maps, and puzzles, the *Companion* helps students discover our ancient heritage. Students will enjoy exploring ancient ideas about government, war, philosophy, literature, heroism, leadership, and aspects of everyday life. Pulling from sources such as Herodotus, Virgil, Plutarch, Suetonius, and Caesar, authors Rosalie and Charles Baker give students a taste of the ancients in their own words. These were the very stories our Founding Fathers read in school, which then helped to shape the new republic that they created. The fledgling American republic was in many ways the child of Greece and Rome.

Without an awareness of this remarkable heritage, students cannot begin to understand the enduring values of western civilization. On the other hand, as students read about the "glory that was Greece and Rome," they also will encounter the conflicts in values that are an unavoidable part of any human society. As they will see, these were warlike societies that conquered and enslaved their neighbors. Along with democracy, the ancients left us a legacy of imperialism and war.

In this second edition of the *Classical Companion*, the authors expand their wonderful sourcebook by adding an original play and student-related activities to each chapter. This volume opens the door to the treasure-trove of ancient history. The collection of engaging readings and activities will whet the appetite of students to explore it and make it their own.

Linda Symcox
Director, UCLA/Options for
Youth Curriculum Laboratory

Introduction

The *Classical Companion* is a sourcebook for students and teachers interested in the ancient civilizations of Greece and Rome. In this revised and updated second edition, we have added five original plays and a variety of activities specially written to accompany each play. One play is a translated excerpt from an ancient Greek comedy; the others are all original plays.

The Companion is divided into five chapters, each centering on a nation whose people succeeded in stopping, albeit briefly, the onward march of Greece and Rome. Chapter I focuses on Persia versus Greece; Chapter II on Greece versus Rome; Chapter III on Carthage versus Rome; Chapter IV on Gaul versus Rome; and Chapter V on Egypt versus Rome.

The first article of each chapter describes the historical events preceding the head-on collision of the two superpowers. The articles that follow give details of the major conflicts, profiles of the generals and leaders, and descriptions of the peoples themselves.

A series of puzzles based on the material is presented at the end of each chapter. In addition, each chapter includes a project with instructions—e.g., the project in Chapter IV is to reconstruct Caesar's famous siegeworks around Alesia.

Each chapter also includes an article to broaden the interest of anyone studying Western civilization. In Chapter V, "On Today's Ancients" describes three current projects designed to duplicate or test past experiences. These projects include the *Daedalus* human-powered airplane, the Greek merchant ship *Kyrenia II*, and the Greek warship *Olympias*.

Prefacing each chapter is a map locating every site mentioned. Foreign names and phrases are highlighted by a pronunciation key near the appropriate word. For delving deeper into a particular subject, a further reading list appears at the end of the book.

Each of the six companion sections presents ideas for additional study. These include topics for comparison, suggestions for essays and written reports, debate topics, and a variety of further activities. Each of the first five companion sections corresponds to a specific chapter. The sixth section at the end of the book includes suggestions relating to all the chapters.

We have especially enjoyed revising the original *Classical Companion,* and we hope you will enjoy using it.

Charles F. Baker III
Rosalie F. Baker

I Persia versus Greece

OVERVIEW

PEEOPLS INVOLVED:
Persians, Greeks

DECISIVE BATTLES:
(all on Greek soil)
Marathon (490 B.C.),
Thermopylae (480 B.C.),
Salamis (480 B.C.),
Plataea (479 B.C.)

GENERALS:
Darius, Xerxes (Persian);
Leonidas, Themistocles (Greek)

HISTORICAL SIGNIFICANCE:
Greece defeats the Persians and becomes the cradle of Western civilization.

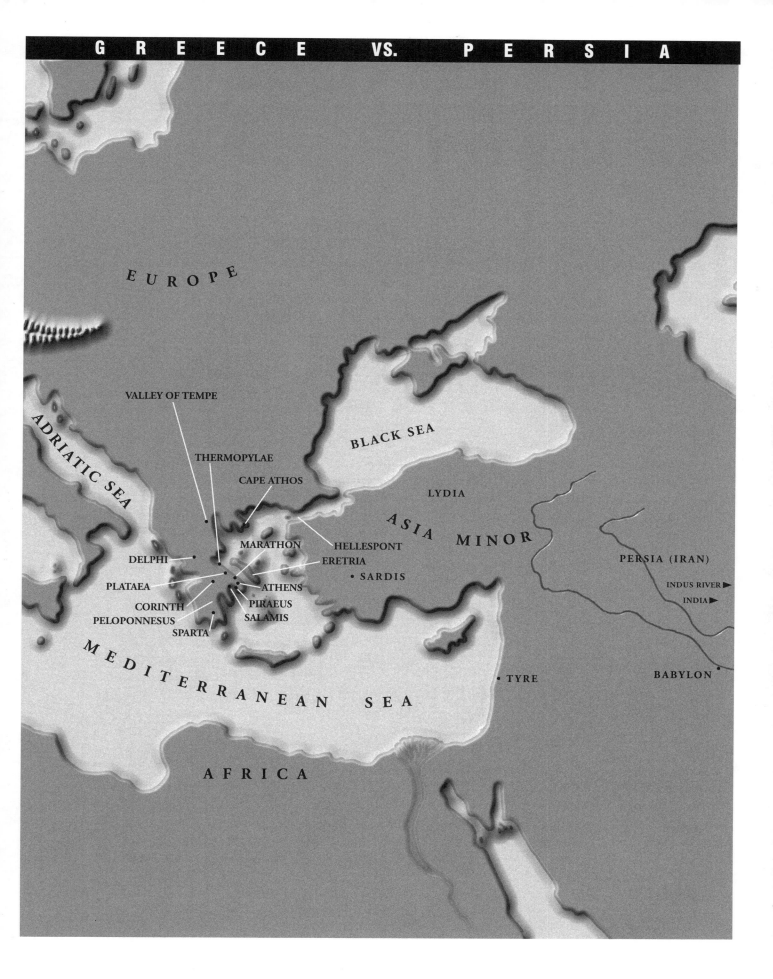

The Persian Threat

By 500 B.C., the Persians controlled most of the known civilized world. Their eastern boundary was the Mediterranean Sea; their western, the Indus River (beyond which lay India). Europe, especially Greece and its well-situated coastal colonies, was their next target. For decades the mere mention of Persia or the names of its three famous kings—Cyrus (560–529 B.C.), Darius (522–486 B.C.), and Xerxes (ZURK sees) (486–465 B.C.)—instilled fear in the heart of every Greek.

From 750 to 550 B.C., Greeks had emigrated from the mainland in search of new homelands. The western coast of Asia Minor (present-day Turkey) was transformed into a major Greek colony composed of numerous city-states, known as the Ionian cities.

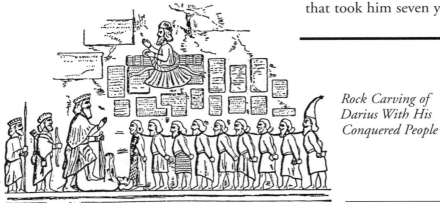

Rock Carving of Darius With His Conquered People

During Darius' reign, this entire area came under Persian control. Yet all was not well. The Greek colonists longed to be free. In 500 B.C., the city-states banded together, defied Persian authority, established a democratic form of government, and began the great Ionian revolt.

Realizing the urgent need for a strong ally, Aristagoras, the leader of the revolt, sent envoys to petition aid from Sparta, Greece's most powerful city-state. After being refused, Aristagoras turned to Athens, the second city of Greece, and was granted a squadron of twenty ships. The Athenians helped Aristagoras because they considered themselves the mother country of the eastern colonies and because they feared treachery at the hands of Hippias, a banished Athenian ruler aligned with the Persians. The city of Eretria (eh REE tree ah), north of Athens, also agreed to help and sent five ships.

In 499 B.C., the Ionian colonists, with the aid of Athens and Eretria, stormed Sardis, the capital of Lydia in Asia Minor, and destroyed the city. King Darius of Persia was incensed and vowed retaliation against Greece. First, however, he had to quell the revolt in Asia Minor, a goal that took him seven years to accomplish.

Darius was then prepared to subdue Greece. He sent heralds to all the Greek city-states demanding their allegiance. Many yielded, fearing the wrath of the Persian king. Athens and Sparta both refused to yield. Darius was not deterred, for he knew that the weakness of the Greeks lay in their failure to unite around a single leader. Darius felt that to conquer Greece, he needed only to proceed slowly, capturing one city-state at a time.

Historians call this the period of the Persian wars. Thousands upon thousands of heroic, duty-bound men lost their lives in these wars, which decided the fate of the Western world.

The Four Decisive Battles

The refusal of Athens and Sparta to pledge their allegiance to King Darius brought Persian troops marching into Greece. The Athenians quickly realized that lack of cooperation among the Greek city-states would mean defeat. They sent envoys to Sparta acknowledging its military might in arms and agreed to follow its commands. Sparta, aware of the urgency of the situation, agreed to help Athens.

As the two most powerful Greek city-states readied themselves for attack, Darius' army slowly approached Greece proper, capturing many of the Greek islands on its drive toward Athens. After landing on the mainland, the Persians marched first to Eretria and destroyed the city. With the banished Hippias as their advisor, the Persians then sailed toward the plains of Marathon, where they planned their attack on Athens. History tells us that their fleet consisted of six hundred *trieres* (an ancient warship with three banks of oars) transporting soldiers, cavalrymen, archers, and support personnel—a combined force of about one hundred thousand men. Athens, however, had an army of only nine thousand soldiers. With the help of neighboring city-state Plataea's (pluh TAY ah) band of one thousand, a total of ten thousand men prepared to meet the Persians.

The Athenian leaders realized they needed Sparta's help. Pheidippides (phi DIH pih dees), a trained long-distance runner, was summoned and asked to make the arduous one-hundred-twenty-mile round-trip journey requesting Sparta's aid. For two days and two nights Pheidippides traveled, swimming rivers, climb-ing mountains, and crossing whatever lay in his path, until he reached Sparta. After making his plea, he returned to Athens with the answer: Sparta had agreed to send a contingent of two thousand men. But for religious reasons, they would not arrive until after the full moon. The Athenians understood and accepted Sparta's terms and quickly sought a plan of action, since the Persians had landed at Marathon.

The Athenians resolved to march to Marathon immediately. To camouflage the size of their army, General Miltiades (mil TEE ah dees) devised a new strategy. He assigned a comparatively few men to the center front lines and heavily armed the wings. In this way, the Greek

Significance of Marathon Marathon marked the beginning of the Greek world's freedom from Persian control. This allowed Athens to become one of the great powers of the ancient world and to produce architects, thinkers, and writers whose works, ideas, and designs have become the basis of Western civilization.

line of battle could be extended to equal that of the Persians. When all was ready, the signal was given and the Athenians charged across the fields. The Persians thought that the Greek army was mad running toward them, but Miltiades knew that his men held the advantage only if they ran. To proceed at a march would have meant that many would fall, pierced by enemy spears.

The Persians overcame their surprise at the manner of the Greek attack as the Athenians neared the front lines. The battle was long and fierce. The Persians easily pushed through the weak center but were overcome by the heavily armed wings of the Athenian lines. The Athenians fought hard to preserve their homeland, their family life, and their democratic way of life. Finally, the Persians began to retreat to their ships anchored in the harbor. The Athenians rejoiced. Victory was at hand. East had met West and lost. After the battle was over, the word "marathon" became synonymous with victory throughout the Greek world.

Pheidippides was entrusted with the honor of announcing the great news of Marathon to the people in Athens. As quickly as he could, the battle-worn runner ran the twenty-two miles from the plains of Marathon to Athens, only to die of exhaustion once he had proclaimed the victory.

To honor those who gave their lives to preserve the Greek way of life, the Athenians constructed a huge mound of earth on the plains of Marathon. Today it remains a visible monument to freedom.

NB The Spartans did arrive, but after the battle was over. Athenian losses were not overwhelming. Only 192 Athenians lost their lives compared to 6,400 Persians.

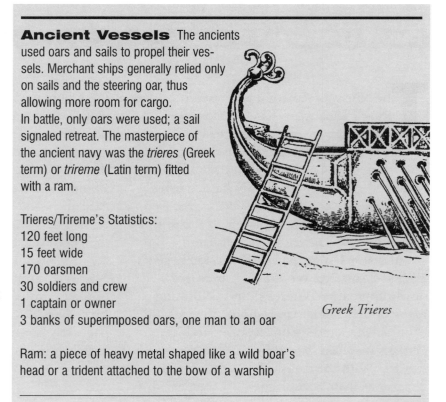

Ancient Vessels The ancients used oars and sails to propel their vessels. Merchant ships generally relied only on sails and the steering oar, thus allowing more room for cargo. In battle, only oars were used; a sail signaled retreat. The masterpiece of the ancient navy was the *trieres* (Greek term) or *trireme* (Latin term) fitted with a ram.

Trieres/Trireme's Statistics:
120 feet long
15 feet wide
170 oarsmen
30 soldiers and crew
1 captain or owner
3 banks of superimposed oars, one man to an oar

Ram: a piece of heavy metal shaped like a wild boar's head or a trident attached to the bow of a warship

Greek Trieres

THERMOPYLAE (480 B.C.)

King Darius of Persia vowed to avenge his defeat at Marathon, but he died before he could fulfill his promise. His son Xerxes succeeded him and arrogantly announced his plans to conquer the Greek peninsula.

The Greeks, in a state of turmoil, could not agree on the best course of action. Even the Delphic oracle, the most sacred of all Greek shrines, did not seem to advise resistance. Her response had been negative, except for her saying, "The wooden wall alone shall remain unconquered to defend you and your children."

Themistocles (theh MISS toe kleez), the great Athenian statesman, believed he understood the oracle's intention. "Greece needs a navy. The wooden wall surely means a fleet of wooden ships. Our land force is well trained and formidable, but defeat at the hands of any comparable power is inevitable unless we command a fleet of ships. Persia must be so humiliated that no Persian will march again against Greece. To do this, Greece needs a navy." Athens and her allies finally agreed, and a fleet of wooden ships was built.

Two problems remained: Who would command the Greeks, and what strategy was best? After much dissension and discussion, the Greek leaders pledged allegiance to Sparta and a Spartan general. The valley of Tempe was marked as the first defense position because of its natural physical features and its proximity to the coast.

To Xerxes, a continent away, no Greek decision was of any importance. His dream was to subdue mainland Greece. He ordered every allied territory and every area under Persian control to prepare and arm troops and ships for his planned expedition. No one dared refuse him.

Xerxes spent the winter of 481–480 B.C. in Sardis mustering his troops and conferring with his generals. The spring of 480 B.C. witnessed the march of the greatest horde of warriors ever assembled. The fifth-century Greek historian Herodotus (heh ROD o tus) recorded the number of the fighting force as more than two and one-half million and the number of the entire Persian contingent as more than five million. While historians today believe Herodotus exaggerated his figures, the actual number must have been quite high because it took seven days and nights of uninterrupted marching to cross the bridges spanning the Hellespont.

As preparations were made to defend Tempe, the Greeks learned that a second path led to the valley and that their forces would be surrounded. They abandoned Tempe and, consequently, northern Greece.

"To Thermopylae!" (ther MAW pih lie) was the call issued by the Greeks as troops were ordered to the front. It was a small force, however, since Sparta and its neighbors were celebrating a religious festival and Athens and the other Greek city-states were involved in the Olympic Games.

After arriving at Thermopylae, Leonidas (lee OWN ih das), the brave Spartan king in charge of the Greek forces, learned that the city, like Tempe, also had a second, little-known pass. Yet he refused to retreat a second time. The fighting went well for two days. Even the elite Persian fighting force, the Immortals, could not break through the pass. The Greeks might have

won had it not been for two unfortunate incidents. First, Leonidas did not know that the Greek fleet, his supporting force, had panicked and retreated. Second, a Greek named Ephialtes (eh phih AL tees) traitorously revealed to Xerxes the little-known pass. When Leonidas learned of the Persians to his rear, he knew the Greeks had been betrayed and defeat was imminent.

The Persian Immortals The Immortals were the best soldiers in the entire Persian army. They numbered exactly ten thousand and were hand-picked. When one died or left, another was immediately chosen to take his place. One thousand of the men were Xerxes' special guard, and each had a golden apple attached to the end of his spear. The other nine thousand had silver apples attached to the ends of their spears.

Persian Soldiers

Reinforcements would never arrive on time. The festivals were just over and preparations had not been made.

Leonidas quickly decided on a plan of action. Everyone was to abandon his position at Thermopylae and return to Corinth, except for himself and his three hundred Spartans. (Leonidas purposely chose his force from men who had living sons, so that in the event of death each family would still have a male heir.) The contingent of seven hundred Thespians also refused to accept defeat and prepared to fight. This small, proud Greek band fought bravely and recklessly against the massive Persian army, each Greek knowing death alone would crown his efforts.

Leonidas' order of the day: Breakfast here, supper in Hades (the underworld).

News of the disaster at Thermopylae spread panic throughout the Greek city-states. Many leaders urged a retreat of all forces to the Peloponnesus (peh lo po NEE sus), south of Athens. But Themistocles realized this action meant abandoning Athens, his city and the main supplier of the Greek navy, to Xerxes. He addressed his comrades: "If the Greek League chooses to fight only at the Isthmus of Corinth and not at Salamis, where the Athenians have retreated, we Athenians shall not lend our support, but seek another homeland." (Athens had been evacuated except for those who chose to sacrifice their lives in one last attempt to save the city.)

The other Greeks understood this threat. They knew the Athenian vessels made the Greek navy. Yet they still considered heading south. Themistocles formed a plan. He summoned his children's tutor and gave him a message for Xerxes. The brave tutor secretly slipped out of the Greek camp and sought Xerxes. He told the great Persian king how the Greek fleet was planning to slip away through the far channel of the Bay of Salamis. If Xerxes wished to trap and defeat the fleet, he had to act immediately.

Xerxes ordered his Egyptian squadron to block the far channel and the main fleet to block the eastern end. "Soon all Greece will be mine," Xerxes cried.

When news of the blockade reached the Greek commanders, they refused to believe it until a Persian vessel defected and corroborated the report. Themistocles had won. He had chosen the battlefield.

At dawn, on September 20, 480 B.C., the Greek fleet of three hundred eighty ships, encouraged and inspired by Themistocles and the other Greek leaders, waited and maneuvered itself so as to force the Persian fleet to enter the narrow straits and expose its flanks to the Greeks positioned to the left. The bold and daring strategy worked. With their confidence renewed, the Greeks effectively rammed and sank numerous Persian ships. They boarded other ships and engaged in hand-to-hand combat. From his silver throne positioned on a mountaintop overlooking the Bay of Salamis, Xerxes watched the defeat of his great fleet in disbelief.

Soon Xerxes began to fear for his own welfare and ordered his troops and navy to retreat. For some time the Greeks did not fully realize the extent of their victory; they thought Xerxes was retreating to regroup. Therefore, the Greeks repaired their vessels and refitted themselves for the next encounter.

On September 22, the Greeks awoke to a quiet sea. Xerxes' fleet had vanished.

Rams Attached to Prows of Warships

Themistocles' interpretation of the Delphic priestess' wooden walls had been correct. The ships had saved the Athenians and Greece.

Leonidas at Thermopylae (by French painter Jacques Louis David, 1748–1825)

All of Greece rejoiced after the victory of Salamis, but not for long. Xerxes' general Mardonius regrouped the Persian forces and, in 479 B.C., marched against Athens and southern Greece. Once more Sparta delayed taking any action, and the Athenians were forced to abandon their homes and seek refuge in Salamis. For the second time, Athens was occupied by invaders from the east.

Finally, Greek patriotism prevailed, and the city-states of the Greek League, including Sparta, sent troops. East again prepared to meet West, this time at Plataea.

The fighting was bitter and fierce. Mardonius, without Xerxes to rally the forces, fearlessly led his troops into battle. He died on the battlefield, and with him went the Persian spirit. The Greeks sensed what was happening and pressed on even harder. Victory was theirs. West had met East and won.

Pheidippides Remembered

"Rejoice, we conquer!" gasped the Greek messenger Pheidippides, as he ran toward the gates of the city of Athens. And the Greek world did rejoice, for its soldiers had defeated the great Persian army on the plains of Marathon.

Unfortunately, the patriot Pheidippides never participated in the hero's welcome given the returning Athenian army. Tradition tells us that he died exhausted from the battle and from his twenty-two-mile run. But for centuries, the spirit and message of Pheidippides have fired the imagination of poets, artists, and historians.

In April 1896, after much discussion and preparation, the Olympic Games were reinstituted. Greece, as the originator of the games, was the host country. The main event was, as it had been in ancient times, a footrace. However, Olympic officials decided to make it a cross-country race instead of the six-hundred-yard stadium dash of the ancients. The Greeks won the event.

The Boston Athletic Association (BAA), which had been responsible to a great extent for organizing the United States Olympic team, decided not to wait four years until the next games for another exciting cross-country race. However, before the BAA determined a location and a time to hold the race, New York sponsored its own in October 1896, a twenty-five-mile run from Stamford, Connecticut, to Columbus Circle in New York City.

Pheidippides on His Way to Sparta (from Comic History of Greece, *by Charles M. Snyder, 1898)*

Meanwhile, the BAA completed the details for its marathon. The twenty-five-mile course ran from Ashland, Massachusetts, to Boston. In 1897, the first Boston Marathon was held on April 19, Patriots' Day, a day commemorating Paul Revere's historic ride for American freedom. Fifteen runners assembled, all dressed in toreador pants and heavy boots. A great tradition had begun. In 1908, the length of a marathon race was standardized at twenty-six miles and three hundred eighty-five yards. As a result, the Boston course had to be lengthened. It now begins in Hopkinton and ends in Boston's Back Bay.

Following Boston's example, other cities throughout the United States and the world have established their own marathons. With every marathon the memory of Pheidippides and the heroic stand of his countrymen are honored today.

Greek Warriors

Themistocles

The Greeks credited Themistocles with engineering the victory at Salamis and as such gave him a hero's welcome. While much is known of the heroic deeds of many ancient Greek leaders, little is known of their personal lives. Several ancient authors refer to Themistocles as an opportunist. He also was portrayed as one who opposed individuals with power. He was accused of corruption and ostracized in 471 B.C. Ostracism, a constitutional reform some say Themistocles introduced, was the method used in Athens to banish for ten years a powerful and influential citizen who had become unpopular. (*N.B. Ostracism did become a political weapon.*)

In his later years Themistocles was accused of organizing an anti-Spartan alliance and of associating too closely with Easterners. After the Athenians condemned him to death, Themistocles fled to Asia Minor and joined King Artaxerxes (ar tuh ZURK sees) of Persia. The Persians treated him well, and he lived grandly until his death at the age of sixty-five. (Some say he committed suicide.)

Themistocles

NB This symbol and the *N.B.* notation within the text is an abbreviation for the Latin phrase *Note bene*, which means "note well" or "take note."

Cyrus, Darius, and Xerxes

CYRUS (560–529 B.C.)

Under Cyrus, Persia became the ruling nation in eastern Asia. His conquests included Babylon and Lydia, the kingdom of the famed Croesus (KREE sus). His tolerance of customs foreign to his beliefs and his ability to govern fairly and wisely won him the respect of his subjects. Even the Greeks praised him in this respect.

DARIUS I (522–486 B.C.)

In 522 B.C., Cyrus' son and successor died and a usurper held the throne. Darius, a nobleman and general who proudly claimed descent from a long lineage of Persians, won control of the sprawling Persian Empire.

Since Darius wanted succeeding generations to know of his great deeds, he had his achievements carved in rock. One record noting his rise to the monarchy was written in three languages. It covers a space fifty-nine feet wide and twenty-five feet high and recounts Darius' victories and ethical views. For historians, this set of inscriptions was a major find because it provided the key to deciphering Old Persian, the language of Darius' time.

Darius' reign was active and productive. He carefully and thoughtfully reorganized the system of governing his vast empire, taking a great interest in reforming the laws affecting each of the various provinces. He revamped the tax system and actively sought effective officials, judges, and government representatives. He also built splendid palaces.

From written records we know that Darius was a good archer and spear thrower, both on foot and on horseback. He also was reported to have been quite handsome, with arms that reached to his knees (a mark of beauty in Persia). His absolute belief in Ahuramazda, the representative of good, governed his treatment of his subjects, conquered peoples, and criminals. Evil and lies were mercilessly punished.

Rock-Cut Tomb of Darius

Xerxes succeeded his father, Darius, to the Persian throne and relentlessly sought to achieve the goal of conquering Greece, especially Athens and Sparta.

Since sea travel along the coast from Asia to Greece was hazardous, especially near Cape Athos, Xerxes had his engineers and laborers dig a canal through the neck of the peninsula of Athos. The mile-and-a-half canal was sixty-five to one hundred feet wide and six to ten feet deep. Two ships were able to pass abreast of each other. To prevent silting, breakwaters were built at each end.

Xerxes considered himself worthy of the greatest respect and expected his every order to be obeyed. Once when he was on a ship with his attendants and some soldiers, a terrible storm arose. Fearing that disaster might be near, Xerxes asked the captain what could be done. "Nothing, my lord, unless we could rid ourselves of some passengers." Without hesitating, Xerxes turned to the passengers and said, "Men of Persia, now is the time to show how much you love your king.

My safety depends upon your actions."

The Persians immediately jumped overboard and drowned. The ship, relieved of its load, rode the waves much more easily. When Xerxes arrived safely, he called the captain to him and said, "Here is a golden coin for saving my life; but because so many of our comrades died as a result of your suggestion, you too must die."

When Xerxes marched into Greece, each area where he rested was ordered to provide him and his men with one meal a day. The great quantities of food severely taxed the resources of each community. It was reported that the valuable silver and gold goblets and the utensils each community used to serve the king and his companions were never returned. It also was said that the enormous Persian contingent completely drained some rivers just quenching its thirst.

What became of Xerxes after his retreat from Salamis in Greece is unknown. He continued to rule over Persia, building extensively. History relates that he was murdered in a royal plot.

Ahuramazda Ahuramazda, the great god of the Persians, ruled all of King Darius' actions. Ahuramazda was the good, the righteous, helping him overcome the evil, the lie.

The Persians believed Ahuramazda created earth and sky, humans and animals. This great power also was responsible for Darius and all the blessings enjoyed by the Persians. Fire and water were sacred. Persians were not allowed to wash in rivers, for the dirt would pollute the water. Cremation was not allowed because the dead body would pollute the fire. According to custom, the Persians buried their dead after first covering them with wax.

The Guardian God of the Persians

Bridging the Hellespont

Transporting the hundreds of thousands of soldiers and camp followers into Greece was a major problem for Xerxes. A land route, crossing only the narrow waters of the Hellespont, was the best course.

Xerxes commanded his engineers to devise a plan for crossing the mile of water separating Asia Minor from Europe. His men eagerly set to work building a bridge made of cables and ropes. But after the bridge had been successfully completed, a terrible storm destroyed the massive work.

Xerxes was so angry that he ordered his soldiers to whip the waters of the Hellespont three hundred times and then to cast chains into the channel. He also executed the designers of the bridge.

His next command was for a second bridge to be built that was more secure and flexible. Construction began with more than six hundred ships moored breastwise in two separate lines, their prows toward the Aegean Sea. Anchors and very long cables secured their prows and sterns. Six lines of cables were stretched over or through each line of ships from shore to shore. A gap was left in three places to allow trading ships to enter or leave the Euxine Sea by passing beneath the cables, which could be tightened or loosened from the shore. Upon this foundation, a causeway of earth and wood was laid. A fence of stakes prevented cattle, used for food and provisions, from seeing the water and stampeding.

Xerxes Lashing the Hellespont

Herodotus on the Persians

Around 450 B.C., the Greek historian Herodotus traveled through Asia Minor as far as Babylon. In his accounts, he noted his thoughts and interpretation of various Persian customs:

The Persians have no images of their gods, no temples, and no altars. The Persians do not believe the gods have the same nature as humans, as we Greeks believe. Rather it is the Persian custom to climb to the peaks of the highest mountains and there sacrifice to Ahuramazda, a name they use to represent all the heavens.

For sacrifices to their gods, the Persians build no altar, light no fire, and pour no libations. There is no sound of the flute, no consecrated cakes of barley (all customs practiced by the Greeks). A Persian brings the animal he plans to sacrifice to a sacred area and then calls the name of the god intended for the offering. Usually the Persian will encircle his turban with a wreath, commonly made of myrtle. The sacrificer is not allowed to pray for blessings on himself alone, but must pray for the welfare of the king and all the Persian people. He cuts the victim into pieces, boils the flesh, and lays it upon tender, green plants. When all is ready, one of the magi (an order of priests)

comes forward and chants a hymn, which they say recounts the origin of the gods. A magi must be present before a sacrifice can be made. After pausing briefly, the sacrificer leaves with the victim's flesh to do with it as he wills.

In general, Persians discuss serious matters when they are drunk. The next day, when they are sober, they consider the decision made the day before. If they agree with the

Persians

decision, they act; if not, they set the matter aside.

If two Persians of equal rank meet on the street, they kiss each other on the lips. If one is of a lower class, the kiss is given on the cheek. If there is a great difference in rank, the one belonging to the lower class lies down on the ground.

The Persians treat their nearest neighbors with the greatest respect. The farther away a particular nation is, the less respect it receives.

The Persians regard themselves as far superior in every respect to all other peoples and rank others in relationship to their geographic location.

No nation adopts foreign customs more readily than the Persians. As soon as they hear of any luxury, they instantly make it their own. Each Persian man has several wives and a harem.

Bravery on the battlefield is the greatest proof of manliness. Being the father of many sons ranks second. Every year the king sends sumptuous gifts to the father with the most sons. Between the ages of five and twenty, boys are taught three disciplines: riding, archery, and speaking the truth. Boys younger than five remain with their mothers, unseen by their fathers. This prevents any attachment if a boy dies of some childhood disease.

No one can be put to death for just one crime. A slave cannot be punished severely if he or she makes one mistake. Punishment is inflicted only if a person's wrongdoings outweigh his or her good deeds.

Persians consider lying the greatest sin; the second greatest offense is to owe a debt, for a debtor must tell lies.

excerpted from History, *Bk I, 131–139*

Zarathustra Zarathustra (za ruh THOOS tra) was revered by the Persians as a holy prophet. Historians believe he lived around 600 B.C. and that his own people did not follow or adhere to his philosophy of dualism (the concept of good and evil and the right and ability of a human being to choose between the two). Disheartened, Zarathustra emigrated to eastern Iran, where the followers of Ahuramazda embraced him warmly. The Greeks referred to Zarathustra as Zoroaster (zo row ASS ter), and in time his beliefs and teachings combined with those associated with Ahuramazda. Zoroastrianism became one of eastern Asia's prominent religions.

On the Ancients' World

GEOGRAPHY IN ANCIENT TIMES

The two great masterpieces of ancient literature, the *Iliad* and the *Odyssey*, written by the Greek poet Homer (fl. c. 700 B.C.), have helped historians form a better idea of how the world looked to early cartographers.

In the *Iliad*, the world is a round plain encircled by the great river Oceanus. The sky is an enormous concave roof propped up by pillars that the mighty giant Atlas supports on his shoulders. Homer knew only the middle section of this large, flat disc. The center of his world was northern Greece, where Mount Olympos, the home of the gods, was believed to be located. His configuration of Greece, the Aegean Sea, and Asia Minor, i.e., the eastern Mediterranean, was fairly accurate, especially when one considers the materials and instruments used at the time. For the western Mediterranean he relied heavily on the mythological beliefs of the time, e.g., Scylla, Charybdis (ca RIB diss), and the Sirens (monsters who preyed on sailors.) To the north were the Cimerii, a race of milk-fed nomads and a mythical

The World According to Homer

people who lived enveloped in constant mist and darkness. To the south were the Lotophagi. They ate a fruit called the lotus, the taste of which was so delicious that anyone who ate it lost all desire to return home. Along the southern shores of Oceanus lived the Pygmaei, people who were only thirteen and one-half inches tall.

In the centuries that followed Homer's time, mainland Greece established numerous colonies in Asia Minor and throughout the eastern Mediterranean. This resulted in an increased number of commercial ventures and an intense thirst for knowledge about what lay beyond the then known world. Around 550 B.C., Aristagoras of Miletus in Asia Minor made the first attempt to outline a map of the world.

By the time of Herodotus (c. 484–420 B.C.), the ancients' concept of the world had changed greatly. Herodotus eliminated the legendary creatures, Italy assumed a much more recognizable form, the Iberian Peninsula and Europe were known.

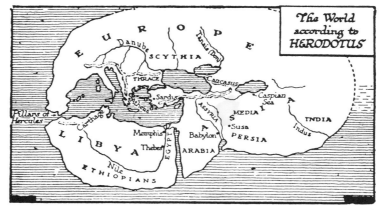

The World According to Herodotus

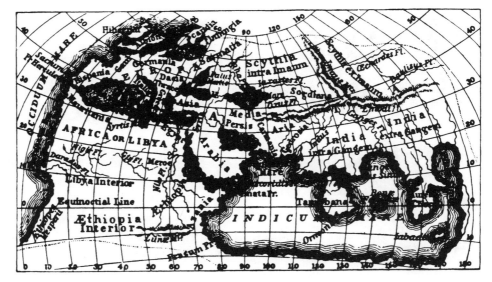

The World According to Ptolemy

With each succeeding generation, the maritime trade of the Greek city-states increased and seafarers became more adventurous as they sought to extend their commercial enterprises into new areas. As was characteristic of the Greek mind, a mere awareness of a world larger than had been previously thought of was not enough. A more comprehensive understanding of the universe and how it functioned was sought. About 350 B.C. Pytheas (PITH eh ahs), from the Greek colony of Massilia (mas SIL ih ah) (present-day Marseilles [mar SAY], France), made an incredible voyage along the western coast of France to England and then circled the British Isles. It is believed that Pytheas was probably the first navigator to have recorded his positions using astronomical observations.

In the East, the campaigns of Alexander the Great of Macedonia (356–323 B.C.) were opening up the lands of Asia to Greek research. One of the countries that prospered under Alexander and his successor, Ptolemy I, was Egypt. Its capital, Alexandria, became one of the greatest centers of research and learning.

Eratosthenes (eh ra TOSS theh neez) (c. 280–175 B.C.) of Cyrene (sigh REE neh) in Libya calculated the circumference of the earth and came within fifty miles of the true diameter. Hipparchos (hih PAR kos) (c. 160–120 B.C.) of the Greek colony of Nicaea (nih KAY ah) in Asia Minor promoted the concept of marking positions on the surface of the earth by using latitudes and longitudes. Only a few modifications have ever been made to Hipparchos' map of the world.

The Romans, despite their powerful intervention in world affairs, produced few good geographers and cartographers. Nevertheless, their expeditions in this field were invaluable. Through conquests and expeditions they extended the borders of the known world into Africa and northern Europe. Under the direction of Emperor Augustus (27 B.C.– A.D. 14), Agrippa measured and mapped the distance between the stations on the military roads that crossed the Roman Empire. Agrippa's work laid the foundation for today's maps.

In the second century A.D., the last significant contribution to geographical science in antiquity was made by the Alexandrian astronomer Ptolemy (TOL eh me). His work, a summary of all Greek and Roman discoveries, remained the acknowledged authority in the field of geography until the thirteenth century and the Middle Ages.

Arbitration

A translated excerpt from the play "Arbitration" by the Greek comic playwright Menander (c. 342 - c. 291 B.C.)

CHARACTERS

Smikrines—*rich but frugal old citizen of Athens, father of Pamphila, father-in-law of Charisios*
Chaerestratos—*friend and neighbor of Charisios*
Simmias—*friend of Chaerestratos and Charisios*
Syriskos—*charcoal burner and slave of Chaerestratos*
Davos—*slave goat herder*
Onesimos—*slave of Charisios*

Habrotonon—*a young professional harpist and slave hired by Charisios*
Pamphila—*daughter of Smikrines and wife of Charisios*
Charisios—*rich young citizen of Athens, husband of Pamphila*
Sophrona—*Pamphila's old nurse*

Scene of Play: *A street on the outskirts of Athens, a city-state in ancient Greece. Backdrop: The facades of Chaerestratos' house and Charisios' house. After a recent disagreement with his wife, Pamphila, Charisios moved in with Chaerestratos. So, too, did Charisios' friend Habrotonon. Charisios' wife is living by herself in Charisios' house. The exit at stage left leads to Athens; the exit at stage right leads to the mountains.*

Act I

Smikrines enters stage left, grumbling about his wretched, high-spending son-in-law Charisios. The old man is so absorbed in his plans to convince his daughter Pamphila to leave her husband that he does not see Chaerestratos, Charisios' friend, leaving his house.

Smikrines: That son-in-law of mine! I just don't understand how he can drink so much when he has to pay for each glass.

Chaerestratos: Here he comes. I knew it. He'll ruin all our fun.

Smikrines: But what's it to me? He's the one who'll lose. Still, there is the dowry. If he spends it, and I'm sure he will, my daughter will have nothing. In fact, I bet he's using it already to pay for that harpist he hired at a very high price.

Chaerestratos: *(aside)* How does he know this?

Smikrines: Why, the money he's using for the harpist would feed a grown man for a whole month and, let me see, six days besides.

(Door to Chaerestratos' house opens. Simmias appears.)

Simmias: Chaerestratos, come in. Charisios is waiting for you. *(points to Smikrines)* Who's that?

Chaerestratos: Pamphila's father.

Simmias: Why is he so glum? I'll speak to him.

Chaerestratos: I wouldn't if I were you. Let him find out about Habrotonon and the rest by himself.

Act II*

Scene 1: *Enter Davos, Syriskos, and Syriskos' wife with a baby in her arms. The two men are arguing about the infant.*

Syriskos: You're not fair.

Davos: You want what's not yours.

Syriskos: Let's get someone to arbitrate this matter. Whom should we ask?

Davos: Anyone will do. *(aside)* How I wish I had never made any deals with this man!

(Enter Smikrines.)

Syriskos: *(pointing to Smikrines)* Will he do as the judge?

Davos: Okay, but I pray that luck will be on my side.

Syriskos: *(to Smikrines)* Ho, there, could you spare a few minutes for us?

Smikrines: For you? Why?

Syriskos: He and I, we have a small disagreement.

Smikrines: Why should I care?

23

Syriskos: We need someone to arbitrate, someone who is impartial. Please help us settle the matter.

Smikrines: You're workmen, laborers—do you presume to talk of debates and legal rights?

Syriskos: So we do. But, please, it's a simple matter. Don't look down on us. Justice should always win, everywhere, and everyone should make it his concern to see that justice wins. It's a duty, an obligation we all share.

Davos: *(aside)* Syriskos here talks on like a true lawyer. Why did I ever do business with him?

Smikrines: *(curtly)* Will you obey my decision, whatever it is?

Syriskos and Davos: *(together)* Yes.

Smikrines: I'll hear the case. *(to Davos)* You, who have said nothing, go first.

Davos: I'll give you some background. About a month ago, I was herding my flock all alone, when I found an abandoned infant in the thick bush near here. Next to it was a necklace and a few other ornaments. *(He shows the jewelry.)*

Syriskos: *(cutting in)* This is what we've been arguing about.

Davos: *(to Smikrines, angrily)* He's not letting me speak!

Smikrines: *(to Syriskos)* Interrupt again and I'll smack you with this stick. *(to Davos)* Go on.

Davos: I picked up the baby and its belongings and returned home. I planned to raise the child myself. But that night I had second thoughts. What did I know about raising a child? How could I afford to? At dawn the next day, I went back to my flock, and this man here *(pointing to Syriskos)* came by to cut some tree stumps. I knew him a little, and we began talking. He noticed how glum I was and asked, "What's wrong, Davos?" I told him everything—how I had found the baby, everything. Then he started pleading and grabbing and kissing my hands. "Let me have the baby," he said. "My wife just lost a baby in childbirth." His wife's the one over there with the baby. *(pointing to Syriskos' wife)*

Smikrines: *(to Syriskos)* You begged him?

Davos: *(to Syriskos)* Well?

Syriskos: Yes, I did.

Davos: I gave them the infant, and that was that. Now he and his wife claim I owe them everything I found with the baby. This jewelry is worth nothing—mere trinkets—but they say it's theirs. He ought to be grateful he got what he got, not go asking for more. I found the baby all by myself, yet you *(to Syriskos)* want everything and leave nothing for me. If you've changed your mind about the baby, then give it back, but don't try to squeeze more out of me. There, I've had my say.

Syriskos: Is he done?

Smikrines: Are you deaf? He said he was done.

Syriskos: All he said is true. Another herder, a friend of his, told me about the baby's trinkets. Here, sir, is my client *(he takes the baby from his wife's arms)* to claim what is rightfully his—the necklace and the birth tokens. You must decide whether this jewelry is to be kept for the child until he comes of age, as his birth mother intended, or whether this baby robber is to be allowed to keep what's not his. Think, too, of this: When this child grows up, these trinkets may help him find his parents. Perhaps they are of a class far above ours. If Davos is allowed to keep them or sell them, the child will never know his rightful parents or his real station in life. *(to Davos)* As for giving the baby back, that would just allow you to play the same deceitful game again. *(to Smikrines)* I'm done. Decide as you wish.

Smikrines: It's a simple case. The baby and all that was with him go together.

Davos: But what about the baby?

Smikrines: By Zeus, I won't give him to you, who wants to cheat him of what's rightfully his. He goes to his rescuer, Syriskos.

Syriskos: May the gods bless you.

Davos: *(furious)* What? I who found all lose all. What a dreadful decision.

Smikrines: *(to Syriskos)* Do you have everything?

Syriskos: I think so.

Smikrines: Unless that petty thief swallowed one while you were pleading your case.

Davos: I don't believe it! *(exit Davos)*

Syriskos: *(to Smikrines)* Good-bye and thanks. How I wish all our judges were such as you. *(to his wife)* Let's sort through all this.

Scene 2: *Onesimos exits from Chaerestratos' house. He sees Syriskos and his wife handling a pocketful of jewelry.*

Onesimos: What are you two doing?

Syriskos: *(still unaware of Onesimos)* Look at this gold-plated ring with a bull or a goat carved on the seal. It has "made by Cleostratos" on it.

Onesimos: *(interrupting)* Let me see.

Syriskos: *(without thinking, hands over the ring)* Here. Wait, who are you?

Onesimos: This is the one.

Syriskos: Who is?

Onesimos: The ring.

Syriskos: What do you mean?

Onesimos: It's my master Charisios' ring

Syriskos: You're crazy. Give me that ring.

Onesimos: *(holding the ring up high)* No way. Where did you get it?

Syriskos: What work it is to keep a baby's belongings together. Give me that ring.

Onesimos: You must be kidding. It's my master's.

Syriskos: I'd sooner die than give it to your master. I'll go to court. *(His wife and the baby go into Chaerestratos' house.)* *(to Onesimos)* Now what were you saying?

Onesimos: My master told me that one night, when he

was drunk, he lost this very ring.

Syriskos: I am one of Chaerestratos' slaves. Take and protect the ring if you wish or give it to me for safekeeping.

Onesimos: I shall guard it. But there's a party going on now, so I'll wait until tomorrow to have someone arbitrate this case. *(Exit Onesimos into Chaerestratos' house.)* Maybe I should take up law myself.

Syriskos: It seems to be the only way a person can make sure everything is kept straight. *(Follows Onesimos into the house.)*

Act III

Enter Onesimos from Chaerestratos' house.

Onesimos: I just didn't have the nerve to show my master this ring. He's been quite upset with me lately. He keeps saying he wished I had never told him his wife had been unfaithful and had had a child. He left her and moved into Chaerestratos' house when I told him that gossip. If he ever makes up with her, he'll throw me out.

(Habrotonon, the harpist Charisios hired, rushes out of Chaerestratos' house. Minutes later, Syriskos also rushes out of the house.)

Syriskos: *(seeing Onesimos)* Give me back the ring or show it to your master.

Onesimos: This is my master's ring, but to show it to him now would surely make him the father of the baby with whom it was found.

Syriskos: How can that be?

Onesimos: He lost the ring at the festival in honor of the goddess Artemis. That's the one the women celebrate at night. It seems that some girl was wronged that night. When she gave birth to this baby, she abandoned it with the ring. We must find the girl; otherwise, the situation will be too confusing.

Syriskos: That's up to you. I'm not making any deals.

Onesimos: I agree.

Syriskos: I'm going into town to do some errands. I'll be back to see what must be done.

(Syriskos exits left. Habrotonon approaches Onesimos.)

Habrotonon: Onesimos, is the baby inside the one found by this charcoal burner who just left?

Onesimos: So he says. The baby was found with this ring, which belongs to my master.

Habrotonon: Are you going to let this child, perhaps your master's son, be brought up as a slave? You should be flogged and killed.

Onesimos: No one knows the mother.

Habrotonon: You say your master lost it at the Festival of Artemis. I was there last year, hired as a harpist, and I heard that a man managed to sneak in.

Onesimos: But the girl, the mother, who was she?

Habrotonon: I can ask around. This girl was beautiful and rich, a friend of the women who hired me. I know I'd recognize her if I saw her.

Onesimos: Did she have this ring?

Habrotonon: Perhaps, but I did not see it. Listen to me; tell your master all.

Onesimos: First, let's find out who the girl is. I need your help.

Habrotonon: I couldn't—not until I know who the girl at the feast was. Maybe it wasn't your master. Maybe one of his friends won the ring from him. Maybe his friend lost it to someone else in a game of cards. Anything could have happened. I don't want to look for the girl until I know for certain who the man is. I have a plan. I'll pretend I was the girl. I'll even take the ring and show it to him.

Onesimos: Keep talking. I'm beginning to understand.

Habrotonon: When he sees me with it, he'll ask where I got it. I'll say, "At the Festival of Artemis." Then I'll pretend I was the girl.

Onesimos: Great!

Habrotonon: If he is the one, he'll recognize facts. He'll begin to fill in the details. I'll let him talk, and I'll agree.

When he's done, I'll say, "Charisios, this is your child," and I'll show him the baby.

Onesimos: What an actress and swindler you could be!

Habrotonon: If my plan works and he is the child's father we'll have plenty of time to find the mother.

Onesimos: You forgot to mention one point. If your plan works, he'll set you free.

Habrotonon: Oh, how I wish he would.

Onesimos: What about me? Suppose you double-cross me and decide not to seek the mother?

Habrotonon: Have no fear. I do not wish to be a mother. I just want my freedom. Do you like my idea?

Onesimos: Yes. But if you play any tricks on me, I'll fight back. Let's see how it goes.

Habrotonon: Hand me the ring, quickly!

Onesimos: *(giving the ring)* Here, take it.

Habrotonon: *(taking the ring)* Goddess of Persuasion, please stand by me and help me speak the right words.

(Exit Habrotonon into Chaerestratos' house.)

Onesimos: *(alone)* She is a clever one. She's sure to win her freedom. She'll find a way, while I, a poor stupid fool, cannot get my brain to function, hence I shall always be a slave. Maybe, if her plan works, she'll reward me, too. I deserve it! Alas, have I lost my mind to think that she would thank me? It is best for me to stay away. If Charisios finds out that the mother of his child is from a good family, he'll leave his wife, Pamphila. Yes, I better keep quiet. No more meddling. I give anyone who catches me chattering about permission to cut out my tongue. *(Smikrines enters stage left.)* Smikrines looks quite upset. Maybe he's heard more about Charisios. I think I'll leave.

(Onesimos exits into Chaerestratos' house.)

NB *Only a few lines of the second half of this act survive. The fragments tell us that Habrotonon's plan works. Charisios acknowledges the baby as his and Habrotonon as the mother. When Chaerestratos leaves his house, Smikrines stops him and vows to rescue his daughter Pamphila from the wretched Charisios.*

Act IV

Pamphila and Smikrines emerge from Charisios' house. Smikrines had been begging his daughter to leave her husband. Pamphila has refused.

Smikrines: Listen to me. Your marriage is ruined. Think of the cost Charisios must bear to support two wives. He'll spend all his money keeping up two houses, two wives, two everything.

(Smikrines leaves. Habrotonon emerges from Chaerestratos' house, holding the baby.)

Habrotonon: I shall take this baby out.

Pamphila: *(to herself, not seeing Habrotonon)* Oh, gods, please take pity on me!

Habrotonon: *(sees Pamphila, recognizes her immediately, and whispers to the baby)* Baby dear, here is your mommy!

Pamphila: *(to herself)* I'll go now.

Habrotonon: *(to Pamphila)* One moment, please.

Pamphila: Are you speaking to me?

Habrotonon: Yes. Look at me! Do you know me? *(to herself)* Yes, she is the one I saw at the Festival of Artemis.

Pamphila: *(suddenly noticing the necklace the baby is wearing)* Where did you get this child?

Habrotonon: *(pointing to the necklace and trinkets)* Do you recognize these? Please tell me. Do not be afraid.

Pamphila: *(confused)* Aren't you the mother?

Habrotonon: I pretended I was—not to be deceitful or to cheat the mother but to gain time to find her. Now I have. You are the girl I saw that night.

Pamphila: Who is the baby's father?

Habrotonon: Charisios.

Pamphila: *(startled)* Are you sure?

Habrotonon: Yes. Thank the gods, for they have shown you mercy. *(The door to Chaerestratos' house opens.)* Someone is coming out. Take me into your house and I'll tell you all the details.

(The two women exit into Charisios' house. Onesimos then emerges from Chaerestratos' house.)

Onesimos: He's going crazy. By god, he is crazy. I mean Charisios, my master. How else can you explain his behavior just now? He listened for the longest time while at the door to his house to hear what his wife's father was saying. Then he hit himself hard on the head and said, "Oh, my dear sweet Pamphila! To think I had such a wife as she and I'm so miserable." Then, when he moved away from the door, he burst into a mad rage and even began pulling out his hair. "I am the guilty one, not Pamphila," he wailed. "I have behaved badly—heartless creature that I was." I'm afraid he'll kill me, for I am the one who told on Pamphila. Here he comes now. I'm done for! Zeus save me!

(Onesimos hides as Charisios comes out of Chaerestratos' house.)

Charisios: *(to himself)* I was the innocent partner. The gods have surely treated me as I deserve. Now everyone will know me for what I am—a pompous, boastful brute. And Pamphila still is willing to forgive me. But her father— what do I care about her father? I'll tell him to follow his daughter's wishes.

(Onesimos comes out, with Habrotonon behind him.)

Charisios: What? You again!

Onesimos: *(trembling)* I'm in trouble. *(to Habrotonon)* Please don't abandon me now.

Charisios: You eavesdropper! You were listening to all I said.

Onesimos: No, by the gods I swear, I just came out.

(Habrotonon comes forward.)

Habrotonon: Charisios, you don't know that whole story.

Charisios: What?

Habrotonon: The baby is not mine. I only pretended that.

Charisios: Not yours! Whose is it then? Tell me now.

Habrotonon: Will you free me if I—

Charisios: I'll send you to Hades if you don't tell me now, quickly!

Habrotonon: Your wife is the real mother.

Charisios: Are you certain?

Habrotonon: Yes. Onesimos, you tell him.

Charisios: Are you two testing me?

Onesimos: By the gods, I swear she talked me into this.

Charisios: (to Habrotonon) You sneak!

Habrotonon: Stop! Your wife is the baby's mother, no one else.

Charisios: How I wish she were!

Habrotonon: The baby is hers and yours.

Charisios: Pamphila's and mine?

(After more explanations and discussion, the three go into Charisios' house to see Pamphila.)

Act V

Enter Smikrines, unaware of all that has happened, with Sophrona, Pamphila's old nurse.

Smikrines: (to himself) Sophrona, are you telling me what to do? I'll bash your head in if you are. You old hag, I know what to do about my daughter. That husband of hers is a scoundrel; he'll use up all her money. Remember that pond we passed. I'll drown you there if you don't agree with me. (approaches Charisios' house) The door is locked. I'll bang on it. Open up!

(Onesimos opens the door but stops Smikrines from entering.)

Onesimos: Who's knocking at the door? It's that grouch Smikrines, coming for his dowry and his daughter.

Smikrines: You're right! You scoundrel. By god—

Onesimos: (interrupting) Smikrines, do you really think the gods have enough spare time to go around parceling out good and bad every day?

Smikrines: What a working day they'd have!

Onesimos: Then are you to say that the gods don't care about us? No! They have given each one of us character as our own commander. It is character that condemns a person or saves him. Treat character kindly, and you'll prosper and live well.

Smikrines: You sneak, are you saying my character is behaving badly now?

Onesimos: Yes, it's ruining you. Can you honestly say it's good to take a daughter away from her husband?

Smikrines: Who's talking about good? It's something that has to be done.

Onesimos: (to Sophrona) You see? This man thinks you must do something bad. Something else, not character, is destroying him. Luck has saved you this time. Everything has turned out well. But let me warn you, Smikrines, don't let me catch you doing anything rash again. I acquit you of all charges. Now go in and hold your daughter's child and give it your blessing.

Smikrines: My daughter's child? I'll have you whipped!

Onesimos: You thickheaded dolt! Sophrona, remember the Festival of Artemis.

Smikrines: What?

Sophrona: I think I begin to understand. This is the best we could have hoped for!

Smikrines: If what you say is true. Then the child—

NB *The rest of the play is lost, but the plot is complete. All ends well: The slaves involved are free. Smikrines realizes his errors, and Charisios and Pamphila are reunited along with their child.*

---

*While less than a quarter of Act II has survived, the play does not suffer, since the main purpose of the lost lines was to introduce the audience to the characters and the plot. This was necessary because the ancients had no playbills and the actors wore stock costumes and masks made to represent a type of character rather than a specific individual. The skill and merit of a playwright depended on his treatment of a subject and his handling of the plot.

Project

BACKGROUND

Clothing styles change quite rapidly today. Fads abound and often control what clothing is produced and worn. Yet this was not always true. Among the ancient Greeks and Romans, a style remained unchanged for generations. Ancient dress was simpler, more natural, and more graceful than modern dress. The ancients did not waste material, although authors do mention men and women who spent enormous sums on special dyes for decorating clothes. Purple was the most costly dye. One pound of the best Tyrian purple wool cost more than one thousand dollars. Pins and brooches were other potential expenses, since most clothes were wrapped around the wearer and needed to be fastened in some manner. The method of wrapping, the color and the trim, and the type of fastener were the three parts of ancient dress that were affected by style and changes. The basic design remained the same.

PURPLE DYE

A small quantity of liquid was extracted from the tiny bladders of two Mediterranean sea animals: the trumpet shell snail *(bucinum)* and the purple shell snail *(purpura)*. The bucinum's liquid was

Roman Dressed in a Toga

scarlet colored and the purpura's liquid was a yellowish white that turned a rich purple color when exposed to sun and dampness. The Tyrians poured quantities of purpura mixed with salt into metal vessels. They then heated the mixture with steam to obtain the dye. Bucinum was usually mixed with purpura to prevent fading. Cloth was dipped into the dye a certain number of times to obtain a particular shade. For a

Purple Dye (courtesy of The Bettmann Archive)

29

brighter and more intense purple color—the true Tyrian purple—cloth was dyed twice: first in purpura and then in bucinum.

At first only the hems of clothes worn by officials were colored with genuine Tyrian purple.

An ordinary person used imitation purple. Later, laws were passed forbidding anyone but the emperor to wear clothes dyed with the genuine Tyrian purple.

GREEK CHITON

a. worn by both men and women
b. similar to a long nightgown
c. made of plain, homespun, undyed wool or linen
d. with or without sleeves
e. length depended on wearer and upon his or her occupation
f. many styles and modifications
g. a belt adjusted length and folds

CHITON—Doric Style

a. length of material one foot longer than height of wearer
b. width of material equal to distance from tip to tip of fingertips when hands extended horizontally

To make a chiton, fold down edges A and B a distance equal to the distance from the wearer's neck to his or her waist.

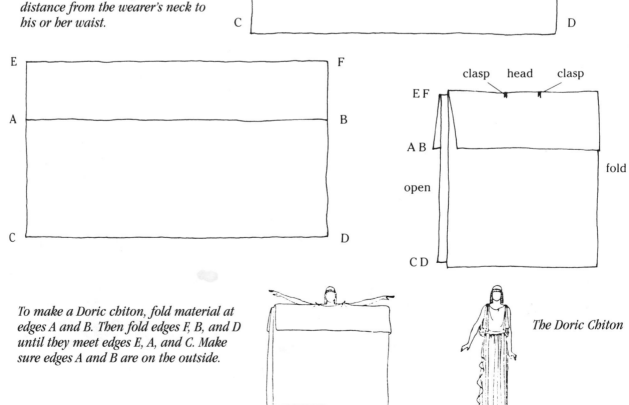

To make a Doric chiton, fold material at edges A and B. Then fold edges F, B, and D until they meet edges E, A, and C. Make sure edges A and B are on the outside.

The Doric Chiton

ROMAN TOGA

a. heavy, white, natural woolen robe
b. worn by Roman citizens
c. official garment until fifth century A.D.
d. symbol of peace—wearer could not move quickly, therefore could not wear toga when fighting
e. used for all special occasions, e.g., when a person became a citizen
f. no foreigner allowed to wear a toga
g. banished Roman citizens not allowed to wear a toga

NINETEENTH-CENTURY RECONSTRUCTION OF TOGA

a. dotted line GC is straight edge of material
b. solid line is cut-out toga
c. FRAB line is a piece of cloth cut out and sewn onto toga
d. dotted line GE equals height of wearer from shoulder to floor
e. GC is a little more than two and one-half times GE

NB *Width of toga at widest point, not counting sewn-in piece, approximately same as GE.*

TO WEAR A TOGA

a. place section E on left shoulder with section G touching ground in front
b. F at back of neck
c. L and M on calves of legs
d. A under right elbow
e. B on stomach
f. carry material to back and under right arm
g. throw material over left shoulder
h. C on top of E
i. OPCA hangs down to ground
j. pull FRA over right shoulder to cover right chest area
k. pull material touching ground in front of left shoulder up away from feet, work it into and around diagonal folds, and let it fall out a little in front. *(See illustration on page 29.)*

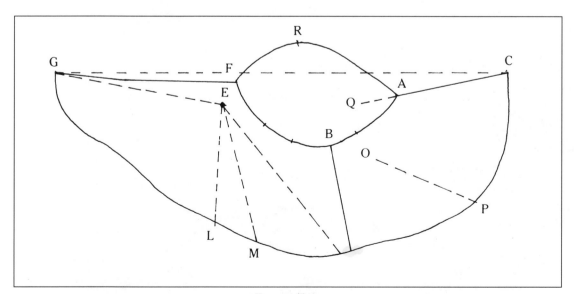

Roman Toga

Puzzle Pages

CROSSWORD PUZZLE

Across

1. Roman word for warship
2. Athenian method of impeachment
4. Attached to prow of Greek warship
6. Type of Greek government
7. What Pheidippides had to swim
9. What Themistocles wanted
10. Ephialtes was one
11. Ahuramazda stood against this
14. Xerxes had thousands of these
15. Best Persian soldiers
16. Ahuramazda represented this
17. Started Persian wars
19. Greeks consulted this oracle
21. Number of miles Pheidippides ran to Athens
22. What Themistocles finally got
23. Themistocles and Miltiades used this to win
24. Greece was divided into these

Down

1. Greek word for warship
3. Race commemorating Pheidippides' run
5. What Greeks fought for
8. Carried by Persian Immortals
12. Wars between Xerxes and Greece
13. What Pheidippides announced
16. Apples of elite Immortals
18. Pheidippides _____ when he reached Athens
20. This race was main event at ancient Olympics

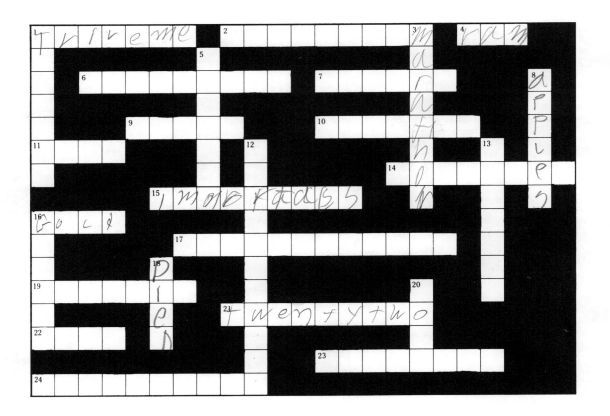

UNSCRAMBLE THE SITES

Unscramble each of the six jumbled sites below to determine the answers to the clues. Place the unscrambled words on the blank lines, then match each letter with its corresponding number to discover where the Spartans bravely died.

1. Sardis was its capital:

   alidy _L_ _ _ _ _d_
        8   10

2. Area of Greece south of Athens:

   sepolnunespo _ _ _L_ _P_ _ _ _ _ _ _ _
          9   7

3. Pheidippides announced this victory:

   rtaoanmh _M_a_r_a_t_h_o_n_
        5   1

4. Xerxes built two bridges across this body of water:

   elotlnepsth _H_e_l_l_e_s_p_o_n_t_
         2   6

5. This city sent five ships to the Ionian colonists:

   rieater _E_r_ _ _ _ _ _
        11 4

6. Xerxes was king of this nation:

   siepar _P_e_r_s_i_a_
        3

Where the Spartans bravely died: _T_h_e_r_m_o_p_y_l_a_e_
               1 2 3 4 5 6 7 8 9 10 11

WORD PUZZLE

Fill in the blanks below using the letters from the Greek runner Pheidippides' name as your clues.

1. Banished Athenian ruler   _ _ _ P _ _ _ _
2. Persian god   _ H _ _ _ _ _ _ _ _
3. King of Lydia   _ _ _ E _ _ _ _
4. Athenian general at Marathon   _ _ _ _ I _ _ _ _ _
5. Greek historian   _ _ _ _ D _ _ _ _
6. Spartan king   _ _ _ _ I _ _ _
7. Greek traitor   _ P _ _ _ _ _ _
8. Fought with Leonidas at Thermopylae   _ _ _ _ P _ _ _ _
9. Greek general   _ _ _ _ I _ _ _ _ _ _ _
10. Persian general   _ _ _ D _ _ _ _ _
11. Persian king   _X_e_r_x_e_s_
12. Zarathustra to Greeks   _ _ _ _ _ _ S _ _ _ _

ON THE ANCIENTS' WORLD WORD FIND

Can you find the thirty words hidden in the maze below? They all can be found in the article "On the Ancients' World" on page 21.

Aegean	Greece	nomads
Agrippa	Greek	Oceanus
Alexandria	Hipparchos	Olympos
Asia	Italy	Ptolemy
Asia Minor	Libya	Pygmaei
Atlas	Lotophagi	Pytheas
Charybdis	maps	Scylla
Cimerii	Massilia	sea
Egypt	Mediterranean Sea	Sirens
Europe	Nicaea	world

```
P Y T H E A S H O N I M A E C W L R
T R O N I M A I S A T S Y N I O O A
O A G R I P P A E E L O B O M R T I
L E E P O R U E A G A P I M E L O R
E A G Y I L S K Y E Y M L A R D P D
M C Y G I U I C H A R Y B D I S H N
Y I P M N A R D Y A T L A S I O A A
D N T A G R E E K L Y O S P A M G X
G R E E C E N S A I L I S S A M I E
S C A I S A S O H C R A P P I H E L
O Y M E D I T E R R A N E A N S E A
```

CAN YOU MATCH?

Match the correct word with the appropriate description.

1. Smikrenes

2. Menander

3. Charisios

4. Habrotonon

5. Davos

6. Pamphila

7. Chaerestratos

8. Athens

9. Onesimos

10. Syriskos

a. Slave who agreed to care for baby

b. Slave who was quite philosophical

c. Believed his son-in-law was a scoundrel and advised his daughter to leave him

d. Greek comic playwright

e. Slave who found the baby

f. A city-state in ancient Greece

g. Baby's father

h. Baby's mother

i. Slave girl who pretended she was the mother of the baby

j. Close friend of Charisios

TRUE OR FALSE?

On the blank line write "True" or "False" about the corresponding statement from the play *Arbitration*.

1. The Greek play *Arbitration* was written as a tragedy. _____

2. The ring and necklace served as clues to the true parents. _____

3. The slaves are portrayed as smarter than their masters. _____

4. Charisios and Habrotonon were the baby's parents. _____

5. All the action takes place outdoors. _____

6. The slave Habrotonon was also a musician. _____

7. Chaerestratos considered his friend Charisios a true scoundrel. _____

8. Habrotonon hoped her role in finding the child's parents would win her her freedom. _____

Topics for Comparison

1. Greek colonists founded numerous settlements throughout the Aegean Sea and Asia Minor. English colonists settled the United States and Canada. Were their reasons similar? Did each set of colonists look at its mother country in the same way? If so, how? If not, explain. Today, centuries later, look at their situations. How does Turkey (Asia Minor) regard Greece, and vice versa? How does the United States regard England, and vice versa? How does Canada regard England, and vice versa?

2. Pheidippides acted patriotically and heroically. He thought more of delivering the message about his country's victory than of himself. Do you know anyone today or in history who has done the same? Compare and contrast the two. *(N.B. The person does not have to die as a result of his actions. A simple comparison could be the Dutch boy who stopped the water from leaking through the dike with his finger.)*

3. After Greece defeated Persia, Athens went on to become a center of learning and a patron of the arts. Why? What happened to produce this effect? Is this characteristic of a country or area that has won its freedom at a terrible cost? Compare and contrast the United States after the American Revolution, France after its revolution, and the Soviet Union after the Bolshevik Revolution.

4. Compare and contrast the heroic stand at Thermopylae in Greece in 480 B.C. with the stand at the Alamo in Texas in 1836.

5. Armies often include one battalion or attachment that is superior to the rest of the troops. The members must first prove themselves worthy of the honor. The Persians had the Immortals with their special insignia, the golden apple. Later the Romans had the Tenth Legion with the golden eagle. Research and explain army insignia. Do our armed forces today use insignia?

6. Ostracism was the approved Athenian method to rid the government of an unwanted politician. It was used on Themistocles. How are such politicians dealt with today? Discuss impeachment, a recall election, and the Senate Ethics Committee.

7. Ephialtes has often been called the Judas of Greece. Why? Compare and contrast his actions with those of Judas Iscariot and his betrayal of Jesus of Nazareth.

Suggestions for Essays and Written Reports

1. What made the ancient Greeks so disunited? Look at Greece's geographical features, the history of its settlement as the result of migrations, and the importance of games and religious festivals to each city-state.

2. Discuss the value of troop size versus strategy on the battlefield. Include examples from Miltiades at Marathon, Leonidas at Thermopylae, and Themistocles at Salamis.

3. Would Xerxes and his brutal, sometimes senseless actions have survived in the West? Why did his subjects follow him when he had practically no regard for human life? Was his power based solely on the fact that in the East the emperor was considered a god?

4. Consider the roles played by the slaves and how each contributed to solving the mystery of the baby's parents. Why do you think Menander left the solution of the problem to the slaves?

5. Reread the play and mark those lines that are humorous. What do you think makes the humor timeless? Next, consider the lines that are philosophical. Is this philosophical advice still applicable today? Why or why not?

Further Activities

1. Map out Persian army routes to Greece using different colors.

2. Do we have any memorial games or events that were instituted by an individual or a group to commemorate an event? If so, when, where, and what are the traditional activities?

3. Try to reconstruct Xerxes' bridge at the Hellespont.

4. Write a play with a plot illustrating the customs of the ancient Persians. Research Persian names for the characters, decide on a setting, and possibly include a Greek traveler as a character.

Remember that in Persia men were important, while women were not, and that bravery on the battlefield was the mark of a patriot.

5. Do further research on the beliefs and traditions of the Eastern religion Zoroastrianism. It is still practiced today by the Ghebers in Iran and the Parsis in India. See if there are any adherents to this faith in your area. If possible, plan to meet with them or visit their place of worship.

6. Research mythological tales about Atlas, Scylla, Charybdis, and the Sirens.

7. Act out the play. Using the footnote (at the end of the play) about masks and costumes as background information, create a mask and costume for each of the characters in the play. Pay special attention to the details of each mask and costume so that the audience can immediately recognize the personality of each character just from the mask and costume.

γνῶθι σεαυτόν

Know thyself.

*written on the wall inside
the temple of Apollo at
Delphi, Greece*

II Greece versus Rome

OVERVIEW

**PEOPLES
INVOLVED:**
Greeks, Romans

DECISIVE BATTLE:
Taras in *Magna
Graecia* ("Great
Greece," or southern
Italy) (280–272 B.C.)

GENERALS:
Pyrrhus (Greek),
Decius Mus (Roman)

**HISTORICAL
SIGNIFICANCE:**
All of southern Italy
becomes subject to
Roman rule after
Taras falls.

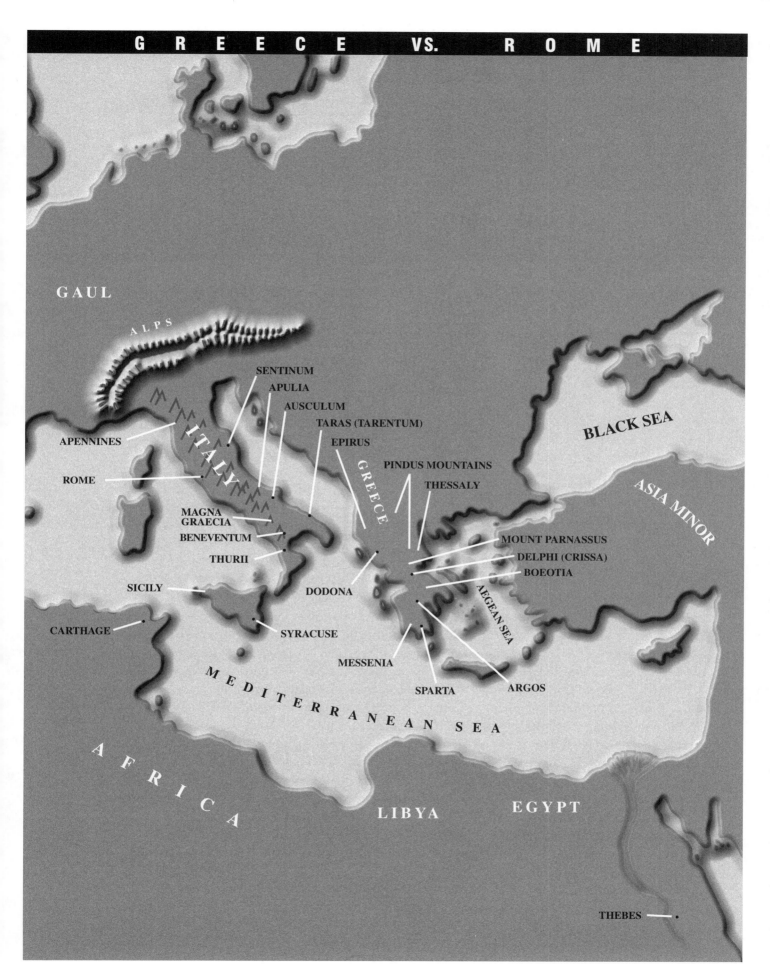

GAUL

ALPS

APENNINES

ITALY

ROME

SENTINUM

APULIA

AUSCULUM

TARAS (TARENTUM)

EPIRUS

GREECE

PINDUS MOUNTAINS

THESSALY

BLACK SEA

ASIA MINOR

MAGNA GRAECIA

BENEVENTUM

THURII

DODONA

MOUNT PARNASSUS

DELPHI (CRISSA)

BOEOTIA

SICILY

SYRACUSE

AEGEAN SEA

CARTHAGE

MESSENIA

SPARTA

ARGOS

MEDITERRANEAN SEA

AFRICA

LIBYA

EGYPT

THEBES

Greek Colonization

Throughout history, hordes of invading tribes have stamped their conquering feet discovering new lands and defeating entire nations. If these marches had not occurred, the course of history would have been unmistakably different. The Greek nation, recognized by generations of historians as the cradle of Western civilization, traces its roots to such invading forces.

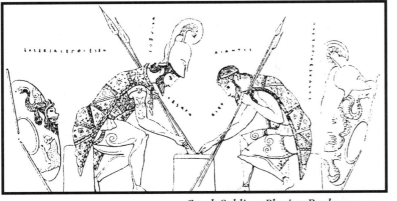

Greek Soldiers Playing Backgammon
(from a Greek vase painting)

Around 2000 B.C., the ancient ancestors of the Greeks migrated from an earlier home somewhere in the East to the lands surrounding the Aegean Sea. These early people, referred to as Indo-Europeans or Aryans (AIR ee un), populated the seacoast and the Aegean islands.

Yet the sea did not become a barrier. Instead, the numerous islands acted as stepping-stones, forming a bridge for travelers and traders to exchange goods, ideas, and customs as they crossed from one shore to the other. While their language and heritage were very similar, each area differed from the other because of the influence of the interior lands on the new coastal communities. Here East did meet West, each exposing the other to its accomplishments and philosophy.

Several generations later, Greece became the home of four main tribes—the Achaeans (uh KEY uns), the Ionians, the Dorians, and the Aeolians (EYE o lee uns).

Around 1100 B.C., marauding tribes from the north began crossing into the lands of Epirus. The inhabitants of Epirus, unable to resist yet unwilling to be conquered, decided to imitate the tactics of their northern neighbors. They crossed the Pindus Mountains, drove out their neighbors, the Dorians, and renamed their new territory Thessaly. Rather than accept defeat, the Dorians also migrated southward, united with the Aeolians, and defeated the Achaeans. The Ionians to the far south resettled with their kinsmen to the north.

These invasions and the accompanying destruction eventually affected, and in some cases completely stopped, Greece's progress as a civilized nation. But the divisions between the regions remained. With these newly established boundary lines, Greece began its influence on Western civilization.

As one tribe displaced another tribe, those who had lost homes or were dissatisfied with their new rulers decided to relocate themselves and their families. The most obvious and logical choice was an Aegean island or an area in Asia Minor, where people with the same ancestry had lived for centuries. In these areas they would encounter no language barrier, and the customs and way of life would be similar. Some Greek colonists, however, did go west to Sicily and southern Italy, which became known as *Magna Graecia* (Latin for "Great Greece").

Conditions in many areas of Greece encouraged colonization. It helped solve several problems plaguing the Greek mainland: poor soil, land ownership in the hands of a few people, primitive plows unable to till the hard soil properly, and the introduction of coinage to replace the barter system, a system especially advantageous to the poor.

Each new colony was recognized as a completely independent state, even by the mother city that had organized the expedition and chose a leader from among the émigrés.

But the new colonies never forgot Greece. The colonists retained their Greek way of life and philosophy. Through its émigrés, Greece slowly became the cradle of Western civilization and was directly responsible for Hellenizing much of the Mediterranean world.

The Colonization of Taras

Colonization was a way of life in early Greece. People emigrated for a variety of reasons: greater freedom and independence, a better life, commercial ventures, and adventure. While most mainland Greek city-states promoted and encouraged colonization, Sparta did not. It had enough land and, as a landlocked city-state, was not interested in commercial ports or adventures. Sparta's firm belief in strict discipline and military fitness instilled in its citizens an unwavering patriotic devotion to the well-being of the city-state.

Early in Sparta's history, around 706 B.C., unusual circumstances arose that did force a group of citizens to exit.

For several years Sparta had been involved in a war with Messenia, an area to the west. The wives of the Spartan soldiers, perhaps

Greek Warrior Receiving Farewell Cup of Wine From a Lady (from a Greek vase painting)

the most patriotic and strictest of all Greek wives, maintained the homeland with fierce pride and dignity. But as time passed, some wives were not faithful to their husbands, and a considerable number of illegitimate children were born. Later, when the women's lawful husbands returned, they appealed to Spartan courts to deny full rights of citizenship to the illegal offspring.

As the children came of age, they banded together to fight this unjust and discriminatory ruling. The circumstances had not been their fault—they were innocent. Sparta had wronged them. Tempers flared, and riots were sure to follow. The rulers of Sparta advised sending a delegation to consult the famed oracle of Delphi. The fate of the illegitimate offspring would rest with the advice of the Delphic priestess.

"Sail west and found your own new colony, where you shall be the masters," was Delphi's advice. And the wronged youths obeyed. They sailed to southern Italy under their leader Phalanthus (fuh LAN thus). There they founded Taras (Tarentum to the Romans). Its position and location—an accessible harbor protected from the Mediterranean Sea by two islands—ensured its prosperity and success both in ancient and in modern times.

NB *The story of Phalanthus and his followers is a legend, but it is believed that Spartans did found Taras. Their exit from the mainland was probably caused by some inequality in the laws concerning the rights of citizens.*

The Battle for Taras

Rome was the growing power in the West, spreading its rule throughout the long boot-shaped peninsula called Italia. Its army was well trained, its government secure, and its citizens patriotic. From one encampment on the Palatine Hill, Rome had spread east and west to the bordering seas and north to the Alps. Its recent victories extended its control southward almost to the "boot." Magna Graecia was still "Great Greece" in name but not in political allegiance. Many southern city-states recognized Rome's power and its inevitable conquest of their lands and pledged themselves to it.

Taras was Magna Graecia's great seaport city. With its impregnable citadel and its strategic location on Italy's instep, Taras began to take offense at Rome's moves. As the possessor of the largest fleet in Italy and of an army of fifteen thousand men, Taras had been and still considered itself the protector of the Greek colonies in southern Italy. Taras even signed a treaty with Rome excluding Roman ships from its waters.

In 282 B.C., Rome ignored this agreement and sent its ships sailing into Italy's instep to protect the Thurii (THU rih ee) who had sought help. Taras was so incensed at Rome's boldness that it attacked the Roman garrison at Thurii and forced it to surrender. When Rome sent envoys to Taras demanding an apology and restitution, Taras insulted the envoys and prepared to wage war against Rome.

The Famous Greek Phalanx
(*from* Comic History of Greece, *by Charles M. Snyder, 1898*)

Taras knew it could not defeat Rome without help. Naturally it turned to Greece and the most powerful of the Greek rulers, Pyrrhus (PIR us) of Epirus. Pyrrhus willingly agreed, rounded up his twenty-five thousand mercenaries, and set sail for Italy.

Pyrrhus easily won his first battle in

280 B.C. His military strategy consisted of a phalanx (FAY langks) of twenty thousand men with their lances and shields interlocked to make the line of battle impenetrable. Pyrrhus also brought with him twenty Indian war elephants. The Roman army met the phalanx bravely, but the elephants routed the Roman cavalry and then the legionnaires themselves. Pyrrhus won the battle, but at a cost of many lives, both Roman and Greek.

In 279 B.C., Pyrrhus again met the Roman army under the heroic Decius Mus near Ausculum in northern Apulia. Again he defeated them, and again he suffered great losses (c. 6,000 men). Pyrrhus sought a treaty with Rome that guaranteed Taras' freedom, but the Romans declined.

Pyrrhus then led his army into Sicily. The reason for this is uncertain; perhaps he hoped to win more territory. His army was victorious across the island, and Pyrrhus became known as the king of Sicily. But during his three-year sojourn on the island, Rome advanced its armies into southern Italy and recaptured every city-state except Taras.

The same was happening in Sicily. Carthage, the north African power that controlled much of Sicily prior to Pyrrhus' arrival, began reclaiming its territories. Pyrrhus left for Italy. This time he did not defeat the Romans. Rome had learned to throw javelins at the elephants, causing them to go wild and turn on their own men.

Finally, with only one-third of his original army as survivors, Pyrrhus marched back to Taras and shortly thereafter sailed home to Epirus. Taras stood alone and in 272 B.C. signed an alliance with Rome. All of Magna Graecia was now Rome's.

NB *Any victory, military or otherwise, that is won at a great cost is called a Pyrrhic victory.*

Pyrrhus

After the death of Alexander the Great in 323 B.C., no single individual arose to command his empire. The lands he had conquered were too vast. Gradually military commanders arose and assumed control of various areas. General Pyrrhus, who claimed to be a cousin of Alexander, won control of Epirus in northwestern Greece.

As a soldier and military leader Pyrrhus was a clever and quick thinker; his tactics and strategies were well thought out and planned. After extending his rule across Epirus and making it one of Greece's largest and most powerful kingdoms, he eagerly sought to expand his territory. When the Greeks of Taras in southern Italy sought his aid, he quickly agreed. His soldiers were mostly mercenaries, men trained for war and paid to fight.

Pyrrhus

Pyrrhus did win decisive victories, first in Magna Graecia and then in Sicily; but he did not follow them up. His long-term goal was a huge empire, but he did not persevere in obtaining it. He won, moved on, won, moved on. By not remaining after a victory to ensure obedience by those he had conquered, he left the defeated free to regroup and attack again. When victory produced huge losses, Pyrrhus lost heart, and, as a result, so did his troops.

Pyrrhus returned to Epirus only to get involved in more power struggles. In a desperate street battle in Argos, he was killed by a tile that a woman threw from a housetop.

Decius Mus

When Pyrrhus, king of Epirus, answered Taras' call for help, Rome prepared for a difficult battle. Decius Mus, one of Rome's consuls and an excellent general, undertook command of the army. Soldiers and statesmen still told of how his father and grandfather (both of the same name, Decius Mus) had heroically given their lives in battle decades earlier.

Young Decius Mus fought well and with great courage but did not have the opportunity to practice *devotio* as his father and grandfather had.

DECIUS MUS—GRANDFATHER (DIED 337 B.C.)

Each of the Roman consuls had a dream the night before the great battle versus the Latins. In it each had been told that the leader of one side and the army of the other side were "devoted" to death. The next morning the consuls agreed that should any of their troops begin to waver or fall back, the leader in charge of that wing would charge headlong into the enemy, "devoting" himself and the enemy's army to death. In the ensuing battle, Decius' left wing began to have difficulties. The courageous consul remembered his vow and charged into the thickest part of the enemy. He fought bravely and heroically to his death. Soon thereafter, the Latins admitted defeat and surrendered to the Romans.

DECIUS MUS—FATHER (DIED 296 B.C.)

In 296 B.C., the Romans were fighting for control of more land in Italy. At Sentinum in the Apennines, the Romans won a battle that confirmed their power on the Italian peninsula. Decius Mus led the left wing against the Gauls, who had allied themselves with the Italians. When his troops began to waver, Decius remembered the example of his father and rushed headlong into the enemy's forces. This diverted their attention and allowed the Romans to regroup and regain their confidence by watching the brave and selfless example of their leader.

Roman Horseman

Two Noble Romans

Roman authors enjoyed recounting the following tales of two Romans who fought against Pyrrhus in the war for southern Italy. Each leader symbolized the patriotic spirit and the integrity of the early Romans.

FABRICIUS

After Pyrrhus defeated the Roman army in 280 B.C., Fabricius was appointed envoy. His mission was to negotiate an exchange of prisoners or, at best, a ransom for the Roman prisoners.

Pyrrhus warmly welcomed Fabricius into his court and tried to win his favor. Pyrrhus offered Fabricius many sumptuous gifts, and even a position in his army, all of which he flatly refused.

In 279 B.C., Fabricius lost another major battle to Pyrrhus. In 278 B.C., after a more favorable battle, Fabricius again negotiated with Pyrrhus. This time the Greek king agreed to leave Italy. The surrender to Pyrrhus of a Greek traitor who had offered to poison him is believed to have been one of the reasons he cooperated so readily with the Romans.

Fabricius had no desire for wealth. He lived simply on the farm he had inherited, refusing numerous bribes and all offers of luxury. Fabricius served when called and served selflessly. The glory and honor of his homeland were his only motives.

CURIUS DENTATUS

Like Fabricius, Curius Dentatus also fought against Pyrrhus, leading armies against Rome's southern neighbors. In 275 B.C., his army defeated Pyrrhus decisively near Beneventum. After Pyrrhus' exit from Italy, Curius Dentatus won many battles against other areas in southern Italy still opposed to Roman rule.

Curius, like Fabricius, refused all presents and bribes. After his military successes and the many resulting honors, he simply retired to the farm he had inherited. The glory and honor of Rome were his two concerns. To preserve them, he would give all.

Roman Devotion to Mars

The Romans loved Mars, their god of war. Before every battle a Roman general and his soldiers prayed to Mars for help and guidance. Whenever a victorious army returned to Rome, everything that had been won in battle was dedicated to Mars at the Campus Martius, Latin for "Field of Mars." All military maneuvers and athletic contests also were held there.

During the cold and snowy winter months, the Romans waged war only if an emergency or a rebellion arose. As warmer weather approached, so did the time for military campaigns. The Romans named the month when the army set out on the field after the god of war. We derive our term "March" from the Latin *Martius*.

Mars had been Rome's protector for centuries. In very ancient times, a terrible epidemic raged through Rome. Fearing that everyone would die, the surviving Romans rushed to the temple of Mars. They prayed and asked Mars for help. A shield fell from the sky, and as it landed, a voice was heard saying that Rome would be safe as long as this shield was preserved. Not only did Mars send this shield, but that same day, March 1, he stopped the plague.

To prevent thieves from stealing this gift, the Romans commissioned a blacksmith named Mamurius Veturius to make eleven exact copies of the original shield. All twelve were placed in the temple of Mars in the Campus Martius, but only the priests of Mars knew which was the original shield.

Roman Army on the March

As a result of this incident, the Romans felt that all military expeditions should begin in the month of March. In fact, before a Roman general left on a military campaign, he always touched the sacred shield with the point of his lance.

A group of twelve priests guarded the shield and conducted the ceremonies held before an army left on a campaign. On March 1, these priests, dressed in embroidered tunics (similar to long T-shirts), bronze breast-plates, and

Salii Carrying Sacred Shield of Mars

pointed helmets, led a procession through the center of Rome. Each priest had a sword at his waist, carried a staff in his right hand, and held a holy shield in his left hand.

The priests stopped at every altar and temple. In full armor, they performed a war dance to expel all the evil spirits that might have entered the city during the winter. Since the Latin verb meaning "to dance" is *salire,* these priests came to be known as the *Salii* (SAH lih ee). Not only did they dance, but they beat on their shields and sang special songs.

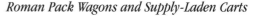

Roman Pack Wagons and Supply-Laden Carts

The procession continued through March 24, ending each day at an appointed place where the shields were kept in special houses until the next morning. At certain times during the three-week period, all horses, shields, and other weapons used in battle were cleaned and made ready for new campaigns.

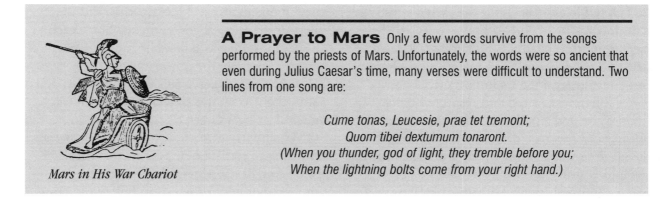

Mars in His War Chariot

A Prayer to Mars Only a few words survive from the songs performed by the priests of Mars. Unfortunately, the words were so ancient that even during Julius Caesar's time, many verses were difficult to understand. Two lines from one song are:

Cume tonas, Leucesie, prae tet tremont;
Quom tibei dextumum tonaront.
(When you thunder, god of light, they tremble before you;
When the lightning bolts come from your right hand.)

The Sacred Greek Oracles

Throughout history, the desire to know the future has been a powerful motivating force. Every generation has discovered and developed numerous ways to predict its destiny. The ancient Greeks believed that the gods willingly and frequently spoke to mortals in unique ways at special sites. A petitioner approaching such a site to ask the particular god's advice was said to be consulting the oracle.

The oldest oracle in Greece was Dodona, located in Epirus, a stormy and mountainous northwestern area. The Greek epic writer Homer (fl. c. 700 B.C.) mentioned Dodona in his *Iliad* and *Odyssey*. Homer described the priests has having "unwashed feet" and sleeping on the ground. Dodona was dedicated to Zeus, king of gods and men. Here the oracle spoke from a sacred oak tree. The noise made by the wind rustling through the trees was believed to be the commands and wishes of the god. Since these sounds often blended together, the ancients hung bronze vases from the tree branches. When the wind blew, the suspended vases moved, sometimes tapping one another. Priests and priestesses were appointed to interpret the various sounds. As the decades passed, another method of consulting the oracle was introduced. The suppliant put his or her question on a leaden strip and placed it in a jar. The question was then given to the priestess to interpret.

In 219 B.C., the temple was destroyed by invading Greek tribes, and the sacred oaks were cut down. The people of Epirus restored the area, but after invading Roman troops destroyed the area for a second time in 167 B.C., Dodona never again regained its importance.

The most sacred and respected oracle was that of the god Apollo at Delphi in central Greece. As was true of most oracular sites, the location of the Delphic oracle was awe inspiring. Delphi is situated on the lofty slopes of eight-thousand-foot-high Mount Parnassus. To the north and east, eight hundred feet above the sanctuary of the god, are two huge mountainous masses separated by a deep gorge through which flows the cool, sacred spring of Castalia. To the south is a ravine made by the Plistus River. In addition, the threat of a rock slide or of a sudden opening of the earth is always present in this earthquake-prone area. One can imagine how dwarfed a suppliant felt as he or she climbed the steep incline to Apollo's temple built on a semicircular terrace. Every petitioner also must have been overwhelmed by the serene beauty of the lush scenery and the sparkling blue water below.

The priests and priestesses at Delphi were consulted by representatives from all the Greek city-states, as well as by foreigners, and often knew more about world affairs than did the rulers of the various governments. Since each Greek city-state was politically independent, the oracles, especially the one at Delphi, helped to unify the Greek people spiritually, morally, and politically. No matter of real importance was undertaken by a Greek city-state or by an individual without consulting an oracle. Before venturing to settle a new colony, the Greeks always sought the approval of the oracle. In time, foreign nations began to follow the same practice.

Origin of the Oracle of Dodona

The origin of Dodona is recounted in this ancient tale. In very early times, two black doves flew away from the Egyptian city of Thebes. One dove flew to Libya and the other to Dodona. The latter perched on the branch of an oak tree and began speaking with a human voice. She instructed her listeners to consecrate the tree and the area surrounding it to Zeus. The dove that flew to Libya did the same, consecrating her area to Ammon, a principal god of that region.

Origin of the Oracle of Delphi

Legend says that Apollo traveled throughout Greece until he arrived in Boeotia (boy O tee a) in eastern Greece. As he prepared to lay the foundation of the temple, the nymph of the nearby stream advised him to seek a location elsewhere. She told him that the constant noise of horses and mules quenching their thirst in the stream had robbed the area of the silence needed for an oracular site. (Perhaps she feared his worship would overshadow her and her stream.)

Consulting the Delphic Oracle (from Comic History of Greece, *by Charles M. Snyder, 1898)*

Apollo then proceeded to Crissa near Mount Parnassus in central Greece, as the nymph had advised. The lush green hills, the magnificent vistas, and the sublime solitude of the area won over Apollo. Yet all did not proceed smoothly. A horrible, slimy serpent had been destroying the countryside mercilessly. After a dreadful fight, Apollo finally slew the serpent with golden arrows. Placing his foot on the dying monster, he cried, *"Puthen!"* (which is Greek for "Now rot!"). The creature then became known as the Python or Pytho; the games celebrated every four years in joyous commemoration of this victory were called the Pythian Games, and Apollo's special priestess at Delphi was named the Pythia (PITH ee uh).

After defeating the serpent, Apollo needed priests for his temple. As he looked out over the sea, he saw a ship sailing from the Mediterranean island of Crete. Immediately Apollo dove into the sea, changed himself into a dolphin, and jumped aboard the ship. Startled and frightened, the crew watched in amazement as the ship, with the incredible dolphin at the helm, seemed to steer its own course. Soon the vessel entered the bay of Crissa.

What was happening? No one knew. Suddenly the strange dolphin lifted upward toward the sky and turned into a blazing star. Before the crew could regain its senses, Apollo again approached them dressed as a young man. Calmly he asked them who they were. Eager for information about the area, they in turn questioned him. Apollo then revealed himself as a god and invited them to become the priests of his new temple. Because he had appeared to them first as a dolphin (in Greek, *delphis*), he requested that his priests and followers call him Apollo Delphinus. Legend also says that for this same reason the name of Crissa was changed to Delphi.

Croesus Consults the Oracle

In the sixth century B.C., the famed Croesus (KREE sUS) ruled Lydia, a country in western Asia Minor (present-day Turkey). During his reign he subdued all the nations between the Aegean Sea and the River Halys (HAY liss), an area that included many Greek colonies. These conquests, in addition to many successful commercial ventures, brought Croesus and his kingdom tremendous wealth. In return Croesus generously supported the arts, sciences, and literature. He also invited numerous philosophers and poets to his court. One was the renowned Athenian lawgiver Solon, whose interview with the king was celebrated throughout antiquity.

Croesus asked Solon to name the happiest person in the world. Solon replied that he could name no living person, for a truly happy individual was one who was content at the time he died. These wise words would later save Croesus' life.

At this time Croesus considered himself blessed by the gods. Yet he did have one problem—the growing Persian Empire in the East. After much discussion as to whether the Lydians should march on the Persians, Croesus decided to send a representative to the oracle at Delphi.

After Croesus' envoy had paid his offering and provided the sacrificial victims, he was informed that the signs were favorable. He then proceeded to the area of the temple where an opening in the stone floor exposed the rough surface of Mount Parnassus. Over the mouth of this opening was a golden tripod on which the Pythia sat. Close beside her was a golden statue of the god Apollo. It was believed by many that vapors arose from the mountainside that helped inspire the priestess. History tells us that the Pythia spent three days preparing for this solemn occasion by fasting, chewing laurel leaves, and bathing in the sacred Castalian Spring.

Apollo never addressed his suppliants directly, but spoke through his priestess. In very early times the Pythia was the young daughter of one of the

Croesus on the Pyre

noble families of Delphi. However, after one beautiful priestess was kidnapped by a young noble, the regulations were revised and priestesses were selected from honorable women over fifty years of age.

Since the Pythia's utterances were delivered in a state of frenzy and were difficult to understand, a priest stood beside her in order to interpret the divine words. The priest's translations, however, were usually quite vague and ambiguous.

Croesus' question "Should I march on the Persians?" was answered in this way: "If Croesus attacks the Persians, he will destroy a mighty empire." Croesus was overjoyed when he was informed of the divine reply. He thought that he would destroy the mighty Persian Empire.

In 546 B.C., the overconfident Croesus attacked the army of the Persian king Cyrus. Croesus' army was destroyed, and he was taken prisoner. As the condemned Croesus sat above the pyre on which he was to be burned, he remembered Solon's advice about happiness. Three times he cried aloud, "Oh, Solon!" Cyrus, who was standing nearby, asked Croesus his reason for calling this name. The Lydian king then told the Persian king of his interview with that wise Athenian. Cyrus was so taken by this definition of happiness that he ordered his men not to light the pyre. But it was too late. Flames were already shooting forth around Croesus. Croesus raised his eyes to the heavens and prayed to Apollo. Immediately the skies opened and torrential rains fell, extinguishing the flames.

Croesus then descended the pyre and approached his conqueror. He asked Cyrus what the Persian soldiers were doing. Cyrus replied that they were stealing Croesus' riches. Croesus simply stated, "This is no longer my city, but yours. Therefore, your men are stealing your treasures." Impressed by such a wise reply, Cyrus engaged Croesus as one of his advisors.

Croesus, however, was still bewildered because of the Delphic oracle's "false" utterance. He sent a messenger to Delphi to express his feelings. The envoy quickly returned with the oracle's reply: "Croesus did attack the Persians and did destroy a mighty empire, his own."

Why the Greeks Called Themselves the Hellenes

The ancient Greeks referred to themselves as Hellenes and to their country as Hellas. According to Greek mythology, Zeus, the king of gods and men, had a son named Hellen. Hellen's three sons (Dorus, Aeolus, and Xuthus) and two grandsons (Ion and Achaeus) became the mythical founders of the four tribes that inhabited Greece: the Dorians, Aeolians, Achaeans, and Ionians. Hellen gave his name to the country and to the people.

It was the Romans who first called the land across the Adriatic Sea *Graecia* and its inhabitants the *Graeci* (GREYE key). Legend says that the first tribes the Romans met when they crossed the Adriatic called themselves the Graeci; hence, the Romans used Graeci to represent all the inhabitants of Hellas.

On Language

LATIN, GREEK, AND ENGLISH

About five thousand years ago, the people living between central Europe and western Asia spoke the same basic language, Indo-European (or Aryan). Sometime between 4000 and 2000 B.C., the various people in this area began a massive campaign to expand their territories. They easily triumphed and assumed control of their newly won lands. Their advantage over their enemies was the horse, which gave them speed, height, and a good overview of any battlefield. The conquests by the Indo-Europeans were swift and absolute.

Soon Indo-Europeans were found in India, Greece, Italy, France, Germany, the Balkans, and Iran. The invaders brought with them their language, which was gradually affected by the native dialects. New languages (modified versions of the Indo-European and native) emerged as rulers and natives sought one common language to represent the combination of people.

Since early Latin was a language spoken by people who fought and struggled for survival, its vocabulary reflected a difficult lifestyle. However, as Rome conquered more lands and became more prosperous, its language changed to meet its needs. Roman soldiers, businessmen, and public officials took their language with them, introducing Latin to people everywhere. The Romans, in turn, were introduced to other languages. Whenever the Romans encountered objects and ideas in foreign lands that were unfamiliar to them, they often found it easier to adopt the foreign word rather than to invent their own. The same was true for the conquered people.

In the first century A.D., Christianity began to spread. As the number of its followers grew, so did the effect on the language they spoke. Since Latin was spoken everywhere throughout the Mediterranean world, Christian leaders chose it as the common language to spread their beliefs. As the years passed and the various forms of Latin continually mixed with native dialects, distinct language patterns began to emerge across western Europe. French was first used officially in A.D. 842. Written Spanish and Italian appeared in A.D. 950 and 960, respectively.

The languages that derive their grammatical constructions and vocabulary directly from Latin are called the Romance languages. These include French, Italian, Portuguese, Romanian, and Spanish.

Centuries later, a reversal occurred. As the nations of western Europe emerged and grew, their peoples began to seek more information about the ancient Greeks and Romans. They began adopting many of the ancients' ideas and words. This process of borrowing, adapting, and adopting eventually resulted in Latin words becoming the basis of more than fifty percent of our English vocabulary and Greek accounting for more than ten percent.

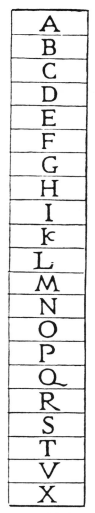

Latin Alphabet

Esperanto: A Universal Language

Language provides us with the ability to communicate and exchange ideas, inventions, and criticisms. In this way language promotes progress. Yet language also can impede progress if communication is not possible because of the inability to understand another language.

Numerous attempts have been made to invent an artificial, internationally recognized language that would be simple to learn and easy to understand. The most widely accepted language has been Esperanto, meaning "one who hopes." It was introduced by Dr. Ludwig L. Zamensky of Poland in 1887. Today, millions of people have studied it and are able to speak it. Some schools teach it. Some radio stations, newspapers, and magazines use it.

The greatest percentage of Esperanto's vocabulary is from Latin and the Romance languages. The Germanic and Slavic (Eastern European and Russian) languages also have contributed some words.

Esperanto, which is pronounced as spelled, has twenty-two English letters (it does not have our q, w, x, y) and the letters ĉ, ĝ, ĥ, ĵ, ŝ, û. Nouns end in "o," adjectives in "a," adverbs in "e," and verb infinitives in "i."

To identify the tense of a verb, an "as" ending indicates the present tense, "is" the past, "os" the future, and "u" the imperative (a command). The definite article "the" is always "la." To change a masculine noun to a feminine form, "in" is inserted before the "o" noun ending. For example, *frato* is the Esperanto word for "brother," and *fratino* is the word for "sister."

Below is a paragraph written in Esperanto. Using the brief rules above as your guide, see if you can translate it.

> *La inteligenta persono lernas Esperanto rapide kaj facile.*
> *Esperanto estas la moderna lingvo por la mondo. Simpla kaj praktika*
> *solvo de la internacia problemo de universala interkompreno,*
> *Esperanto meritas vian seriosan konsideron. Lernu Esperanto.*

Αα	Ββ	Γγ	Δδ	Εε	Ζξ	Ηη	Θθ	Ιι	Κκ	Λλ	Μμ
ALPHA	BETA	GAMMA	DELTA	EPSILON	ZETA	ETA	THETA	IOTA	KAPPA	LAMBDA	MU

Νν	Ξξ	Οο	Ππ	Ρρ	Σσς	Ττ	Υυ	Φφ	Χχ	Ψψ	Ωω
NU	XI	OMICRON	PI	RHO	SIGMA	TAU	UPSILON	PHI	CHI	PSI	OMEGA

Greek Alphabet

Archimedes and the Siege of Syracuse

A play about the weapons and strategies devised by Archimedes to outsmart the enemy

CHARACTERS

Archimedes—*great mathematician and inventor*
King Hieron—*king of Syracuse*
Prince Gelon—*son of Hieron*
Prince Hieronymus—*grandson of Hieron and son of Gelon*
Hippocrates—*traitor who seized control of Syracuse*
Marcellus—*Roman commander*
Roman Lieutenant
Roman Engineer
Roman Soldiers

Syracuse, a peaceful and thriving city on the island of Sicily, a colony of Greece off the southern coast of Italy, was the home of the famous mathematician and inventor Archimedes. During the reign of King Hieron (some sources spell the name Hiero), Syracuse found itself affected by a fierce conflict between Rome and Carthage, a powerful city-state on the north coast of Africa.

The Romans and the Carthaginians were vying for control of the Mediterranean Sea. Carthage already had colonies in Spain and claimed all of the western Mediterranean and most of Sicily except for Syracuse. Rome's armies had been capturing the Greek city-states in southern Italy. It was not unreasonable to expect that Syracuse, because of its location, would be caught in a war between the rapidly growing powers.

Act I

It is the year 220 B.C. Syracuse has an alliance with Rome, but King Hieron is wondering how long this will last. Carthage has a great fleet of ships, and the Romans are involved militarily on many fronts and cannot be relied on for protection. King Hieron needs a plan to defend his vulnerable city and turns to his longtime friend and kinsman Archimedes for advice and help.

Scene 1: *The royal palace of King Hieron. The king and his son, Prince Gelon, have received news that the Romans are angry at the Carthaginians because they cannot trade in Sicily. Carthage has recently gained control of the Strait of Messina, which separates Sicily and Italy. The king has just sent for his friend Archimedes.*

King Hieron: My son, I fear for the safety of our city. Rome will not tolerate the aggressive actions of Carthage, and there will be a war.

Prince Gelon: I agree. This is a dangerous situation. Rome will be cut off from its own ports in eastern Italy. The Romans cannot even sail around Sicily because Carthage also controls the western Mediterranean. All-out war is inevitable, and we will be caught in the middle.

King Hieron: We must prepare to defend ourselves, even though we have an alliance with Rome. They could not possibly come to our rescue against the

Carthaginians. They are already fighting in many different areas and cannot spare the soldiers or ships to protect our city.

Prince Gelon: I would not trust the Romans to continue to be our allies. They are an ambitious nation, and I am sure they will want to add our prosperous city to their growing empire.

King Hieron: I think you are right. That is why I want to build up our defenses. It is my hope that I will leave a strong, independent city for you and my grandson, Prince Hieronymus, to inherit. I have sent for Archimedes so that we can discuss this serious situation with him. I value his advice.

Prince Gelon: I also have great respect for Archimedes, but how can he help to defend our city? He is a mathematician, not a soldier.

(Archimedes enters the royal chamber and hears Prince Gelon's statement.)

Archimedes: You are right, Your Royal Highness. Since I returned to Syracuse from Egypt many years ago, I have dedicated my life entirely to mathematical research.

King Hieron: You know as well as I do, my friend, that you also have become famous for your clever mechanical inventions.

Archimedes: They are only the diversions of geometry at play, and I attach no importance to them. I regard the business of mechanics as vulgar and despicable.

King Hieron: Syracuse is in danger of becoming involved in the war between Rome and Carthage.

Archimedes: So I have heard.

King Hieron: Having been at peace for so many years, we have not bothered to maintain our defenses. We forgot that our city was once taken by siege years ago. I do not want that to happen again. Archimedes, I implore you to use your wealth of scientific knowledge to prepare for me offensive and defensive engines that can be used in every kind of siege warfare.

Archimedes: I do not like the idea of using science to destroy people.

King Hieron: Why can't you use some of your scientific knowledge to defend the city that has sheltered you and given you the freedom to do your mathematical research for so many years? I should think that you would be anxious to prove that science can provide a better means to defend Syracuse than an army can.

Archimedes: You have won. I will begin at once to devise plans for all sorts of engines to use against any besiegers.

King Hieron: We will all be grateful for your expertise.

Scene 2: *Several months later. King Hieron, Prince Gelon, Prince Hieronymus, and Archimedes are standing on the battlements of Syracuse inspecting the newly built war machines designed by the famous mathematician. Once Archimedes set his mind to this project, he drew plan after plan, and each machine was constructed by the king's workmen.*

War Machines of Archimedes

King Hieron: I am very pleased by your fast and productive work, Archimedes. I knew we could rely on you to strengthen our city with your clever inventions.

Archimedes: Thank you, Your Majesty. I used all the knowledge about mechanics that I have gained over the years.

Prince Gelon: Would you describe the functions of some of these war machines to us? My son, Hieronymus, and I are curious as to their use. They all look so ingeniously made.

Archimedes: I would be happy to, Your Royal Highness. *(pointing to the various machines)* Those are catapults that can fling heavy stones at long or short ranges. Over there are machines that can discharge showers of missiles through holes made in the walls.

Prince Hieronymus: Why are those poles jutting out beyond the walls?

Archimedes: Some of them are to be used to drop heavy stones or pieces of lead on enemy ships.

Prince Gelon: What are those objects hanging from some poles that look like the beaks of cranes?

Archimedes: They are iron claws that will be lowered to grapple the prows of ships, lifting them into the air and swinging them until the sailors fall out, then dropping the vessels onto the rocks, where they will be smashed.

Prince Hieronymus: What are all those mirrors for?

Archimedes: I intend to use them to direct the sun's rays at the attacking ships, blinding the sailors so that they become confused and cannot fight back. They can be effective only if the sun is shining intensely, of course.

King Hieron: Our city should be safe from any attack by our enemies. Until we are besieged, I command that these machines be stored away but kept in perfect working condition. The ropes must never become frayed, any rotted wood is to be replaced, and none of the metal can be allowed to corrode in the salt air. I also command that we always have men trained to operate the machines, even if it is years

before we need to use them. Let us return to the palace. Knowing that my city is well protected, I can now sleep in peace.

Act II

It is about 212 B.C. King Hieron died in 215 B.C.; his son, Prince Gelon, died soon after. His grandson, Hieronymus, then became king of Syracuse.

Hieronymus did not stay king for long. He was soon murdered by a treacherous man named Hippocrates, who had been bribed by Carthage. When Hippocrates took control of Syracuse, he broke the alliance the city had had for many years with Rome almost immediately. He then made a new alliance with his friends in Carthage.

Naturally, Rome was very angry at losing such a valuable ally and immediately declared war on Syracuse. Marcellus, a famous Roman general and a personal enemy of Hippocrates, was sent with a large fleet of ships and an army to seize Syracuse from the Carthaginians. He was determined to gain control of the Strait of Messina so that Roman ships could finally use it safely.

Scene 1: *The battlements of Syracuse. A large Roman fleet is approaching the city, and the frightened people are pleading with Hippocrates to protect them. He has called upon Archimedes to ready his war machines. The mathematician does not like the traitor who now rules his city, but Archimedes must think of protecting his fellow citizens.*

Hippocrates: Archimedes, I beg you to use your war machines to repel the Roman besiegers. Their army surrounds us on land, and their fleet of sixty ships is about to attack us by sea.

Archimedes: Where are your friends from Carthage?

Hippocrates: We cannot wait for their help. We must stop the Romans now before it is too late.

Archimedes: The machines have been kept in excellent condition since they were first built, and the men trained to operate them are ready.

Hippocrates: What is that harp-shaped contraption

built on a platform on those Roman ships? It looks frightening.

Archimedes: That is called a sambuca, after the musical instrument it resembles. It carries a broad scaling ladder that, when pulled up, makes it possible for the men to scale the walls.

Hippocrates: Swarms of Roman soldiers will be pouring into our city if we do not destroy the sambuca first.

Archimedes: Do not worry. The cranes I have constructed on the walls will drop large stones on the ships before the soldiers can climb the ladders.

Hippocrates: How shall we stop the land forces that are approaching?

Archimedes: I have created engines that will shoot all sorts of missiles and large quantities of stones with great speed at the invading army. The soldiers will be knocked down and thrown into confusion.

Hippocrates: The stories I have heard of your cleverness are true. You have contrived all sorts of war machines to use against our enemies. Let us prepare them for action at once.

(The two men leave immediately, for the invading forces will soon be upon Syracuse.)

Scene 2: *The camp of Marcellus, just outside the walls of Syracuse. The Roman commander is conferring with his officers and engineers after a devastating attempt to besiege the city.*

Marcellus: *(looking up at the walls of Syracuse)* We are certainly up against a formidable foe. All that I have heard of this Archimedes must be true. *(turning to his engineers and officers)* How do his war machines work?

Roman Lieutenant: Some of my men think that they are fighting against the gods because many missiles are thrown at them so rapidly.

Roman Engineer: The machines have been contrived by a man who has studied mathematics extensively. Archimedes has made great engines that are working models of geometry and mechanics. He uses levers and pulleys, cranks and cogwheels, and screws, as well as his knowledge of balance and centers of gravity.

Marcellus: How are they powered?

Roman Engineer: By manpower, air power, and water power.

Roman Lieutenant: These war machines destroy our ships and kill our soldiers so effectively that my soldiers become frightened whenever they see a rope or piece of wood projecting from the walls of the city. They run away shouting that another machine is appearing to kill them.

Marcellus: *(turning in jest to his own engineers)* Let us stop fighting this geometrical Briareus* who treats our ships as if they were cups to ladle water from the sea, has destroyed our sambuca, and has shot many missiles against us, outdoing the hundred-handed monsters of mythology.

Roman Lieutenant: Look! Archimedes is aiming one of his engines at us. We must flee.

Marcellus: *(turning to his lieutenant)* I command that we end all fighting and assaults on the city and retreat to safety. Instead we shall begin to prepare for a long siege and conquer the other areas of Sicily that are held by the Carthaginians.

Syracuse remained unconquered for some time while Marcellus captured the ancient city of Megara; took the camp of Hippocrates at Acrillae, killing eight thousand men as they were building entrenchments; and overran much of Sicily. He was victorious everywhere he led his army.

Marcellus returned with the intention of blockading Syracuse by land and sea. He came upon the city as the citizens were celebrating a festival in honor of the goddess Artemis. He noticed that a tower and wall had been left poorly guarded and promptly had his men build ladders to scale the wall at night and take the city by surprise. At dawn Marcellus ordered trumpets to sound, and the startled Syracusans fled in terror, thinking that the entire city was being overrun by the Romans.

Syracuse was soon in Marcellus' possession, and as he surveyed the noble and beautiful city from a high point, he wept because he knew its impending fate. As was the custom in those days, the city was sacked by the conquering army, but Marcellus would not allow any free citizens to be killed or enslaved. He was especially anxious to save the life of Archimedes, for whom he had developed much respect, and he immediately sent for him.

Scene 3: *The house of Archimedes in Syracuse. The mathematician is concentrating so intently on a diagram he has drawn in glass dust that he has not heard the clamor created by the invading Romans, not even the blaring of trumpets. A soldier sent by Marcellus enters the house with orders to bring Archimedes to the Roman commander at once.*

Roman Soldier: *(bursting into the house)* Is this the home of Archimedes?

(Archimedes ignores the soldier, his mind and eyes too involved with the problem he has drawn in the tray.)

Roman Soldier: *(shouting)* Old man, are you Archimedes?

Archimedes: *(barely glancing up at the soldier)* Yes, I

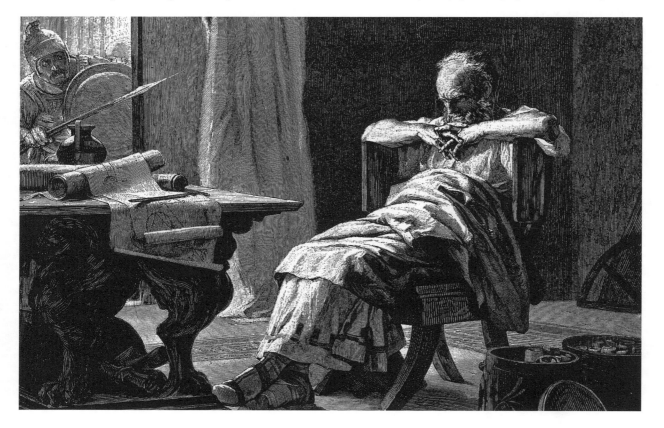

am Archimedes. Do not bother me.

Roman Soldier: I have orders to bring you to my commander, the Roman general Marcellus.

Archimedes: Leave me alone. I refuse to go anywhere until I solve this problem.

Roman Soldier: *(drawing his sword)* If you do not come with me, I will kill you at once!

Archimedes: Wait for a moment. I do not want to leave my problem incomplete and unsolved. The wonders of science are more my concern than the affairs of generals.

Furious, the soldier kills the old man. When Marcellus learns that Archimedes is dead, he has the soldier executed for murder. To pay tribute to the man he wished to meet, the Roman commander has the famous mathematician buried with much ceremony and also honors his friends and relatives.

During his lifetime, Archimedes had requested that on his tomb there should be engraved the drawing of a cylinder circumscribing a sphere within it, together with an inscripton giving the ratio of the cylinder to the sphere (3:2). He regarded his discovery of this ratio as his greatest accomplishment, a much more important achievement than the invention of any war machine. Marcellus granted this wish as a tribute to the greatest mathematical genius of antiquity and possibly the greatest that the world has ever seen.

* Briareus was one of the three mythological Hecatoncheires, or hundred-armed giants, who were the sons of Uranus and Gaia

Project

A ROMAN MARCHING CAMP

BACKGROUND

Camp was home to the Roman soldier. Whether on the march, fighting a war, or stationed in an area, he spent his nights safely in a fortified, well-planned, and organized camp that he had helped build. A camp was built even if a com-

Roman Soldiers Fortifying Their Camp

mander planned to stay in a particular area for only one night. Each soldier had his assigned task, and in three to four hours the job was done. Winter camp and summer camp were identical, except that in winter wooden huts with thatched roofs replaced tents. Sheds were built in the winter for the baggage animals.

Whenever possible, the campsite was on a gentle hill with the rear toward the summit. Ideally the camp faced the direction in which the army would march the following morning or, if in battle or awaiting a battle, the camp faced the enemy. The best site had a stream or marsh at the foot of the hill, affording further protection from an enemy attack. Nearby was a river or stream with fresh water for washing and drinking and woods with timber for cooking and building.

An advance guard defined the camp's outlines. The cavalry patrolled the surrounding area while the soldiers set to work building the camp. Each soldier carried with him whatever tools the building required.

After the camp was built, it was suppertime. At sunset, musicians sounded the call that began the night watch. Reveille was sounded approximately twelve hours later. If the army was to march, the musicians gave three signals: the first to strike the tents, the second to load the baggage animals, and the third for the army to move out.

MATERIALS NEEDED

FOR THE CAMP
- one large box (bottom section only); the larger the box, the easier the construction
- box (top and bottom) about three inches high and approximately four inches shorter and narrower than the large box
- flat board or cardboard the size of the smaller box
- dirt, clay, or plastic
- water
- dowels or twigs (with no forked branches)
- twigs with forked branches
- Popsicle sticks
- spoons
- knives and spatulas

FOR THE TENTS
- paper or cloth rectangles (tan or brown)
- tacks, string, and dowels

FOR THE ALTAR
- very small empty spool of thread

N.B. This plan is for a marching camp, not a permanent camp, which required more fortification.

FOR THE VEXILLUM (FLAG)
- one-and-one-half-inch square piece of red cloth or paper
- string or tape
- bits of red yarn
- glue
- one 6-inch stick
- one 2-inch stick

Roman Soldier on the March
N.B. Branch for fortification wall.

PROCEDURE

DITCH AND RAMPART
1. Center the small box inside the large box. (If a second box is not available, use packed dirt.)
2. Place the flat board on the small box.
3. Construct a ditch three inches deep by four inches wide with dirt, clay, or plasticine around the flat board. (The ditch may have both sides sloping, the side away from the camp sloping, or both sides vertical.)
4. Use the dirt or clay scooped out of the ditch for a rampart or mound around the camp. Slope the inner side (camp side) of the rampart.
5. Lay twigs or dowels along the sloping side of the rampart in a steplike manner (see illustration).
6. Place Popsicle sticks to form a fence at the top of the rampart, along the side facing the ditch.
   N.B. A fence was a boundary line, not a defensive structure.
7. Cut some Popsicle sticks to make gaps in the fence for soldiers on watch to look out.
   N.B. Sometimes wooden towers were erected at regular intervals along the fence.
8. Bind the sticks together with string.
   N.B. Leave space between the camp tents and rampart to allow room for troops to defend the wall and to prevent any enemy weapons from hitting the tents.

THE CAMP
With a pen or marker outline the plan of the camp on the flat board or cardboard according to the directions and illustration on page 61.

1. Divide the board crosswise into three sections.
2. Make each crosswise line (there will be two) a street approximately three inches wide. Name the streets Via Principalis and Via Quintana.
   N.B. Main Roman camp streets were sixty feet wide.
3. Divide the board lengthwise into two sections.
4. Make another street named Via Praetoria approximately three inches wide from Via Principalis to the rampart.
5. Leave four openings for the entrance and exit gates (see illustration). Keep the openings small—about one inch.
   N.B. There were few actual gates in a marching camp.

6. Scoop out a short ditch in front of and behind each gate, i.e., inside the walls of the camp.

7. Between Via Quintana and Via Principalis use a dividing line as a guide for the large rectangular Praetorium, which housed a commander's tent and headquarters, an altar, and a law court.

8. Between Via Quintana and the rear rampart use a dividing line as a guide for the large rectangular Quaestorium, which housed administrative staff, hostages and prisoners, animals' food, and booty.

KEY TO CAMP DIAGRAM

⊠ = cavalry quarters
⊡ = general, staff, and troop quarters
☐ = archer and slinger quarters
$\boxed{1_5}$ $\boxed{1_4}$ = cohort quarters
Aux. = auxiliary quarters
Equit. = *Equites* ("cavalry") quarters
Legat. Trib. = *Legati* and *tribuni*, ("special messenger" and "government-appointed army officer") quarters

TENTS

1. Use paper or cloth to set up a simple tent with flap entrances on two sides.

2. Use string, dowels, tacks, and toothpicks to make and secure the tent.

3. Place several tents in rectangles reserved for cohorts.
   N.B. The area given to each cohort division $\boxed{1_5}$ *was 180 by 120 feet. Each tent was 10 feet square with 4 feet between tents. Each tent housed eight men and always faced the street. Animals were always housed in the rear.*

PRAETORIUM

Place the empty spool of thread in the Praetorium to represent an altar. A commander regularly offered sacrifices to the gods and sought their advice.

VEXILLUM

1. Attach the two-inch stick to the six-inch stick with string or tape.

2. Glue bits of yarn to one end of the red cloth.

3. Tape or tie the red cloth (yarn hanging at bottom as fringe) to the crossbar on the stick.
   N.B. Traditionally, when a commander's red vexillum was placed outside his tent, it was the signal of a battle or march.

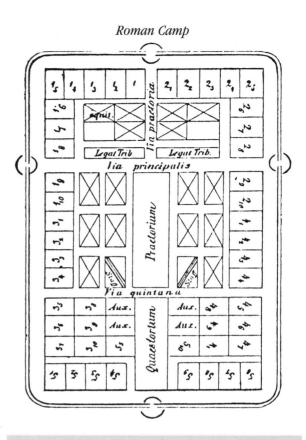
Roman Camp

Caesar's Men Attacked While Making Camp The six legions who had arrived at the proposed campsite area marked out the camp and began construction.

The main army of the enemy (the Nervii of Belgium) suddenly dashed out and climbed the hill to our campsite while my men were busily fortifying it.

I had to do everything immediately—raise the flag (vexillum), which signaled prepare for battle, sound the trumpet, call back the men working on the fortifications and those who were searching for rampart material, marshal the troops into battle formation, encourage the soldiers, and, finally, give the signal to attack.

I really had no time to give all these orders because the enemy was approaching so fast. The knowledge and experience of the soldiers helped and the fact that I had ordered the officers of the legions to stay with their troops until the camp was fortified.

The battle was so intense that it became a crisis situation with no reserves available. Since I had no shield, I snatched one from a soldier in the rear and went straight to the front line. My arrival gave the troops hope.

Julius Caesar's *Gallic Wars*, Book II, excerpts from Chapters 19–21 and 25

Puzzle Pages

CROSSWORD PUZZLE

Across

1. Priests of Mars
3. Pyrrhus claimed to be his cousin
5. Name of Delphic priestess
7. Athenian lawgiver
9. Son of Hellen
13. One of Greece's four main tribes
14. Greek king from Epirus
15. Roman god of war
17. One of Greece's four main tribes
19. Interviewed by Croesus
22. Noble Roman patriot
25. One of Greece's four main tribes
26. Croesus marched against these people
27. Son of Hellen
28. Decius _____
29. What Greeks called them selves

Down

2. One of Greece's four main tribes
3. Principal god in Libya
4. Oldest Greek oracle
6. Greek epic writer
8. What Romans called Greeks
10. Curius and Fabricius
11. Greek king of gods and men
12. Monster killed by Apollo
16. Founder of Dorians
18. Also called Indo-Europeans
20. Rich king of Lydia
21. Son of Hellen
23. Greek name for Greece
24. Persian king

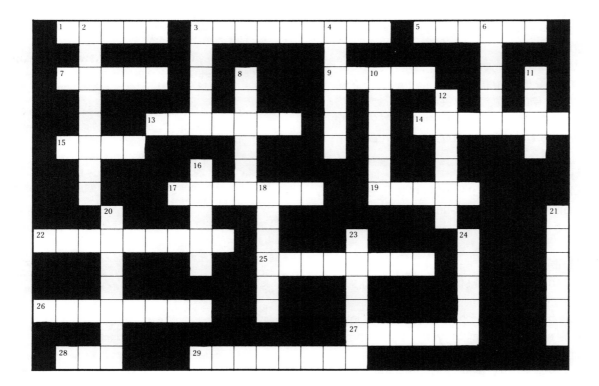

Unscramble each of the six jumbled words below to determine the answers to the clues. Place the unscrambled words on the blank lines, then match each letter with its corresponding number to discover where many ancients went for advice.

1. Decius Mus I and II both performed this:

   viodeto __ __ __ __ __ __ __
          1   8

2. Apollo assumed this shape when he approached the sailors he wanted for his priests:

   inhpold __ __ __ __ __ __ __
         12 5

3. Pyrrhus used this type of battle formation:

   alhpan __ __ __ __ __ __ __
      4   10

4. Pyrrhus used these soldiers in battle:

   casneeemrir __ __ __ __ __ __ __ __ __ __ __
        9 11   2

5. Victory at a great cost:

   picrhry __ __ __ __ __ __ __
          6 7

6. This killed Pyrrhus:

   liet __ __ __ __
      3 13

Ancients consulted: __ __ __ __ __ __ __   __ __ __ __ __ __
               1 2 3 4 5 6 7   8 9 10 11 12 13

Fill in the blanks using the letters of the Roman name for southern Italy, *Magna Graecia* ("Great Greece"), as your clues.

Clue	Answer
1. Growing power in Italy	__ __ M __
2. Greece borders this body of water	__ __ __ __ A __ __ __ __
3. Powerful city in Africa	__ __ __ __ __ __ G __
4. Roman name of Taras	__ __ __ __ N __ __
5. Colonists from here founded Taras	__ __ A __ __ __
6. Her people founded many colonies	G __ __ __ __
7. Phalanthus founded this colony	__ __ R __ __
8. Delphi was once called this	__ __ __ __ __ A
9. Home to Pyrrhus	E __ __ __ __ __
10. Pyrrhus also fought and won here	__ __ C __ __ __ __
11. Where the Pythia live	__ __ __ __ __ I
12. Where Pyrrhus was killed	A __ __ __ __ __

ON LANGUAGE WORD FIND

Can you find the twenty words hidden in the maze below? They all can be found in the articles "On Language" and "Esperanto: A Universal Language" on pages 52 and 53.

Aryan	French	Italian
Asia	German	Italy
English	Greece	Latin
Esperanto	Greek	Roman
Europe	horse	Romance
France	India	Zamensky
frato	Iran	

```
        Y K S L S I
      S T Y E A A B N N A L K
  N U F E N K U I F D A R Y L A T I H
  A L R C A S R S I R K N T H O R S E
  M A E N Y N O A I N A I L A T I Y E
  O T N A R E P S E M L N K Y L S H P
  R I C M A M E M R G A G C G R E E K
  L N H O E A U E Y K B O N E M A T L
      R R Z G R E E C E C H K
        O T A R F C
```

CAN YOU MATCH?

Match the correct word with the appropriate description.

1. Marcellus — a. Soldiers used these machines to fling heavy stones at enemy

2. Carthaginians — b. A Roman device that allowed its soldiers to scale enemy walls

3. sambuca — c. Ruler of Syracuse when Romans attacked

4. Archimedes — d. People of North Africa who sought control of the Mediterranean Sea

5. catapults — e. Roman commander who wished to meet Archimedes

6. Hippocrates — f. Ruler of Syracuse who was determined to keep his city free of Roman control

7. Rome — g. Island off the coast of southern Italy

8. Syracuse — h. Devised ingenious devices to keep the Romans from capturing Syracuse

9. Sicily — i. Greek colony

10. Hieron — j. A city in Italy whose leaders were intent on extending their power into Sicily

On the blank line write "True" or "False" about the corresponding statement.

1. Archimedes refused to help Hippocrates against the Romans. _____

2. Hieron wisely kept his war machines ready for action at a moment's notice. _____

3. The Roman soldiers feared the strange war machines of the Syracusans. _____

4. Marcellus ordered Archimedes killed. _____

5. One of Archimedes' war machines involved the use of mirrors to blind the enemy. _____

6. Carthage and Rome fought as allies for control of Syracuse. _____

7. Archimedes considered his greatest achievement the discovery of the ratio of a cylinder to a sphere. _____

8. King Hieron of Syracuse allied himself with the Romans, not the Carthaginians. _____

9. The Romans were prepared to counteract all of Archimedes' "war machines." _____

10. Archimedes used his knowledge of geometry to help him build war machines. _____

Topics for Comparison

1. A Roman general always touched the point of his lance to the sacred shield sent by Mars. We look at this superstition and wonder. Yet we are also superstitious. List some commonly observed superstitious practices and give examples—e.g., knocking on wood for good luck.

2. The Romans believed that Mars, their god of war, sent them a shield. They kept it in a special place and treated it with great honor. Many religions practice the same type of custom. Think, read, and inquire about the various religions today and compare the origins, history, uses, and honor of their sacred artifacts (e.g., the Torah in Judaism).

3. Why did migration and resulting invasions almost stop Greece's progress as a civilized nation? Compare Greece to nations involved in war and destructive tactics today where the arts also have difficulty surviving.

4. Ancient Greece was always sending out colonists. England did, too. Compare and contrast their reasons, the sites chosen, and the relationships between colony and "home." Mark Greece's colonies on a map of the ancient world. Mark England's colonies on a map of the modern world. Compare the two maps.

5. Rome was an ancient superpower. If an ally called for military aid, Rome responded with force. The consequences were usually war. The United States and Russia are modern superpowers. (England and France also can be used as examples.) These countries also are called on for military aid. Do they follow Rome's example? When, where, and with what results? Are the situations comparable? Some possible examples are Grenada, Afghanistan, Honduras, South Africa (England), and Vietnam (France).

6. The Romans made a special point of saying that patriots Fabricius and Curius returned from their civic duties to their farms. We do the same with the president, who retreats to his country compound for vacations. Why the country?

Suggestions for Essays and Written Reports

1. Do you agree with Solon's answer to Croesus that a truly happy person is one who is happy at the time of death?

2. Why do armies loot and burn cities they conquer? Why should they read Croesus' answer to Cyrus?

3. Did the oracles really control the political situation with their answers? Why did foreigners go to the oracles if the priests and priestesses were Greek?

4. Why do you think Apollo chose to assume the form of a dolphin to attract his priests to his oracular site? Was it because of the dolphin's characteristics or because Apollo spotted a ship at sea with appropriate sailors for his priests?

5. Should superpowers send military aid to allies or just humanitarian aid? What are the consequences of each choice?

6. Would Pyrrhus have given himself to *devotio* as Decius Mus was willing to do? If yes, why? If not, explain.

7. Why does a country need patriots, even in peacetime?

8. Why did other nations seek peace treaties with Rome after the defeat of Pyrrhus? Did the nations see Rome as a trading partner? What kind of trade agreements would have been beneficial to these other nations?

9. Find Rome, Carthage, and Syracuse on the map on page 39. Then, using the information given in the introduction to the play "Archimedes and the Siege of Syracuse," locate the areas under Carthaginian control and those under Roman control in 220 B.C. Discuss why both Carthaginians and Romans would have seen control of Sicily and of Syracuse critical to their winning control of the Mediterranean Sea.

10. Make a list of the various devices Archimedes invented to oppose the Romans. Then research battle techniques today—best to take a specific battle—and list the devices and/or strategies used. Compare the two lists as to their effectiveness. Are any of the principles on which Archimedes based his inventions involved in today's devices or strategies? Explain.

11. Write an essay discussing whether you agree or disagree with this statement: Archimedes won his battle against the Romans as much through the fear he instilled in them as through the effectiveness of his devices.

Further Activities

1. Reconstruct the oracle of Dodona. You will need trees, branches, or sticks, a fan (electric or paper) to create wind, bronze vases (or metal containers), and a jar. Hang the vases on tree limbs and have a "priest" or "priestess" interpret the sounds. In addition, have a visitor give the priest a jar with a question written on a piece of lead or metal inside. For extra effect, hang a cut-out picture of a black dove on the tree limb and have a narrator explain the scene. Ask everyone to submit questions to the oracle.

2. Oracular sites were awe-inspiring. Is there an area near you or one you have visited that would make a good site for an oracle? Take pictures and bring them to school. Explain your reasons for choosing the site. How would your priest or priestess convey your god's message?

3. Using a map of Greece and the Aegean Sea, plot migration routes into Greece, through Greece, and across the Aegean to Asia Minor. Use different colors for each tribe.

4. March is named for Mars. Research the derivatives of the other eleven months and give their stories: January, god Janus; February, *februare* (Latin for "to purify"); April, *aperire* (Latin for "to open"); May, goddess Maia; June, goddess Juno; July, Julius (Caesar); August, Octavius (later Augustus); September–December, the numbers seven through ten (Latin: *septem, octo, novem, decem*).

5. War destroys the arts. Peace promotes them. Go to the library and research authors, composers, sculptors, and scientists who flourished in the United States during war. Research those who flourished after and before each war. Then look at the works written, composed, and crafted and the discoveries made and see how they reflected the age.

6. Romans loved to retell patriotic tales. Every country has some. Research tales about U.S. patriots and heroes.

7. Go to your library and check for books or magazine articles written in Esperanto.

8. Archimedes used his knowledge of mathematics to help his city. Think of two problems (potential or real) affecting the school or city/town in which you live. Consider what you might do to correct these problems using some skill or area of knowledge in which you excel. Examples: (a) There is a shelter experiencing a shortage of food. You play an instrument. Talk to your music instructor and hold a recital with admission a can or box of food that will be presented to the needy shelter. (b) A few students in the younger grades are having difficulty with their lessons. You understand the material. With your teacher, organize a "help" session for you and fellow classmates to work a brief period each day/week with the younger students on a specific lesson or subject.

Possunt quia posse videntur.

They can because they believe they can.

Virgil,
Roman poet
(70–19 B.C.)

III Carthage versus Rome

PEOPLES INVOLVED:
Carthaginians, Romans

DECISIVE BATTLES:
Zama in Africa (202 B.C., ended Second Punic War), Saguntum in Spain, Cannae in Italy (Carthaginian victories)

GENERALS:
Hannibal (Carthaginian), Regulus, Scipio (Roman)

HISTORICAL SIGNIFICANCE:
Rome's defeat of Carthage in the Second Punic War made Rome the controlling power in the West and a recognized world power.

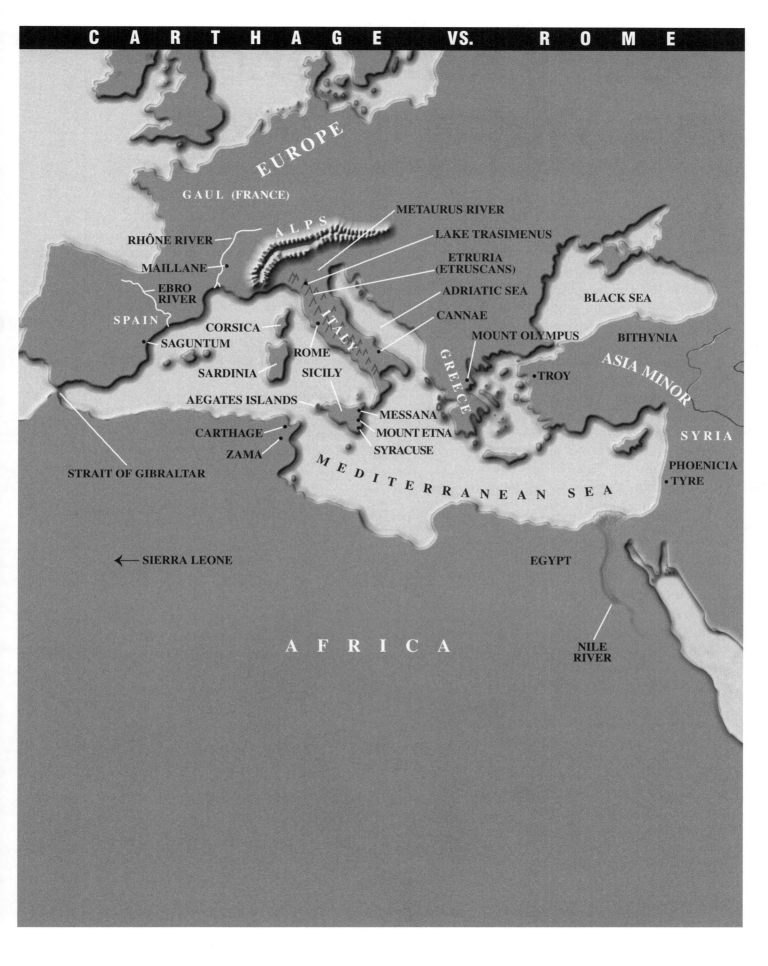

Rome's Emergence as a Western Power

After 272 B.C., the area from the Mediterranean Sea to the Alps in Italy was Rome's. Some tribes had the rights of full Roman citizenship, some had only partial rights, others were colonies, and a great many were dependent allies. Rome's defeat of the Greek king Pyrrhus sent a signal to all the prospering nations surrounding the Mediterranean that a new and formidable power was emerging.

Soon Rome began to feel and notice the effects of its new position. War booty, fines imposed on subject states, and taxes all provided new money to build temples, aqueducts, and the like. Prisoners of war greatly increased the number of slaves in Rome and, as a result, altered the lifestyle. Rome felt the urge to extend its control beyond the peninsula.

The Gauls to the north, although defeated and driven back by Rome, were still fierce. Mainland Greece also was too powerful to attack. Greece had a navy; Rome did not.

To the south lay Carthage in northern Africa. Its commercial interests in Sicily, Sardinia, and Corsica and its early alliance with the Etruscans (ee TRUSS kun) to the north had brought this growing power closer and closer to Rome. Circumstances would soon make war inevitable.

The ruling class in Carthage included merchants, whose commercial fleets needed safe ports for their ships to resupply and for their crews to rest. Travel across the Mediterranean Sea was dangerous. Sailors could depend only on sails and oars. Carthage's soldiers were mercenaries, men paid to fight. The Carthaginians themselves were exempt from the military so that they could concentrate on commercial ventures.

Carthage's wealthy merchant class did not seek conquest on any grand scale. Its main concern was safe seaports.

Rome, on the contrary, was an agricultural nation. It did not seek commercial ventures and had never possessed a fleet. Rome's army and leaders fought for the glory and honor of Rome. Military service was a privilege and mark of status granted only to those who owned enough property and money to equip themselves for duty.

These two rising powers met for the first time on the battlefield in Sicily, neither foreseeing the lengthy and bitter struggle ahead, a struggle that would change Rome forever.

Corvus and Boarding Bridge on a Roman Warship

Carthage Versus Rome

The *Poeni* (po A knee), as the Romans called the people of Carthage, were receiving constant reports of trouble in Sicily. Their garrison in Messana had been expelled for no reason. The Mamertines of Messana asked for Carthage's help against Hiero II, ruler of the powerful Sicilian city Syracuse. Some Mamertines, however, were convinced Rome would be a better ally and sought its help.

Rome's leaders debated the request. Sicily was not considered part of Italy. Interaction in Sicily could lead to war with Carthage. Both points were carefully considered. Finally the senate and the assembly decided to send an army. Carthage joined forces with Hiero II.

The Roman soldiers and their commanders, well trained and seasoned, soon won several battles. Hiero II rethought his position, abandoned his Carthaginian allies, and sided with the Romans. It was Rome versus Carthage—the beginning of the great duel.

For the first time, Rome saw the possibility of gaining complete control of Sicily if it defeated the Carthaginians. But Rome did not have a navy. Carthage was an experienced naval power. Without a fleet, a Roman victory was impossible.

Using a conquered Carthaginian *quinquereme* (kwin KWEH ream) (a type of warship) as a model, Rome built a fleet of approximately one hundred forty ships within months. Because the Romans realized their strength lay in hand-to-hand combat, they attached *corvi* (KOR vee) (heavy iron spikes that resembled beaks[1]) to their ships. In battle they threw the corvi across the sea to hook the enemy ships. They then let down hinged wooden boarding bridges that were tied by a rope to the mast.

These bridges allowed soldiers to cross onto the enemy ships and fight. Despite their inexperience on the sea, the Romans won several naval victories. In 249 B.C., however, Rome's fleet lost a major battle. The survivors then suffered a shipwreck in a terrible storm on the way home to Italy.

Undeterred, the Romans commissioned another fleet to be built and, in 241 B.C., decisively defeated the Carthaginians at the Aegates Islands off the coast of Sicily. Carthage, seeking peace, agreed to leave Sicily, to return all prisoners of war, and to pay considerable fines over the following ten years. Rome had won its first war beyond Italy's borders, but at a great cost: More than one hundred thousand men had died, and more than five hundred warships had been destroyed.

Carthage had lost the war, but it quickly began preparing to increase its area of influence. This time it looked to Spain. General Hamilcar Barca began the venture, which was continued by his son-in-law Hasdrubal (HAZ droo bal) and later by his son Hannibal.

Rome knew of Carthage's actions and kept abreast of new developments. But the Carthaginians assured the Romans that they would not go north of the Ebro River.

But, in 221 B.C., the situation changed. Young Hannibal had assumed command and attacked Saguntum, a town south of the Ebro that had resisted offers of friendship. Saguntum appealed to Rome for aid.

When Saguntum fell to the Carthaginians, Rome sent ambassadors to Carthage demanding Hannibal's surrender. Carthage refused. The Second Punic War had started.

Rome prepared to send an army to Spain and defeat the insolent young general, but Hannibal moved swiftly. He organized his mercenaries, prepared his elephants, and performed the impossible. He crossed the Alps in early autumn. Snow had already fallen. When ice hindered his passage, Hannibal poured vinegar over it. The vinegar reacted with the frozen water and cracked it.

Hannibal's forces suffered many losses and

---

[1] *Corvus* (pl: *corvi*) is the Latin word for "crow."

much fatigue crossing the Alps. But with recruited Gallic tribesmen and his forces, he crushed the Roman army at Lake Trasimenus in 217 B.C.

Hannibal easily continued his march through Italy. Rome's allied towns could not stop him, but they did not join him. In 216 B.C., near the city of Cannae to the south of Rome, Hannibal again met a Roman army and annihilated it. The loss of life was tremendous, but Rome still did not concede defeat. Hannibal had fought hard and well, but time was beginning to turn against him.

Hannibal set up camp and waited. Since no major seaport was under his control, Hannibal could not easily resupply or reoutfit his army while on foreign soil. Rome had the advantage. All the reasons for Hannibal's inactivity at this time are not clear. Perhaps he just intended to wait for his brother Hasdrubal's troops to march into northern Italy. Then the two brothers could crush Rome in a pincer move.

Meanwhile, the Romans had fared better in Sicily and in Spain, where they had won major skirmishes. However, in 211 B.C., the Scipio (SKIP ee o) brothers, who ably led the

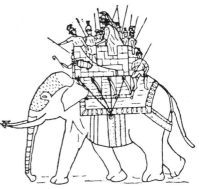
War Elephant

Roman army against the Carthaginians, were both disastrously defeated and killed. A younger Scipio, the son of one of the commanders, had fought alongside his elders. His leadership qualities and his brave feats on the battlefield led to his appointment as the new commander.

The young Scipio immediately tried to prevent Hasdrubal from leaving Spain to meet Hannibal in Italy. Scipio did defeat Hasdrubal in battle, but he was unable to stop him from crossing the Alps in 207 B.C. Hasdrubal reached the Metaurus River in northern Italy that same year but was crushed by an advancing Roman army.

Hannibal learned of the disastrous defeat when Hasdrubal's head was thrown into his camp. Hannibal realized his dream of capturing Rome was now impossible. He retreated to southern Italy and then to Carthage, where the young Scipio had crossed and was preparing to attack.

The final battle was fought at Zama in 202 B.C. Scipio won; Hannibal lost. Carthage lost its territorial possessions, its fleet was limited to ten ships, and it was required to pay fines to Rome for fifty years. Rome was now the controlling power in the western Mediterranean.

Hannibal on His Elephant Crossing the Alps. N.B. Both have colds.
(*from* Comic History of Rome, *by Gilbert A. Beckett, 1870*)

In the Carthaginian Senate The Roman historian Livy described the scene in the Carthaginian senate when Rome demanded Hannibal's surrender:

The Roman ambassador Fabius, with his hand holding his toga at his breast, said, "Here (pointing to his heart), we bring you peace and war. Take which you will."

The Carthaginians immediately replied, "Whichever you wish, we do not care."

The Roman ambassador, allowing his gathered toga to fall, answered, "We give you war."

Hannibal of Carthage

When Hannibal was nine years old, his father, Hamilcar Barca, made him pledge to fight the Romans until he defeated them. Hannibal never forgot this vow. His life was ruled by it.

Hannibal

In 237 B.C., Hannibal accompanied his father to Spain. Carthage authorized Hamilcar to capture territories to compensate for its loss of Sicily after the First Punic War. Hamilcar eagerly went. He had fought bravely against the Romans and had almost won.

Fate was not with him in Spain. In 229 B.C., Hamilcar drowned. His son-in-law, Hasdrubal, took command and continued the conquest. In 221 B.C., Hasdrubal was murdered and the command passed to twenty-six-year-old Hannibal.

The Spaniards liked Hannibal and considered him fair and just. They willingly followed him, all except the people of Saguntum, an ally of Rome. Hannibal remembered his oath and attacked Saguntum.

This was Hannibal's first decisive move. For the next fifteen years, he ably led his army against Rome. With little help from his home government, he almost annihilated Rome's forces and Rome itself.

Hannibal maintained strict discipline, both for himself and for his troops. His fearless attitude encouraged his men on the difficult trip across the Alps. His ambush tactics and blitz attacks won him his men's admiration and approval. His strategy of surrounding and crushing his opponent in a series of carefully planned and synchronized maneuvers by his infantry and cavalry defeated several Roman armies. He bravely endured all hardships, even losing the sight of one eye from an infection caused by the bitter cold temperatures while marching through Italy.

If Hannibal had fought for Rome, whose people and government, unlike Carthage's, fully supported and backed their military commanders, his story would have been quite different.

After his defeat at Zama in 202 B.C., Hannibal remained in Carthage and became one of its political leaders. He instituted several wise constitutional reforms, reorganized the treasury, and encouraged trading and farming. Hannibal's political enemies, fearing his ambitions and popularity, reported to Rome that he was secretly plotting against Rome with King Antiochus of Syria.

When Rome sent envoys to Carthage, Hannibal fled to Syria, where he did support Antiochus against Rome. After Antiochus lost, Hannibal fled to King Prusias of Bithynia. In 183 B.C., when he learned that Prusias had agreed to surrender him to Roman envoys, Hannibal drank poison. He was approximately sixty-four years old. One of the world's greatest generals was dead. Rome could finally rest.

Hannibal Crossing the Rhône

Regulus

During the First Punic War, the Roman general Regulus sailed with his army from Sicily to North Africa. Unexpected and therefore unopposed, Regulus marched almost to the walls of Carthage, made camp, and offered terms of peace. His terms were so strict that Carthage refused and prepared to fight.

Unfortunately for Regulus, Carthage had elephants that tore through his army's flanks. Carthage's cavalry, meanwhile, encircled the Roman army, and the result was disastrous. Few Romans survived, and Regulus was taken prisoner.

Rome sent a fleet to rescue Regulus. When the mission failed, the fleet returned home only to sink in a terrible storm at sea. Carthage felt victorious. It sued for peace and sent envoys to Rome. Regulus asked to accompany the envoys. He promised to return to Carthage if Rome declined the peace terms.

Roman historians wrote of how Regulus strongly counseled his countrymen to accept neither the peace terms nor the exchange of prisoners. He explained how he was prepared to return to Carthage because he had already been given a slow-working poison. The Roman government agreed to follow Regulus' advice.

The heroic Regulus returned to Carthage, where he met a savage and cruel death.

Regulus

Regulus Returning to Carthage (by 19th-century Italian painter Vincent Camuccini)

Scipio Africanus

Scipio, like Hannibal, followed in his father's footsteps. Each descended from a distinguished line of patriotic and heroic military men. Each sought the total destruction of the other's nation. Prior to this period, Rome's leaders and soldiers were almost nameless. When a general assumed control of the army, he fought for the glory of Rome. So, too, did the Scipios, yet their deeds mark a turning point in Rome's history—individual leaders were becoming more prominent, and their lives began to manipulate and control the destiny of Rome.

While Hannibal victoriously fought his way through Italy, his brother attempted to defeat the Roman army led by two brothers, Gnaeus Scipio and Publius Scipio. The Scipios were two of Rome's best generals. They won several major battles and did succeed in delaying Hasdrubal's march to Italy to meet with his brother. Unfortunately, in 211 B.C., Hasdrubal decisively defeated and killed both Scipios.

Publius' son had accompanied him to Spain and ably led the troops in several skirmishes. When his father and uncle were killed, he was made general, and the war immediately began to turn in Rome's favor.

Scipio loosened up the ranks and gave each section more independence. Some historians credit Scipio with the adoption of the heavy, well-made Spanish sword and the improvement of the javelin. He carefully studied the tactics and strategies of the Carthaginians and of Hannibal and developed his own counterdefensives and counteroffensives. His men respected and admired him. Under Scipio's ten-year command, the Roman army became much more professional.

At Zama in Africa, where he met Hannibal on the battlefield, his strategies foiled the Carthaginians. It was Scipio's cavalry that broke the draw and won the day.

Because of this stunning defeat of Hannibal in Africa, the Roman senate granted Scipio the right to add the word "Africanus" to his name. This made Scipio the first Roman to be known by the name of the country he conquered.

Scipio

Swords: (a) and (b) most commonly used by Roman soldiers, (c) handle of Roman officer's sword, (d) elaborate scabbard—probably awarded as an honor to a Roman general

The Founding of Carthage

My dear wife, flee as quickly as you can. Your life is threatened! Look at my chest. See the blood and the gaping hole left by that wretched steel sword. Your jealous brother Pygmalion killed me. His desire for riches consumes him. Flee, my beloved Dido."

Dido bolted upright in her bed. "Sychaeus (sih KAY us), my dear husband. Pygmalion told me that you had left on some urgent journey and that you would return as soon as matters allowed you time. Oh, my dear husband, lead me, tell me what to do!"

"Come quickly. Let me show you my buried treasures. Pygmalion killed me hoping to steal my riches, but he will never find them. I always knew what he was like and prepared for the day when he might decide to kill me. Come, my dear, come quickly."

Dido hastily wrapped herself in a cape and followed the pale ghost of her dead husband. She was glad to learn the truth but wondered if she was imagining the tale to answer her many questions about Sychaeus' mysterious disappearance.

Slowly they descended a narrow flight of stairs to an unused room in the cellar. Sychaeus pointed to a spot on the floor. Dido bent down and saw a small ring. She pulled it up, and the lip popped off. Within lay untold treasures.

"Take them, and with trusted friends set sail for a new land far from here, far from Pygmalion."

Dido looked up to speak and saw no one. She looked down again. The riches were still there. It had not been just a dream.

Quickly but stealthily she retraced her steps to her own room. She called together her most trusted friends and formed an escape plan.

In the dead of the night, Dido and her companions descended to the treasure room, loaded it all into simple containers, and made their way to the harbor. Seizing a boat at anchor, they quickly cut the lines and set sail.[1]

Sentries saw the escaping boat and reported Dido's actions to Pygmalion. But Dido escaped. Pygmalion never caught her or the riches he desperately wanted.

Dido sailed until she reached a little African peninsula jutting into the Mediterranean Sea. She sent scouts to discover whose land it was and whether she might buy some. The native Africans replied that she could have as much land as a bull's hide would cover.

"A bull's hide! Why, that's not enough for anything," retorted Dido's companions. But they could not persuade the natives to sell more land.

Dido, however, heard the news and smiled. "Wonderful! Let's find the biggest bull's hide we can." When they did, Dido took her knife and cut it into the tiniest strips imaginable. She then placed each strip end to end on the land she wished to own. When she was finished, her new city, encircled with strips of bull's hide, covered a fairly large area. Dido's companions looked with pride and astonishment at their new queen. They called the city Carthage, and under Queen Dido, it became the most prosperous in northern Africa.

Loading and Weighing a Shipment of Silphion (a carrotlike plant) in a Greek Seaport on the Northern Coast of Africa

[1] Dido's home was in Tyre (TIRE), Phoenicia (foe KNEE shuh).

Dido and Aeneas

The tale of Dido and Aeneas is one of the more famous love stories ever written. Book IV of the *Aeneid,* the epic poem written by the Roman poet Virgil (70–19 B.C.), retells their tragic story in great detail.

Wearily but eagerly the storm-tossed crew sought refuge in the sheltered harbor opening up before them. They did not know where they were or who ruled the area. They had no choice but to land. The angry seas had wrecked their vessels.

Aeneas was the leader of the crew, refugees from Troy in Asia Minor (present-day Turkey). Their great city had fallen to the Greeks. They had escaped captivity and death. Yet the gods had not made their sea travel easy. They sought to land in Italy, where they planned to found a new home, a nation that would eventually rise above all others.

Such concerns were far distant from their minds when Aeneas bid the crew remain by the shore while he scouted the interior. Suddenly Aeneas' mother, Venus, the goddess of love and beauty, came across his path and told him he was in northern Africa, near the bustling city of Carthage. She also told him about Queen Dido and bid Aeneas seek her help. "Dido, too, is a refugee from the East. Her husband, Sychaeus, was murdered by her greedy brother, and she fled to this hospitable land. Go, she will aid you!"

Aeneas took his mother's advice and entered Carthage. She wrapped him in a special cloud so that no one could see him, but he could see all. Aeneas marveled at the wonderful city and at how industrious the inhabitants were. He noted how respectfully everyone treated Dido.

When the cloud disappeared and Dido saw Aeneas, she stood motionless. Aeneas immediately won her heart, a fact she refused to admit. Dido warmly welcomed the stranger and told him to bring his crew to her court. Aeneas eagerly accepted her hospitality.

Aeneas With Dido in Carthage
(by French artist Pierre Guérin, 1774–1833)

Months passed, and Aeneas still remained with Dido, who had slowly allowed her emotions to rule her mind. She forgot about her subjects and her royal duties. It was Aeneas, in fact, who tended to many of them.

As time passed, Dido feared more and more that Aeneas would leave her to found a new Troy. She sacrificed constantly to the gods, repeating any unfavorable sacrifice. She even begged Aeneas to take her with him.

Finally the gods on Mount Olympus intervened. Mercury, the messenger god, appeared to Aeneas, reminding him of his duty: Aeneas must leave Carthage and continue the course of his destiny. Carefully, but secretly, Aeneas obeyed and prepared to leave. One night he and his men boarded their repaired vessels and sailed from Carthage's harbor. When Dido awoke the next day, she saw sails on the horizon and knew the reason.

Dido ordered all of Aeneas' belongings to be burned. "I shall destroy every trace of that thankless traitor," she said.

While everyone hurried to follow her orders, Dido climbed to the top of the mound of belongings, taking with her the sword Aeneas had given her. Then, before anyone could stop her, Dido plunged the sword deep into her heart and died.

From the deck of his ship at sea, Aeneas saw smoke rising from the palace area and sadly realized what had happened.

Carthaginian Merchants in a Roman Villa

The Aeneid Book VI of the *Aeneid* tells of Aeneas' journey to the underworld to visit his father and to learn more about the nation he will found. To reach his father's place, he had to travel through various areas reserved for dead spirits. In one, known as the Wailing Fields, are the shades of all those whom cruel love has destroyed. There he saw the dead spirit of Dido.

Tears filled his eyes as he tried to explain his actions. He grieved over her death and begged her forgiveness and understanding. Dido did not answer him, nor did she even acknowledge his presence. She merely turned and walked away into the arms of her loving husband, Sychaeus.

The Carthaginians

Carthage's central position on the northern coast of Africa made it a natural spot for early colonization. The little peninsula reaching out to the islands of Sicily, Sardinia, and Corsica and to mainland Europe, the steep hills protecting the coast from the interior, and the large port sheltered in a long, narrow bay were sure to attract the attention of both merchant and adventure ships.

Colonists from Phoenicia's leading city of Tyre first settled Carthage in the eighth century B.C.[1] For almost a century, Carthage remained a colony. After declaring its independence, the republic gradually became one of Africa's more powerful nations. Its land was fertile with abundant produce, but its power and money came from many overseas commercial ventures, especially the export and import of metals, viz., gold, silver, and tin.

Carthage's religious beliefs often caused much anger and outrage. The Carthaginians believed in human sacrifice. History records that other nations did request a stop to this barbarous practice, but with little success. Under Roman domination, Carthage was forced to yield to Rome's laws but on occasion reverted to its old beliefs.

In war, the Carthaginian mercenaries presented a formidable line of attack. Carthaginian generals remained with the army from year to year, unlike Roman generals, who were elected officials and had to return to Rome for the annual elections. Yet Carthaginian generals had a more difficult problem. A defeated general was often crucified, while a victorious one often came to be suspected of possible future ambitions. For this reason, Carthage reluctantly sent reinforcements to its generals.

[1] Tyre was famed for its purple dye. The bays of southern Italy to the north of Carthage had great quantities of the seashells that provided the base for the dye.

Carthaginians Sacrificing Humans to Their God Baal

The Elephant of Maillane In the late eighteenth century, sometime around the year A.D. 1777, Barthélemy Daillan was digging in the cellar of his house in the town of Maillane, in southern France. He found a medallion made of copper and the skeleton of a creature twelve feet long. After analyzing two of the molar teeth found in the skeleton, it was identified as the remains of an elephant. The bones were broken as they were being extracted from the earth. Where they went is unknown. Daillan used the medallion to decorate the handle of his pick. Mrs. Daillan kept at least one of the molar teeth.

In the early 1800s, a theory was proposed that the skeleton was the remains of one of Hannibal's elephants. Since a coin had been found with the animal's remains, probably placed there intentionally at the time of the burial, the researchers concluded that the skeleton did not belong to a prehistoric animal.

If the coin could be traced, it could probably be analyzed and dated, thereby providing positive proof of the time period of the skeleton's remains. Scientific analysis of the teeth and bones also would prove extremely helpful. Unfortunately, nothing remains except the story. We will probably never know if Hannibal buried one of his precious elephants in Maillane, an area in the Alps through which he certainly must have passed on his way to Italy.

Nineteenth-Century Representation of a War Elephant in Combat

Chronology of First and Second Punic Wars

264 B.C.	Romans cross into Sicily to aid Mamertines of Messana vs. Syracusans and Carthaginians	218 B.C.	Hannibal leaves Spain and begins march to Rome
260 B.C.	Romans build first fleet and win first naval victory over Carthaginians	—	Hannibal annihilates three Roman armies in northern Italy
251 B.C.	Romans under Regulus defeat Carthaginians	217 B.C.	Hannibal defeats Romans at Lake Trasimenus north of Rome
247 B.C.	Hamilcar Barca, Hannibal's father, assumes control of Carthaginian forces	216 B.C.	Hannibal annihilates Roman army at Cannae, southeast of Rome
241 B.C.	Romans defeat Carthaginians; First Punic War ends	—	Hasdrubal, Hannibal's brother, completes march from Spain to northern Italy and defeats Roman forces led by the Scipio brothers
237 B.C.	Hamilcar Barca (with Hannibal) enters Spain	207 B.C.	Roman army crushes Carthaginians and kills Hasdrubal at Metaurus River in northern Italy
228 B.C.	Hamilcar Barca dies; son-in-law Hasdrubal assumes command	202 B.C.	Scipio Africanus defeats Hannibal at Zama in northern Africa
221 B.C.	Hasdrubal dies; Hannibal, age twenty-six, assumes command	201 B.C.	Second Punic War ends
219 B.C.	Hannibal lays siege to Saguntum in Spain		

Romans Boarding Carthaginian Ship. N.B. Rams on Prows (early 20th-century representation)

On Vocabulary

COMMONLY USED ABBREVIATIONS

The abbreviations listed below appear in this sourcebook.

A.D.—*anno domini* (in the year of the Lord)
A.M.—*ante meridiem* (before the middle of the day)
c.—*circa* (around, about)
e.g.—*exempli gratia* (for the sake of example)
etc.—*et cetera* (and the rest)
fl.—*floruit* (he/she flourished, he/she lived)
i.e.—*id est* (that is)
N.B.—*Nota bene* (Note well, take notice)
P.M.—*post meridiem* (after the middle of the day)
viz.—*videlicet* (namely)
vs.—*versus* (turned toward, against)

ENGLISH-LATIN PLURALS

Some Latin terms retained their plurals when they entered the English language.

addendum—addenda
alumnus—alumni
axis—axes
datum—data
radius—radii
stratum—strata

LATIN WORDS IN ENGLISH

Many Latin words entered English without a change.

animal
aquarium
curriculum
forceps
formula
index
pauper
ultimatum
vacuum

Two Figureheads from Carthaginian Ships

FORMING ENGLISH WORDS

LATIN PREFIXES

ab (away from)

ad (to, toward)

cum, con (with)

de (down from)

e (out of)

in (in)

inter (between)

intra (within)

intro (within)

per (through)

post (after)

prae, pre (before)

pro (forward, on behalf of)

re (back, again)

sub (below, under)

trans (across)

LATIN VERBS

(Four main principal parts)

dico, dicere, dixi, dictus—to say

duco, ducere, duxi, ductus—to lead

capio, caere, cepi, captus—to capture

facio, facere, feci, factus—to make, to do

fero, ferre, tuli, latus—to bear, to carry

iacio, iacere, ieci, iactus—to throw

mitto, mittere, misi, missus—to send

porto, portare, portavi, portatus—to carry

scribo, scribere, scripsi, scriptus—to write

video, videre, visi, visus—to see

EXAMPLE: The Latin verbs "duco" combines with several of the Latin prefixes above to form English words:

LATIN PREFIX	+	LATIN VERB	=	ENGLISH WORD
ab	+	*duco*	=	abduct
ad	+	*duco*	=	adduce
cum	+	*duco*	=	conduct
de	+	*duco*	=	deduct
in	+	*duco*	=	induce
intro	+	*duco*	=	introduction
pro	+	*duco*	=	produce
re	+	*duco*	=	reduce

EXAMPLE: The Latin verb "capio" combines with several of the Latin prefixes above to form English words:

LATIN PREFIX	+	LATIN VERB	=	ENGLISH WORD
ad	+	*capio*	=	accept
cum	+	*capio*	=	concept
de	+	*capio*	=	deception
in	+	*capio*	=	inception
inter	+	*capio*	=	intercept
pre	+	*capio*	=	precept
re	+	*capio*	=	receive

Note: The final b, d, or m of the Latin preposition often changes to agree with the first letter of the verb. Not every prefix combines with every verb. Check out the other Latin verbs listed above and see how they combine with Latin prefixes to form English words.

GREEK CAN HELP YOU

GREEK WORDS IN ENGLISH
Several Greek words entered English without a change.
> amnesia
> catastrophe
> enigma
> orchestra
> pentathlon
> thesis

GREEK PREFIXES IN ENGLISH
Greek prefixes are often used in English.
> *anti* (against, opposite): antislavery, antiseptic
> *auto* (self): automation, automobile
> *neo* (new): neoclassical, neophyte
> *para* (beside, beyond): paradox, parallel

GREEK ROOTS IN ENGLISH
Greek words are often used as the base of English terms.
> *grapho* (to write): phonograph, telegraph
> *logos* (word, speech): biology, theology
> *monos* (alone): monogram, monologue
> *onoma, onyma* (name): homonym, synonym

LATIN AS THE MOTHER TONGUE

The charts below list words that represent the identical concept in each of the Romance languages. Although the words are pronounced differently, notice the structural similarities of the phrases.

ENGLISH: GOOD BREAD
> Latin: *bonus panis*
> French: *bon pain*
> Italian: *buon pane*
> Portuguese: *bom pão*
> Romanian: *bun paîne* (or *pîine*)
> Spanish: *buen pan*

ENGLISH: ONE THOUSAND
> Latin: *mille*
> French: *mille*
> Italian: *mille*
> Portuguese: *mil*
> Romanian: *mie*
> Spanish: *mil*

Hannibal and His Elephants
Conquerors of the Mountains That Reach the Sky

A play about Hannibal and his daring decision to cross the Alps and advance on Rome

CHARACTERS

Hannibal—*Carthaginian general from a noble family*

Hasdrubal—*one of Hannibal's officers (not his brother) and the one in charge of military siegeworks and the like*

Magol—*elder chieftain of the Boii in northern Italy*

Mago—*one of Hannibal's officers*

Maharbal—*Hannibal's cavalry commander*

Cornelius Scipio—*Roman consul*

Sempronius—*Roman commander*

Hannibal chose not to approach Italy by sea, but by land. He left his brother Hasdrubal in charge of Carthaginian interests in Spain and set out to cross the Pyrenees from Spain into France. He then planned to ford the Rhône River and cross the Alps into Italy. With him were thousands of foot soldiers and horses, as well as thirty-seven elephants. Most of the elephants were African forest elephants that stood not much higher than a horse, only about eight or nine feet at the shoulder. Their concave back, large ears, and ribbed trunk distinguished them from the larger African bush elephants and Indian elephants. Hannibal used elephants against cavalry because the horses were terrified of their smell, trumpeting noises, and strange appearance. If all went well, Hasdrubal would later follow Hannibal to Italy, and the two brothers would take Rome.

Act I

It is the middle of August. The march to Rome is foremost in Hannibal's mind. He has decided not to approach Italy by sea. Instead he is anxious to cross, for he has to get through the passes of the Alps before they are closed by the approaching autumn snows.

Scene 1: *Hannibal's camp in a dense forest near the bank of the Rhône. A steady rain and the smoke from the fires of wet wood cast an element of gloom over the tired, melancholy troops. The trumpeting of the restless elephants and the noise of fierce Gallic warriors on the opposite bank add to the tenseness of the situation. In a large tent, Hannibal and his officers are deep in discussion. Their concern is the morale of the men.*

Hannibal: I sense that the men are uneasy. Why is this so when we have come so far with practically no loss of life? We have traveled sixty-four hundred stadia* from New Carthage, and we have only twenty-six hundred stadia more to go before we reach the first Italian river valley.

Hasdrubal: My dear general, you must remember that our men, mostly Africans from Carthage and Iberians from Spain, are used to an arid, open land. The dense forests that surround us and this damp weather are very oppressive.

Mago: This is true. I've even heard that some of the men scattered ashes around the camp to ward off the evil spirits of the dark, cloudy sky.

Hannibal: We cannot change the weather. As for our surroundings, we can solve that problem by breaking camp, crossing the river, and continuing on over the

Alps. There are no dense forests there. But if we do not hurry, the passes will be filled with snow instead. Then we will have something else to worry about. We have no time to lose. Fall will soon be here.

Hasdrubal: That brings us to another concern. The men have heard rumors that the mountains touch the sky, the realm of unknown gods. Even I have my doubts about this venture.

Maharbal: Hannibal, Magol, the elder chieftain of the Boii, is here to greet you. He has journeyed through the Alps many times. Perhaps he can reason with the men.

Hannibal: Call him in so we can speak to him.

(Magol enters, fully armed, and stands before Hannibal and his officers.)

Magol: On behalf of my people, I come to offer our assistance. We, too, hate the Romans.

Hannibal: Thank you. We have much need of your services. Can we travel through the Alps with our men and beasts before winter sets in?

Magol: Yes, our tribes have made this trip often. It is not an easy road, but it can be done. The mountains are not too high. People even live on them and grow crops. Your only enemy now is time. You must beat the snows.

Hannibal: I am anxious to resume our march. We will rely on you to show us the way.

(Magol leaves and returns to his tent.)

Mago: There are rumors that the Romans have sent an army by sea to stop us. How do we explain this to the men?

Hannibal: There are Roman armies throughout the world. Should we wait for them to conquer us? We are on our way to Rome to destroy their power to make war. Tell your men that we must succeed so that their

families will be able to live freely anywhere they wish. Enough of these fears. We must think ahead. Maharbal, take the infantry northward along the river. I will remain with my cavalry to get the elephants across. We have to protect them by any means necessary, for they will be one of our greatest weapons against unfriendly natives, as well as against the Romans. The rest of you, have your men cut down trees and make rafts to transport the elephants.

The officers leave and begin preparing a large number of rafts, each about fifty feet wide. These are then bound together to form a two-hundred-foot pier that projects into the river. At the end of the pier, two large rafts are attached with towlines connected to several rowboats. Soil is laid on all the rafts, and the elephants are led onto them by making the females go first.

The elephants panic as they are towed across the river. Some are too frightened to move, while others jump into the water. They begin walking on the river bottom, using their trunks as snorkels.

All thirty-seven elephants are saved, although some of their mahouts¨ drown. Hannibal immediately leaves with them and his cavalry to join the main infantry that is already marching north toward the

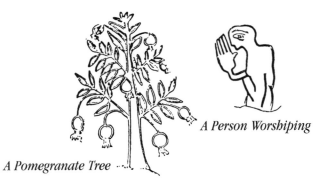

A Pomegranate Tree

A Person Worshiping

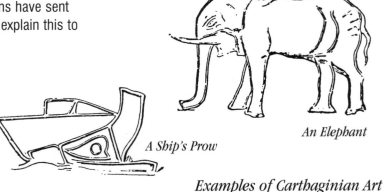

A Ship's Prow

An Elephant

Examples of Carthaginian Art

Alps. Some of the hostile Gauls flee from the Carthaginians when they see the elephants. Many retreat when they realize that Hannibal is only passing through their territory with no intention of harming them. Several join his forces.

Scene 2: *The Roman camp on the bank of the Rhône River, a short distance below the site Hannibal has chosen to cross the river. The Romans have just arrived from Italy in sixty ships under the command of the Roman consul Cornelius Scipio. It has been an uncomfortable trip. The men are exhausted from seasickness and the cramped quarters on board the ships. The leaders have no idea that Hannibal is so close as they plan their next move.*

Cornelius Scipio: Hannibal may still be on the other side of the Pyrenees for all we know.

Sempronius: We cannot be too careful about such a cunning man. Rumor has it that he plans to cross the Alps. He must be nearby if he intends to undertake such a dangerous journey before winter.

Cornelius Scipio: I will send three hundred horsemen up the river on a scouting expedition. The other troops will stay here and rest after our arduous voyage.

Sempronius: I will reorganize the army when the men have recovered so that we can move fast if we have to.

Cornelius Scipio: Remember that Hannibal has many elephants with him. Prepare the men, for they have never seen these awesome beasts before. The cavalry will have to control the horses as well as their own fears because the appearance, smell, and trumpeting will be strange to them.

Sempronius: That will be our most difficult task. Let us hope that Hannibal will lose his elephants when he crosses the Rhone or when he attempts his foolhardy trek across the Alps.

Cornelius Scipio: Let us hope that we also lose Hannibal and his army in the mountains. Sometimes I think only the gods can stop this madman from reaching Rome.

As the three hundred Roman horsemen slowly approach the Rhône, Hannibal sends five hundred of his cavalry down the river to scout the area. Neither of the troops is aware of how close they are to each other. They meet suddenly, and a long and bloody battle is fought. Many men are killed, about an equal number of Romans and Carthaginians. Both sides claim victory and retreat back to their camps.

Having crossed the Rhône, Hannibal decides not to pursue Scipio and heads for the Alps. Scipio, meanwhile, returns to Italy to join other legions and march north to the Po River. There the Romans will take a stand against Hannibal when and if he appears.

Act II

It is September, and Hannibal and his army push north along the left bank of the Rhône and then swing along the Isére toward the Alps, leaving Scipio and his troops behind. Along the way are many Gallic villages, where the Carthaginians get a supply of woolen garments, leg wrappings, and sturdy hide shoes for the difficult mountain terrain and cold weather ahead. The soldiers look forward to fighting the Romans in Italy, but they dread the Alps. It is Hannibal's courage and energy that give them the strength and enthusiasm to continue.

Scene 1: *Hannibal's camp at the end of a valley leading deep into the mountains. Torrents of water from the steady rainfall descend from precipices, and the ascending road is very steep and unsafe. Rugged cliffs and snow-covered peaks tower above the men and beasts. Scores of unkempt armed mountain men called Allobroges perch on the crags ahead, ready to hurl rocks and roll boulders upon the*

Examples of Carthaginian Art

The Ears of the God "Who Hears" and His Mouth, "Which Blesses"

A Chariot on Wheels

A Palm Tree With Two Clusters of Dates, Flanked on Both Sides by Two Pikes Representing Ensigns

Carthaginians and their animals. Hannibal halts his army and orders the men to make camp. He confers with his officers and Magol, the friendly Gallic chieftain.

Hannibal: Magol, you have led us to this valley. We did not anticipate the hostile barbarians who are confronting us. What do you know of them?

Magol: They are defenders of the mountains who call themselves Allobroges. They are protecting their territory. But they are also attracted by your obvious wealth.

Hannibal: How do you suggest we deal with them?

Magol: They retire to their hovels at night, knowing that no one would be foolish enough to travel through such a treacherous pass in the dark.

Hannibal: They underestimate me. Hasdrubal, before the sun rises, take a group of men and have them climb to the cliffs that the barbarians left. We will take them by surprise at dawn.

Hasdrubal: I will choose our strongest and most nimble soldiers.

Hannibal: Mago, even though we are short of wood, keep the campfires burning tonight so the mountain men will not suspect anything. Maharbal, order the men to prepare to decamp. We are going to move as many of our soldiers, supplies, and animals through the pass as possible before dawn.

Maharbal: In what order should we march?

Hannibal: Position your cavalry at the head of the column, with the heavily armed infantry at the rear. We must protect the supply wagons and the elephants at all costs. How are the elephants faring?

Mago: They seem to be enduring the cold, and they are able to make their way over rough terrain. However, it will be difficult for the horses laden with baggage and supplies to climb on ice and rocks in the dark.

Hannibal: We must take our chances.

Maharbal: How will we know when to begin?

Hannibal: I will climb with my bodyguard to a cliff above the pass and signal with a torch when you are to set the column in motion. Let us all begin preparations immediately.

(The officers leave to do as they are commanded.)

At sunrise the Allobroges return to find their niches occupied. In anger they attack the supply wagons and pack animals that have not made it through the pass. Several of the horses panic, causing man and beast to stumble to their deaths. Hannibal and his bodyguard descend from above, and infantrymen rush from the rear to protect the supplies. The strange sight of the elephants and the fierce charge of the Carthaginians send the mountain men fleeing.

Hannibal then leads his men down to the deserted valley, where the barbarians have their homes, crops, and pastures.

Scene 2: *An abandoned fort of the Allobroges. Hannibal meets with his officers to discuss the strategy for the rest of their crossing of the Alps and the descent into the Po River valley of northern Italy.*

Hannibal: We will rest here before we continue our march. The marauding parties of men that I have sent out have returned with enough cattle and sheep to feed our army for three days. We also will use up their stores of grain.

Hasdrubal: When we do move on again, I think we should put the elephants at the head of the column. The enemy will not dare attack because the beasts frighten them.

Mago: I have noticed that the elephants instinctively seem to pick out and follow the easiest path.

Maharbal: They are also a great help clearing the way of boulders that have fallen during landslides.

Hasdrubal: Hannibal, your decision to include the elephants in our adventure was certainly a wise one. I admit that I had my doubts about bringing them along.

Hannibal: We will especially need them against the Romans. Their defeat is the purpose of this venture. Magol, I am sending you and your men on to the Po River valley to prepare for our arrival in Italy. We can manage without your guidance now.

Magol: You need only continue on in the direction of the sunrise. Soon you will begin to descend and see in the distance the vast plains of my country.

Hannibal: (Raising his jeweled sword and pointing it at the snow-covered mountains around him.) These are the walls of Italy that we have conquered. Beyond them, east beneath the sunrise, is the city of Rome. All that we have achieved will be for nothing if we do not complete our journey with a victory over the Romans. Let us regain our strength, for the battle is yet to be won.

On the twelfth day, Hannibal broke camp, and the army, led by his elephants, marched down the steep, slippery, snow-covered path. Progress was made slowly and with much danger.

By the thirteenth day, they passed the snow line and moved into a forest. Huge rocks blocking the trail were removed by building fire on them and then pouring on vinegar that caused cracks to form. This made it easier for the men to split and pry apart the rocks with wedges and crowbars. The elephants, having recovered their strength by eating fresh green foliage around them, moved the crumbled stones. The column finally reached the plains of Italy on the fifteenth day.

Many men and animals had been lost to hostile attacks, exhaustion, exposure to the elements, and crossing swollen rivers. Only a few of the elephants survived. Although the final victory had yet to be won, the noble beasts had proved their worth. They and the Carthaginians had defied the unknown gods of the mountains that were thought to reach the skies.

---

*A stadium was a unit of Greek measurement. One stadium equaled approximately 600 feet. Stadia is the plural of stadium.

**A mahout is a keeper and driver of an elephant.

Project

The Roman calendar included many holidays and festivals. Some were private and celebrated at home by individuals and families. Others were public, organized and funded by the state. The rituals for some were elaborate and lasted for days, while other rituals were simple and took only hours to complete.

TERMINALIA—February 23

February 23 was the special day dedicated to Terminus, the god of boundaries. As the Romans emerged from a small community to a world power, property and property lines became increasingly important to them.

Legend says that around the sixth century B.C., a king of Rome ordered a temple built to Jupiter, the king of gods and men. He chose the Capitoline Hill as the site. All of the other gods who were worshiped in this area yielded their spots to Jupiter; all except Terminus.

The king did not become angry at Terminus or resort to force. He accepted his decision because removing a boundary stone was illegal and forbidden. Therefore, Terminus' shrine was not moved. Jupiter's temple was built around Terminus' shrine. An opening in the roof of the temple was made directly above Terminus' stone, since by custom any

Roman God Terminus

sacrifice made to Terminus had to be under the open sky.

Boundary stones were sacred to Terminus. The important ritual of placing or "planting" a new boundary stone was accompanied by a specific ceremony. An animal was sacrificed, and its blood and ashes, together with vegetables, fruits, honey, and wine, were placed in a hole made by the owners of the two adjacent properties. A stone or stump of wood—the boundary marker—was then put in place to cover the hole.

TO CELEBRATE TERMINALIA

MATERIALS NEEDED
- large stone, block of granite, wood stump, fence, or stone wall for the boundary marker
- leaves and vines
- flowers and ribbons (optional)
- two square stones, boxes, or cartons for the altars
- scraps of red, yellow, and orange paper to simulate fire
- twigs and branches
- corn (use popcorn)
- honeycombs (use bits of sweet cookies or cake)
- basket for corn
- wine (use grape juice)
- blood (use water colored with red food dye)
- white clothes for all those watching the rite

PEOPLE NEEDED TO PERFORM CEREMONY
- two owners of property
- two wives
- two old servants
- two young sons
- two young daughters
- family members or friends

LOCATION
- anywhere inside or outside

CEREMONY

1. If there is an audience, have someone narrate the background of the festival of Terminalia.
2. Choose a boundary stone. It can be a stone brought into the classroom, a marker in the school yard, or a fence or wall of your property.
3. Choose two property owners, one to represent land on each side of the stone.
4. Each owner places a garland made of leaves and vines on the boundary stone (flowers and ribbons optional).
5. Each owner sets an altar before his or her side of the boundary marker.
6. The old servant breaks twigs and branches and places them near the altar.
7. The young son takes a handful of corn from his basket and throws it into the fire. He does this three times.
8. The young daughter places some honeycomb on the altar.
9. Family members and friends place goblets of wine around the altar.
10. Attendants should be dressed in white and remain silent throughout the ceremony.
11. The owners sprinkle the boundary stone with blood.
12. Conclude the ceremony with a banquet and sing songs to Terminus.

N.B. The banquet depends on time and your situation. You can follow the Roman banquet activity on page 162 or just have a small party with refreshments and songs.

LEMURIA—May 9, 11, 13

The Romans honored their ancestors and even worshiped some as household gods. Hence, festivals honoring and placating the dead were very important. Lemuria was one such festival. It was

held on three odd days, since even days were considered unlucky. Lemures was the Latin name for "wandering spirits of dead people," spirits that returned to visit and sometimes to threaten

Statues of Roman Lares ("good spirits of the dead")

their living relatives. The Roman author Ovid (42 B.C.–A.D. 18) described in detail the rites of Lemuria as practiced by Roman families.

TO CELEBRATE LEMURIA
MATERIALS NEEDED
- alarm clock
- bed
- water
- washbasin
- black beans
- white sheets for ghosts
- metal pans, cups, or candlesticks

PEOPLE NEEDED TO PERFORM CEREMONY
- master of house
- people to act as ghosts

LOCATION
- any room or series of rooms made to resemble a house
- one area of the room or one room designated as the bedroom

CEREMONY
1. If there is an audience, have someone narrate the background of the festival.
2. The festival begins when the clock strikes midnight.
3. The master rises from his bed in his bare feet.
4. The master closes his fingers around his thumb and then turns closed fists outward.
5. The master washes his hands in the washbasin.
6. The master walks through his house (or room).
7. As he walks, the master spits black beans out of his mouth. He does not look to see where they fall, and he never turns around. He says nine times: "I redeem myself and my family with these beans."
8. Several ghosts follow the master (unseen by him) and pick up the beans.
9. The master again washes his hands.
10. The master hits together some metal pans.
11. The master says nine times: "Ghosts of my father, get out."
12. The ghosts leave the room.
13. The master then looks behind him, and the beans and ghosts are gone.
14. The master returns to bed.

N.B. This same ritual should be repeated each of the three nights.

Puzzle Pages

CROSSWORD PUZZLE

Across

1. Home of the Scipios
3. Sea bordering Italy
5. Carthaginians were to remain south of this river
8. Hiero II was ruler here
10. Ptolemy was king here
11. Carthaginians had colonies here
12. Dido's home
13. Italy and Greece belong to this continent
14. Volcanic mountain in Sicily
17. Elephant remains found here
18. This nation had alliance with Carthage
20. Powerful city in Sicily
21. Land north of Italy
22. Modern name of Gaul
25. Where Rome is located
27. Hasdrubal defeated here
28. Hannibal left Carthage for here
29. Hannibal defeated Romans here
30. Carthage had seaports here
31. _____ of Gibraltar

Down

1. River of France
2. Home of Mamertines
4. Islands off coast of Sicily
6. Hannibal died here
7. Home of the gods
9. Founded by Dido
15. Aeneas was from here
16. Rome first met Carthage here
19. Lake where Romans lost to Hannibal
21. Land east of Rome
23. Carthage had seaports on this island
24. Where Carthage was located
26. Hannibal crossed these

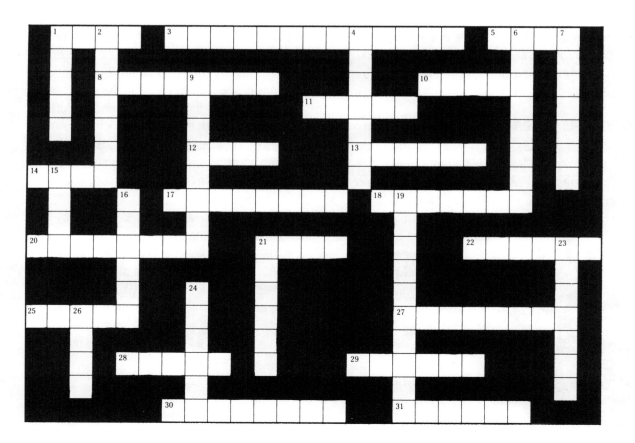

UNSCRAMBLE THE CLUES

Unscramble each of the six jumbled words below to determine the answers to the clues. Place the unscrambled words on the blank lines, then match each letter with its corresponding number to discover where Dido finally rested.

1. Romans tried to abolish this Druid ritual:

   maunh farciseci   __ __ __ __₂ __ __₁₃ __ __ __ __ __₈ __ __ __

2. Name given to the great struggle between Carthage and Rome:

   cupin swar __ __ __ __₃ __ __₁ __ __ __ __

3. Both Aeneas and Dido were this:

   feeguser   __ __₁₀ __ __ __₇ __ __ __

4. These were an important part of Hannibal's army:

   helpsenta __ __₄ __ __ __ __₆ __ __

5. Mercenaries in an army are actually this:

   droeliss __ __ __ __₁₂ __₉ __ __ __

6. Roman soldiers under Scipio Africanus used this weapon:

   nevajil __ __ __ __ __₁₁ __₅ __

Dido rested here:__ __ __ __ __ __ __   __ __ __ __ __ __
                1   2   3   4   5   6   7   8   9 10 11 12 13

WORD PUZZLE

Fill in the blanks by answering the clues. The letters in the squares will tell you the name of Dido's brother.

1. What the Romans called the Carthaginians   1.☐ __ __ __ __

2. Greek king   2.__☐ __ __ __ __ __

3. Roman general who kept his promise   3.__ __☐ __ __ __ __

4. Killed Sychaeus   4.__ __ __☐ __ __ __ __ __

5. Trojan leader   5.__ __ __☐ __

6. Roman poet   6.__ __ __ __ __☐

7. Appealed to Rome for help against Syracuse   7.__ __ __ __ __ __☐ __ __

8. These two peoples fought each other from 246 to 201 B.C.   8.__ __ __ __ __ __ __☐ __ __ __

9. Names of the two Scipio brothers killed by Hannibal's forces   9.__ __ __ __ __ __ __ __☐ __ __ __ __

95

Can you find the nineteen words and eight abbreviations in the maze below? They can all be found in the article "On Vocabulary" on page 84.

addendum	catastrophe	radius	etc.
alumnus	enigma	strata	fl.
anti	forceps	synonym	i.e.
aquarium	grapho	thesis	N.B.
auto	homonym	vacuum	viz.
axes	neo (2)	A.D. (4)	vs.
axis	para	e.g.	

```
                              C
                          D   A   H
                      A   X   T   Q   O
                  M   E   H   A   O   U   M
              U   S   E   T   S   C   H   A   O
          D   U   S   V   T   T   Y   E   P   R   N
      N   I   I   A   R   M   R   X   N   T   A   I   Y
  E   D   S   C   A   N   E   O   N   E   O   C   R   U   M
D   A   S   U   T   U   F   L   P   B   G   E   N   I   G   M   A
D   R   V   U   A   I   T   N   A   H   V   I   Z   I   Y   A   R   A   P
A   L   U   M   N   U   S   O   S   P   E   C   R   O   F   E   M   S   I   X   A
```

CAN YOU MATCH?

Match the correct word with the appropriate description.

1. Hannibal

2. Allobroges

3. rafts

4. Sempronius

5. Hasdrubal

6. mahout

7. Maharbal

8. Magol

9. Mago

10. Cornelius Scipio

a. An officer under Hannibal

b. Roman consul who led an army to oppose the Carthaginians

c. Hannibal's trusted commander of the cavalry

d. Leader of the Boii who offered to help Hannibal

e. Used to transport elephants across the Rhône

f. Carthaginian general who took his battle against Rome into Italy itself

g. Tribe that opposed Hannibal and threatened to stop his passage across the Alps

h. The driver and keeper of an elephant

i. Carthaginian officer with the same name as Hannibal's brother

j. One of the commanders under Cornelius Scipio

TRUE OR FALSE?

On the blank line write "True" or "False" about the corresponding statement.

1. After crossing the Rhône River, Hannibal decided to leave his elephants in Gaul. _____

2. All the Gauls supported Hannibal. _____

3. The Romans under Cornelius Scipio marched north to attack Hannibal in Gaul. _____

4. Hannibal began his march to Italy with the cavalry in front and the heavily armed infantry in the rear. _____

5. Hasdrubal advised Hannibal to have the elephants head their marching column. _____

6. Without Hannibal, the Carthaginians would never have made it across the Alps. _____

Topics for Comparison

1. Rome treated its subjects differently. Some had full citizenship rights, some partial, some none at all. Each ally and province had its rights and rules. Is this true with the United States? Compare the two powers taking the following into account: the American colonies under England, the United States prior to the Civil War, the United States prior to the Civil Rights Act, Alaska and Hawaii prior to statehood, Puerto Rico and the District of Columbia today, the Mariana Islands in the Pacific Ocean, and the United States' allies in NATO.

2. Carthage and Rome both wanted control of the western Mediterranean. Were their reasons similar? Could either survive without control? Could an agreement have been made that would have appeased both sides?

3. Compare the terms of the treaty at the end of the First Punic War with those of the Second Punic War. Discuss what attitude change occurred in Rome. What were Rome's intentions in regard to each treaty?

4. Compare the lives and goals of Hannibal and Scipio Africanus.

5. If Rome sought complete control of the Mediterranean, why were its terms so lenient for Carthage at the end of the First Punic War? Also, why did Rome agree to let Carthage control Spain south of the Ebro? Is dividing a country ever successful? Make comparisons with divided countries today.

Suggestions for Essays and Written Reports

1. Many historians believe that Hannibal was one of the greatest generals who ever lived. Discuss his handicaps (e.g., foreign soil, new recruits) and describe his personality as you see it through history.

2. Hannibal annihilated many Roman armies. Yet the majority of Rome's allies continued to back Rome, not Hannibal. Why? Was it the cultural differences, religious beliefs, or something else?

3. Historians offer many reasons for Hannibal's stay at Cannae after defeating the Roman army. No one knows for sure why Hannibal did not continue battling Rome to an almost certain victory. What do you think?

4. Why was Scipio Africanus' strategy of crossing to Africa clever? Would it still have been clever had he lost? What would have happened had he stayed in Italy and lost?

5. Why did Scipio Africanus succeed where so many Roman generals before him had failed?

6. Did Dido avenge Aeneas' treatment of her when she dismissed his requests in the underworld?

7. Why do you think Hannibal chose not to continue fighting Scipio at the Rhône River? Why do you think Scipio chose to return to Italy? Had each chosen to stay and fight, how might this decision have affected the course of history, especially the history of Western civilization?

8. Why do you think the Romans never used elephants on the battlefield?

Further Activities

1. Take an ice cube or a block of ice. Pour vinegar over it and see the results.

2. Reenact the scene in the Carthaginian senate (see page 74). Dress the Romans in togas. Research garb for the Carthaginians.

3. Write a play about Hannibal or a scene in his camp. Use the Carthaginian names of his family, have the characters discuss Hannibal, and have someone question Hannibal about his plans.

4. Reenact Dido's story of the ghost and her flight to freedom. Start with a darkened room with one light on Dido asleep in bed. Sychaeus (in sheet) then reveals all to Dido. The two characters stealthily walk to an area of the room and lift a board to find a treasure chest below. Use a large appliance box or an upside-down table as the ship Dido and her companions used to escape.

5. Stake out a piece of land. Take a piece of leather, felt, or cloth and make it into the shape of a bull's hide. (Make several the same size for a contest.) Place the bull's hide on the ground and mark out the area with chalk. Have each contestant cut his or her bull's hide into strips and then encircle the area. Have a contest to see who can encircle the greatest area.

6. Go to the library and research the geographic area of Carthage. Is the area still important as a seaport? Is it still prosperous?

7. Write a modern-day scenario for the elephant of Maillane. Would you invite the media? How would the elephant be preserved carefully and methodically? Would tests discover if the elephant was one of Hannibal's? Should a museum be built around the remains? Would the area become a tourist attraction?

8. Refer back to the article "On Vocabulary" on page 84. If any words are unfamiliar, look them up in a dictionary. Write a sentence or paragraph to include each abbreviation. Use Latin-based verbs and prefix combinations in a sentence. Combine other Latin verbs with prefixes. Use them in sentences. Write sentences using English words with Greek prefixes.

9. Research the differences between African forest elephants, African bush elephants, and Indian elephants. Look for pictures of the three types and find out where and how they are of use today.

Topics for Debate

1. Rome, a foreign power, was not right in sending forces to Messana to aid the Mamertines (Doves vs. Hawks). Carefully research the events leading to the Mamertines' request for aid. Consider Carthage's long-time interest in Sicily. For effect, participants can even dress in togas for the debate (see page 31 for toga instructions).

2. Regulus was right to return to Carthage. How could he have continued living in Rome had he not kept his word?

IV Gaul versus Rome

> A person's life is only a point of time. Therefore, let us enjoy it while it lasts and use it purposefully.
>
> *Plutarch,*
> *Greek philosopher and biographer*
> *(c. A.D. 50–c. 120)*

OVERVIEW

PEOPLES INVOLVED:
Romans, Gauls (ancestors of the French)

DECISIVE BATTLE:
Alesia in Gaul (52 B.C.)

GENERALS:
Julius Caesar (Roman),
Vercingetorix (Gaul)

HISTORICAL SIGNIFICANCE:
Gaul loses its freedom and becomes a Roman province

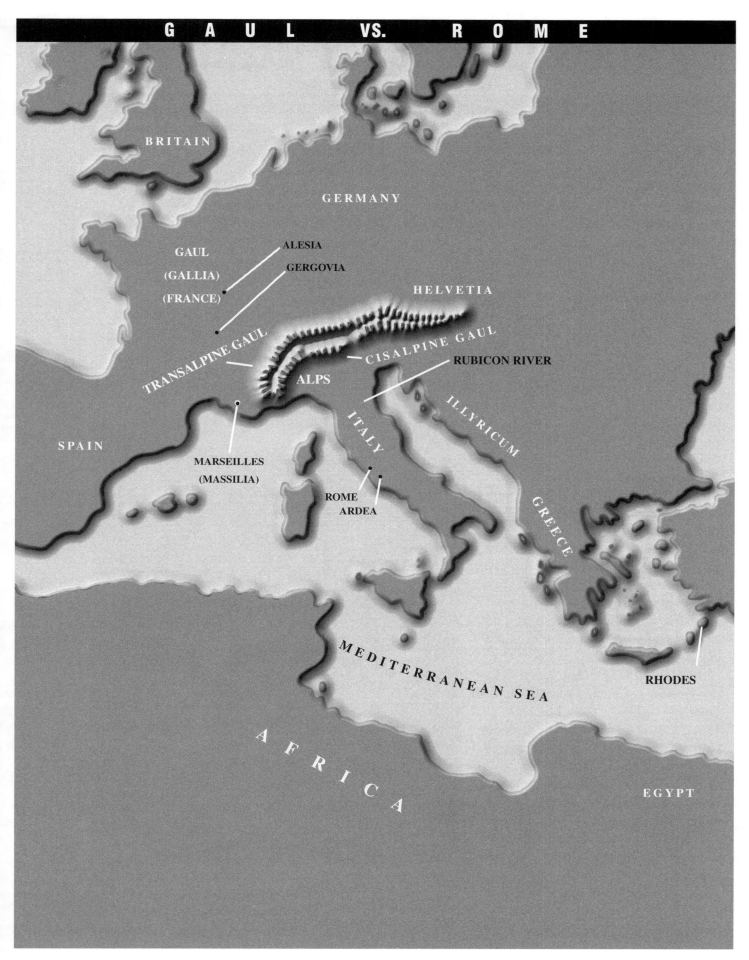

Rome's Battle for Gaul

Since few rulers are content with boundaries on their power, conflicts are inevitable. Yet no people, no country, and no ruler has ever governed forever. Each begins, rises, flourishes, and then falls—some slowly, some gracefully, some tragically.

Rome was not the first power, nor would it be the last, to seek world conquest. Conquered people meant a ready supply of workers and a continual flow of tax money. Conquered lands symbolized power.

In 59 B.C., Rome ruled the Mediterranean. Only Egypt and the western coast of Africa were not totally under its sway. Rome had had several major defeats in the more than five hundred years since its founding on April 21, 753 B.C. (the traditional date) but had overcome each. Now its goal was to subdue the enemies attacking its inland borders.

The Gauls to the north (the ancestors of the French) had been Rome's enemies for centuries. About 387–386 B.C., invading Gauls destroyed the city of Rome. Avenging that terrible day was the Roman dream. This dream became the goal of the Roman statesman and military leader Julius Caesar. If he could conquer such a foe, all of Rome would rejoice and follow him.

In 59 B.C., Roman law stated that no one individual could rule Rome, that the power was to be shared by two elected individuals known as consuls. This law was passed in 509 B.C. to prevent anyone from becoming king of Rome. By law, at the end of a term each consul was given a Roman province outside of Italy to govern for a year. Such regulations were passed to make sure than no one individual became too powerful.

However, as Rome entered the first century B.C., several individuals were not content with this arrangement. Personal gains and glory became more important than the glory of Rome. Julius Caesar grew up in this atmosphere and absorbed this thirst for more control and power.

As Caesar neared the end of his consulship in 59 B.C., he saw to it that his subsequent post was the governorship of Gallia, specifically Transalpine and Cisalpine Gaul. His term, however, was not for the normal one year, but for five years. Helping him obtain such a post were the astute general Pompey and the wealthy financier Crassus.

When the Aedui tribe in central Gaul asked Rome for help against the Helvetii (the ancestors of the Swiss), Caesar knew he had his chance.

The Gauls Invading Rome
(Three Gauls approach an old senator who refused to flee.)

The Helvetii were planning a large-scale migration through central Gaul and would probably choose the route that passed through Transalpine Gaul. The Helvetii were aware of Rome's power and, not wanting to antagonize the Romans, assured them that their passage would be peaceful. Caesar, however, took the opportunity to advance his legions to Transalpine Gaul and defeat the Helvetians. For the next five years, Caesar "helped" the Gallic nations friendly to Rome subdue other unfriendly Gallic, British, and German nations. Gaul was Caesar's, as was the fame of the conquest.

Yet all was not well. Gaul wanted to be a friend not a subject of Rome. In 52 B.C., a Gaul named Vercingetorix (ver sin JET o riks) led the great revolt against Roman rule. Caesar was

there to meet him on the battlefield of Alesia (ah LEE see a) in central Gaul.

The Helvetians Planning Their Migration

Vercingetorix Versus Caesar

The Gallic chieftain Vercingetorix faced Julius Caesar at Alesia in the final battle for Gaul. Vercingetorix had accomplished what no other Gaul had before him: He had won the loyalty and friendship of Gallic tribes throughout all of Gaul. "Death to the Romans; freedom for the Gauls!" was the battle cry heard among the Gallic warriors. Vercingetorix had given them hope. Defeat and surrender were not inevitable. Gaul could be free to rule itself. A unified army fighting for the very land on which it stood could surely defeat an intruder by cutting off its food supplies and reinforcements.

Yet such had not been the case. The Gauls fought bravely and with honor, but their adversary Caesar was a wily general. He did not use one set of tactics or a basic fighting strategy. He carefully scouted his enemies and learned their battle and encampment procedures. Then he

devised new tricks and plans to outwit and outmaneuver them.

Yet even the heavy losses did not deter Vercingetorix. The Romans had suffered heavy losses, too. Alesia, a hill town, was impregnable and would surely prove too much even for Caesar—or so Vercingetorix and his followers hoped.

But the defeat and slaughter of many of the famed Gallic cavalry—superior even to the Roman—cast a desperate gloom over those left to defend Alesia. Before Vercingetorix ordered the gates of the town closed, he sent the remainder of his cavalry home to their tribes to collect supplies and food for the coming siege.

Caesar quickly realized the natural strength of Alesia's position and that storming the hill town would result in the wholesale slaughter of his legions. A blockade and siege were the only possibilities. Caesar then began the incredible task of surrounding Alesia with trenches, pits, and spikes to prevent any Gallic escape or entry. Alesia was under siege.

The days passed quickly, and soon Alesia was without food. The situation was desperate, yet the Gauls did not surrender. When the Gallic relief forces did arrive, they bravely attacked the Romans, giving great hope to those besieged within Alesia's walls. It was a short-lived hope, for after a victorious beginning, the tide of the battle turned and the Romans forced the Gauls to retreat on all sides.

Vercingetorix Before Caesar

Gauls Fleeing Before the Advance of Caesar

Still the Gauls did not yield or surrender, but made preparations for the final battle. Every man was used, every device employed. The fighting was fierce, and the Roman defense system was strained to its utmost. The Romans were besieged on two fronts: by the relieving Gallic forces and by those setting out from Alesia itself. Caesar himself went from battle line to battle line encouraging his men, altering plans, and sending reinforcements to those forces having the most difficulty. Suddenly, as members of the Roman cavalry appeared in one area, the tide began to turn. Soon the Romans had the edge. Slaughter and retreat followed.

Those from Alesia retreated once more within the walls. Vercingetorix called a council meeting. The relief forces, what was left of them, had fled; the food supplies were gone; hope was gone. Vercingetorix offered himself as the prize. He told his fellow leaders: "Surrender me, this body, to Caesar, dead or alive." The Gallic leaders accepted his offer and sent a message to Caesar.

Caesar stood before his camp as the heroic Vercingetorix, dressed in full armor, approached on horseback. The Gallic chieftain circled his adversary once, dismounted, threw off his armor, and surrendered. The battle for Gaul was over. Caesar had won. Six years had passed since Caesar had first entered Gaul to help friendly tribes repel an invading enemy. Now, in 52 B.C., Caesar stood the master of all of Gaul.

Colonel Stoffel and Alesia Napoleon III, nephew of Napoleon I and emperor of France from A.D. 1852 to 1870, greatly admired Julius Caesar. He carefully studied the Roman general's strategies and incorporated some of them into his own.

Napoleon III was very interested in archaeology. He believed that beneath the topsoil across France lay countless relics of the past. He placed one of his trusted men, Colonel Stoffel, in charge of tracing Caesar's routes in Gaul and of locating the exact site of Alesia. Colonel Stoffel also was commissioned to excavate and record whatever traces he could find of Caesar's famous siegeworks.

Using Caesar's *Gallic Wars* as a guide, Colonel Stoffel did locate Alesia and clearly described and illustrated his interpretation of Caesar's strategies. Stoffel found the remains of Alesia on Mount Auxois, near the modern-day town of Alise Ste. Reine. Napoleon III incorporated Stoffel's finds into his comprehensive biography on Caesar, *Histoire de Jules César.*

Vercingetorix

Little is known about Vercingetorix prior to his stand against Caesar. His father had been the leader of the southern Gallic people known as the Arverni. He was killed, however, by his fellow countrymen when he attempted to become king. This was done according to the provisions of a Gallic law passed to prevent any individual from creating a monarchy.

In 52 B.C., a delegation of Gauls representing the resistance movement elected Vercingetorix their leader. He led his troops heroically, even routing Caesar's legions on several occasions. An eloquent speaker, he gave unity of purpose to his followers and taught them discipline and the value of hard work. His basic strategy against Caesar was to burn Gallic towns and supplies so as to starve the Roman troops. His military strategy was similar to guerrilla warfare.

Vercingetorix

Even in defeat, he kept his courage and urged others to do so. Yet at Alesia, when he realized all hope was lost, he nobly offered himself as the prize. His colleagues did not offer to join him, nor did they dissuade him. They willingly accepted his offer.

Caesar had Vercingetorix sent to prison, where he remained until 46 B.C., when Caesar led his prizes of war in a magnificent triumphal procession through Rome. Vercingetorix was his grand prize. After the march, Vercingetorix was led back to the dungeon and killed.

But Vercingetorix was not forgotten. He is a French national hero, and the Frenchmen of the resistance movement in World War II made him their symbol. Today a statue of the patriotic leader stands high in Alesia, and a nearby marker tells visitors of his heroic stand against an invading foe.

Astérix Le Gaulois (Astérix the Gaul) On October 29, 1959, Astérix, a short, stout, mustached cartoon figure dressed in garb worn by the ancient Gauls, first appeared as a comic strip in the French comic weekly *Pilote*.

The creators of the strip, René Goscinny (text) and Albert Udergo (art) originally set Astérix and his exploits in a little village in Armorique, one of the last areas to hold out against the Roman army under Julius Caesar. In later comic strips Astérix ventured outside Gaul—e.g., to Egypt, Britain, and the Olympic Games.

The basis for Astérix's power lies in a magic potion given to him by a Druid, a potion that made him invulnerable. The Romans in the comic strip are portrayed as unintelligent and cowardly. Little Astérix constantly outwits Julius Caesar and his Roman legions.

Profile: Gaius Julius Caesar

Julius Caesar

100 B.C. Caesar is born into the Julian family, which traces its roots to Iulus (U luss), son of Aeneas (eye KNEE us) (Rome's legendary ancestor) and grandson of Venus, the goddess of love and beauty.

87 B.C. Appointed special priest of Jupiter, the king of the gods, by his uncle-in-law Marius, a famous Roman general and leader.

84 B.C. Caesar marries Cornelia, the daughter of Cinna, Marius' colleague and successor.

81 B.C. Sulla, Marius' bitter enemy, names himself dictator of Rome and demands that Caesar divorce his wife. Caesar refuses and goes into hiding. Sulla later relents.

— Daughter Julia is born.

81–76 B.C. Holds various minor political positions; serves with honor in Asia.

75 B.C. Leaves for the island of Rhodes to study oratory (public speaking). En route he is captured by pirates.

73–62 B.C. Returns to Rome; holds various offices.

69 B.C. Wife Cornelia dies.

67 B.C. Marries Pompeia, granddaughter of Sulla.

65 B.C. Serves as *aedile* (EYE deal) (in charge of public buildings, corn supply, and public games). His endeavors are supported financially by the wealthy Roman Crassus. His actions as aedile win Caesar tremendous popular support.

63 B.C. Elected Pontifex Maximus, chief priest of Rome, for life.

61 B.C. Holds office of propraetor (pro PRY tor) in province of Hither Spain.

60 B.C. Caesar joins with Crassus and Pompey (the powerful Roman general and statesman) to form the First Triumvirate in order to advance their political fortunes. Caesar is elected consul.

59 B.C. With the help of Crassus and Pompey, the senate awards Caesar the proconsulship of Cisalpine Gaul, Transalpine Gaul, and Illyricum, strategically and economically important provinces. *N.B. A proconsulship was usually for one year. Caesar's was for five years.*

58–52 B.C. Caesar wins Gaul for Rome.

56 B.C. The triumvirs extend Caesar's proconsulship for another five years.

54 B.C. Caesar's daughter, Julia, dies. Her marriage to Pompey had kept the two Romans on friendly terms.

53 B.C. Crassus dies in battle.

49 B.C. Caesar and his legions cross the Rubicon River, the southern boundary of Cisalpine Gaul, and head for Rome, thus declaring war on Pompey and the Roman senate, which had demanded that Caesar disband his troops before entering Italy.

48 B.C.	Caesar defeats Pompey's forces at Pharsalus in Greece. Pompey flees to Egypt and is assassinated. Caesar follows Pompey to Egypt.
47 B.C.	Caesar sides with Cleopatra against her brother for control of Egypt. Cleopatra is made queen of Egypt.
46 B.C.	Caesar consolidates his power in Africa and crushes Pompey's sons' forces.
45 B.C.	War in Spain; Caesar destroys surviving forces still loyal to Pompey.
45–44 B.C.	Initiates numerous administrative reforms; appointed dictator for life.
44 B.C.	Assassinated on March 15.

NB *Dates according to Matthias Gelzer,* Caesar, *Harvard University Press, Cambridge, MA, 1968.*

Suetonius on Caesar It is said that Caesar was tall, fair complected, well formed with a rather full face and keen black eyes, and healthy except for nightmares and sudden fainting spells in his later years. He was quite careful about his appearance. His baldness bothered him a great deal, and he made it a habit to comb forward the few locks on the crown of his head.

excerpted from Lives of the Caesars: Julius Caesar, *by the Roman biographer Suetonius (sway TOE knee us) (fl. c. A.D.. 120)*

A Heroic Roman Centurion

As Marcus Petronius, a centurion (Roman soldier), tried to cut down one of the enemy's gates, he was overwhelmed by a great number of Gallic soldiers. He shouted to his fellow soldiers following behind him, "I cannot save myself and you, too. But I can at least help you because it was my desire for glory that got us into this situation." He then bravely charged into the midst of the enemy, killed two Gauls, and pushed the others a short distance from the gate. When his comrades tried to help him, he said, "You cannot help me. I have lost far too much blood, and my strength is failing. Get out while you have the chance and return to your legion." Petronius then continued fighting. A few minutes later, he fell dead. But he had saved the lives of his fellow soldiers.

—*as told by Julius Caesar in* Gallic Wars, *Book VII, Chapter 50*

NB *This incident took place during the siege of the Gallic town of Gergovia.*

Roman Soldiers (each with a Spanish sword at his waist)

Caesar and the Pirates

Sea travel in ancient times was quite risky. There were no steam engines, motors, or radar, only sails and oars. If the seas were too choppy, you stayed in port or made for the nearest port. If there was no wind and your oars were few, you stayed in port or waited patiently for a breeze to come. But these problems were minor in comparison with the one great danger of sea travel: pirates. These ruthless bands terrorized the coastal cities of the Mediterranean and all sailing craft in their path. Various countries and kingdoms had sent fleets to destroy the pirates and their strongholds in island bays and caves, but no nation had ever succeeded in wiping them out.

In 76 B.C., Caesar was aboard a ship sailing east when pirates overtook and captured his vessel, its crew, and its passengers. Realizing escape was impossible, Caesar kept calm and reserved. The pirates, noticing Caesar's fine clothes and manners, singled out the young passenger as a member of a wealthy Roman family.

"He'll bring us a good ransom. Just look at his clothes. Let's ask for twenty talents!" (A talent was a unit of Roman money.)

Caesar merely smiled and said, "You really are not very smart. Don't you know who I am? Twenty talents is too little. Ask for fifty talents."

The pirates could hardly believe the prisoner's audacity. "Fifty, you say. But if the money is not raised, death will be your reward!"

For thirty-eight days Caesar lived among his captors. Yet he suffered little. He demanded they provide him with quarters worthy of his position.

If they made too much noise, he ordered them to be quiet. He had them run races with him for exercise. When he felt the urge to divert himself, he read them his poetry and made them listen. Again and again he ridiculed their habits and customs. He promised to kill them as they deserved. The pirates listened and laughed.

Finally the ransom money arrived, and Caesar was freed. He went immediately to his friends who had raised the money and asked for a ship and a crew to avenge his capture. With great eloquence and the promise of much booty, he finally calmed their fears and won their approval.

Without further delay, he headed for the

A Greek pirate ship attacks a Greek merchant ship. N.B. The pirate ship has a ram and is propelled by oars. It is also low and long. The merchant ship has a mast for a sail and no oars. It is also higher and bulkier.

pirates' cove and captured the entire crew without a single loss on his side. He confined the crew to prisonlike quarters on his ship and confiscated the ransom money and other treasures.

Yet prison was not enough. The pirates could escape, or some greedy governor could ransom them. Death was the only method of dealing with such outlaws. Caesar took it upon himself to issue the sentence: Each pirate was to be hanged first and then crucified (so as not to cause him too much pain).

Plutarch on Caesar There was no danger to which Caesar did not willingly expose himself, no task that he shunned. He could endure incredible hardships and yet he was a thin man and subject to epilepsy. He never used his size or illness as an excuse, but rather worked harder to overcome both. He traveled long distances without tiring. He ate a coarse diet and often slept outdoors. He was an expert rider. As a child, he had trained himself to ride at full speed with his hands joined behind his back. He also learned to dictate letters to two people at once while on horseback.

excerpted from Parallel Lives (Lives of the Noble Romans): Caesar, *by the Greek biographer Plutarch (c. A.D. 50–c. 120)*

A Crafty Gentleman

Crassus was a wealthy Roman who helped finance Julius Caesar's career. The Greek biographer Plutarch (c. A.D. 50–120) wrote the following story about Crassus.

In the city of Rome, there lived a powerful and wealthy man named Marcus Licinius Crassus, or Crassus the Rich. Everyone knew him and admired him, for he was a generous man willing to befriend anyone in need. His lifestyle was simple and his home modest. But he had one fault: He was very greedy. He never had enough money. There were many stories about how he first amassed such wealth, but perhaps one of the better known and more credible involved a particular group of slaves whom Crassus had bought.

Early in his career, Crassus realized how susceptible the city of Rome was to fire. The height of the buildings and the lack of space between them made fire fighting extremely difficult. Often structures were completely destroyed before any official fire brigade could be assembled. The crafty Crassus thought of a clever scheme.

He attended many slave auctions, buying men who were builders and architects until he had a force of more than five hundred. He told them of his plan and waited.

They did not wait for long. As soon as Crassus smelled smoke, he called his force together and headed for a burning apartment building. Nearby he saw a man in great distress. Rome's fire department had not yet arrived, and the building was ready to fall.

"Is this your building?" asked Crassus calmly.

"Was it, you mean," answered the man in despair.

"Will you sell it to me?" asked Crassus.

"Sell it to you? My good man, hardly a wall remains, and you wish to buy it?"

"Yes," answered Crassus. "I cannot pay you much, for as you say, barely a wall survives; but I will pay you now."

"It is yours," exclaimed the owner, still con-fused why anyone would want to buy such a wreck. His despair had now turned into joy. Crassus also was happy and instructed his workmen to do as they had been trained.

His five hundred men swarmed around the building, each with an assigned task. Bucket followed bucket, and soon the fire was extinguished. Whatever could be recovered from the interior was removed to be sold or refurbished by his craftsmen.

Crassus was now ready to implement the next stage of his plan. He ordered his architects to redesign the structure and instructed the builders on how to proceed.

Even though many Romans watched all these undertakings with great interest, no one imagined the extent of Crassus' crafty plan until the day when the workers placed a "For Sale" sign on the front of the property. Their surprise was even greater when they heard the high price. The building had been carefully and properly restored by trained architects and builders.

Crassus' plan had worked, and within a short period of time, he had greatly increased his wealth by buying and selling many of Rome's buildings.

Roman Apartment House

The Day the Geese Saved Rome

In 387 B.C. (some sources say 386 B.C.), Rome was fighting for its life. Gallic tribes had marched boldly across the Alps through northern Italy and into the city of Rome. The Roman consul Manlius and several of his colleagues had fled to a fortress atop the Capitoline Hill. There they successfully resisted every Gallic attempt to capture the heart of Rome. However, as the siege continued and the food supply dwindled, the situation became desperate.

Manlius managed to send a message to Ardea, a town south of Rome, asking the exiled Roman ruler Camillus to return and help break the siege. Camillus put aside his anger at having been exiled and agreed to come, but on the condition he be appointed formally by Roman citizens on the Capitoline Hill.

Cominius volunteered for the dangerous mission of bringing Camillus' answer to Rome. Slowly and stealthily Cominius crept through the enemy's lines until he arrived at a hidden passage that led up the Capitoline Hill into the fortress. After delivering his message and obtain-

Can You Find the Geese? (from Comic History of Rome, *by Gilbert A. Beckett, 1870)*

ing Camillus' appointment, Cominius left by the same route.

Later that day, as the Gallic sentries were manning their posts, one soldier noticed several broken branches. After carefully surveying the area, the Gauls realized that they had discovered a path that would lead them into the fortress.

All was readied for the attack. The air was filled with anticipation. Victory was near. Quietly each Gallic soldier picked his way up the brush-covered hill. As the entire force reached the entrance to the fortress, all that could be heard was the cackling of geese.

The sacred geese in the temple of the goddess Juno on the Capitoline Hill had heard the approach of the enemy. The high-pitched shrieking of the geese awakened the sleeping Roman soldiers, who rushed to their battle stations. There they bravely and forcefully repelled the intruders, and the Gauls were quickly defeated. Later, Camillus and his troops joined the Capitoline Romans and routed the entire Gallic army.

Rome was free, but its people never forgot that fateful day. To avenge so bold an attack was the Roman dream—a dream Julius Caesar fulfilled when he conquered Gaul approximately two hundred thirty years later.

Rome Saved by the Cackling of Geese

Gyptos Chooses a Husband

THE STORY OF MARSEILLES, FRANCE

In ancient Gaul a woman chose the man she wished to marry. But after the marriage ceremony, the husband had the power of life and death over his wife.

When a Gallic chieftain's daughter came of age and was ready to marry, her father often would host a great banquet and invite all the eligible bachelors in the area. According to custom, at the end of the feast the young maiden would take a goblet of wine and walk around the hall carefully assessing each suitor. After making her choice, she would give the goblet to her future husband and settle the marriage contract.

According to legend, a Gallic chief named Nann prepared such a feast for his daughter Gyptos (JIP tos). His territory, which bordered the northern coast of the Mediterranean Sea, was a frequent port of call for Greek ships. It so happened that a Greek ship was in port at the time of the feast, and Nann invited the visitors to his banquet.

Later that evening as Gyptos paraded around the room with her goblet of wine, she stopped before a Greek named Euxenes and presented him with the goblet. His surprise and astonishment soon gave way to assent, and the two were married.

Together they founded a new town, Massilia, the ancestor of today's Marseilles. It prospered and became a widely known seaport. Many Greeks came to settle in the area, spreading their culture and civilization throughout southern Gaul. (Massilia also aided Rome against Hannibal in the Second Punic War.)

In later years Marseilles allied itself with Rome and became a principal city in one of Rome's most important provinces, Transalpine Gaul.

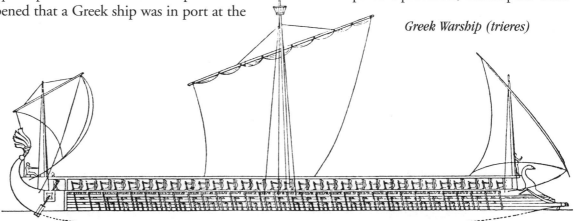

Greek Warship (trieres)

Cisalpine Gaul and Transalpine Gaul Cisalpine Gaul refers to the "nearer" province of Gaul, or the Gaul closest to Rome, on this side of the Alps (northern Italy). Transalpine Gaul refers to the "farther" province of Gaul, or the Gaul farthest from Rome, on the other side of the Alps.

The Healing Waters of the Gauls

The Romans conquered many lands and peoples, imposed their laws, and levied taxes, but rarely did they persecute foreign religions. It was Roman policy to adopt and adapt the religious practices of newly won territories. They believed the new, foreign gods might help them also.

After Caesar won Gaul for Rome, this policy of religious tolerance continued, but with two exceptions: Rome eliminated the Druid practice of human sacrifice (Druidism was the religion practiced by most Gauls) and slowly eliminated Druid priests because they held too much authority.

Since the early Druids left no known written records, it is difficult to fully understand their religious practices. Artifacts unearthed by archaeologists and the writings of the Romans have helped to unravel the mysteries of this people.

From these findings we can see how Roman and Gallic deities often merged or were worshiped together, each retaining characteristics of his or her origins.

One interesting merger of deities concerns water. The Romans loved their baths. This special, prolonged ritual preceded the evening meal and could last for hours. Bathing establishments offered a variety of baths, exercise areas, shops, and libraries. Mineral waters and hot springs fascinated the Romans, and many spas were built throughout Italy.

The Gauls also were partial to hot springs and mineral waters. But they believed that these waters, which seemed to possess miraculous powers, had to be under the power of some deity. Consequently, they worshiped and spoke with the divine spirit presiding over each sacred spring whenever an ailment or physical problem afflicted them.

Gauls traveled great distances to a spring known for curing a particular affliction. They brought with them as offerings models of the afflicted area (e.g., head, arm, etc.) with the effects of the disease graphically illustrated. Thousands of these votives, as they were called, have been unearthed. The models, made of wood or stone, provide a vivid link to some trusting, hopeful pilgrims of the past.

In many of these areas, the springs still flow and modern spas have replaced the ancient buildings.

Julius Caesar's Name Today Julius Caesar's name has been used in a variety of ways to form new terms. Because of Caesar's great popularity, many cities and areas throughout the Roman Empire were called Caesarea. One such place was an island in the English Channel (the body of water separating England and France). In time, the name gradually changed in spelling and pronunciation to "Jersey." In the 1600s and 1700s, when the English were colonizing the New World, they used many names from their native land. They preceded some of these names with the word "new," hence the name of the state of New Jersey.

The phrase "Caesarean section" traces its roots to Caesar, who was believed to have been born in this manner.

Because of Caesar's military prowess, many countries throughout the world have used his name for their word denoting a supreme leader and ruler. The Russians used the terms "tzar" and "tzarina" (also spelled czar and czarina) for their emperors and empresses, while the Germans called their ruler "kaiser."

On Archaeology

Excavation sites can be found throughout the world both on land and underwater. *Archaeology,* a magazine published by the Archaeological Institute of America, includes in its March/April issues a travel guide to the ancient world that lists excavations in progress and restored sites that are open to the public.

UNCOVERING THE PAST

Have you ever wondered how and why objects were covered? Wind, rain, violent storms, floods, and tides all shift the sand, rock, and water that cover the earth. People through the centuries also have done their share as they have cleared or filled in land for homes, farms, harbors, factories, and public buildings. Dig down almost anywhere on the earth and you will find treasures, some of no value and others priceless. Some sites are easily accessible; others, covered by later structures, might never be accessible.

EXCAVATING A SITE

The archaeologist first must determine the site to be excavated. The reasons for choosing an area might include other important discoveries found close by or passages from ancient books and records suggesting something of importance in a particular location. Sometimes when old foundations are dug for new structures, archaeologists check these particular areas. Also, burrowing animals frequently unearth pieces of objects that appear significant. After the site is chosen, a team is selected. Depending upon the type and the location of the "dig" (a term used to refer to an area of excavation), there is generally only one archaeologist accompanied by specialists in various fields, helpers, and volunteers.

A survey is then made of the area both on the ground and from the air. Photographers, using stereo cameras and infrared film, take pictures of the site from airplanes or helicopters. The photos provide a good indication of what may lie beneath the ground or of what took place in an area. For example, aerial photography helps to distinguish the areas where crops grow at a faster rate over filled-in pits and ditches as opposed to areas where crops grow at a slower rate over stone foundations.

The excavators also use scientific instruments such as resistivity meters to measure moisture (a lack of moisture indicates walls, floors, or some structure), proton magnetometers to detect iron objects and ovens (which cause variations in the earth's magnetic field), and sonar equipment to understand sound waves (a lack of these waves indicates a sunken vessel or objects hidden in monuments such as the pyramids of Egypt).

The archaeologist then uses all the data gathered from these instruments to map out the area. Care must be taken, because once a site is uncovered, it can never be reexamined. Archaeologists must do it correctly the first time. Usually partial or sample excavations are done to see what lies below. Only if major finds are expected are trenches dug.

As each object is discovered, its exact position must be noted. Therefore, a grid is made, i.e., the site is marked by strings or wires resembling the lines on a piece of graph paper. This makes describing the discovery site much easier. Archaeologists also must record the depth at which objects are found. The basic law of archaeology is that the deeper the object is found, the older it is.

Computers are being used more often to store information about archaeological finds, to help in the comparison of artifacts found at different excavation sites, and to interpret the quantitative and qualitative patterning that some artifacts, especially those composed of stone and ceramics, provide. A computer's ability to rapidly sift through vast amounts of information and find the needed artifact or paragraph makes it an invaluable tool for the researcher and archaeologist.

BALLOON ARCHAEOLOGY

A new method of surveying an area for traces of ancient ruins has gradually become more widely accepted. Balloon archaeology developed from the realization that the perspective you have of an object or area increases tremendously when you are raised a distance above a certain artifact or location. For example, think of an ant's view of a plowed field and of your own view. Then imagine the view from a balloon.

When archaeologists want an aerial picture of a site, they first attach cameras to a tethered balloon. The balloon is then allowed to float above the specified area. By walking and pulling on the rope, the ground crew can adjust the position of the balloon and their cameras. New types of film can magnify shots, detect variations in soil colors that reveal underground structures and features, and penetrate water to take shots of submerged objects.

A balloon operates best from 10 to 800 meters (1 meter equals 39.37 inches) above the area being photographed. This method has several advantages. The camera can be held fairly stationary above an object, and its distance from the object from a vertical position allows for clear, accurate photographs of a small or a large area.

WORKING AT THE SITE

To reach the treasures, various tools are needed. As no one knows where or when an artifact might be found, strainers of wire mesh are used to sift the soil carefully, especially if bone splinters, seeds, or tiny objects such as jewelry are expected. Sometimes containers are filled with water to "wash" the soil and thus allow light objects such as seeds to float to the surface. Soft camel's hair brushes and toothbrushes also are used. In some areas, trowels, picks, shovels, spades, and even bulldozers are necessary. When a team is working in an underground vault, oxygen masks are often worn. In locations where rooms or chambers lie beneath the surface, inverted telescopes are sent down so that archaeologists can have a look before excavating.

EXPLORING THE OCEAN'S FLOOR

Underwater archaeology also is important. We have learned much from submerged objects, shipwrecks, and even cities that have been covered by water. The principles governing land excavations apply to underwater sites as well. In addition, deep-sea divers are needed to reach some sites; small submarines help survey the area; underwater telephones are used to communicate with those on ships at the surface; decompression chambers allow divers to remain underwater longer; and balloons inflated by divers underwater are attached to wire baskets to lift objects to the surface.

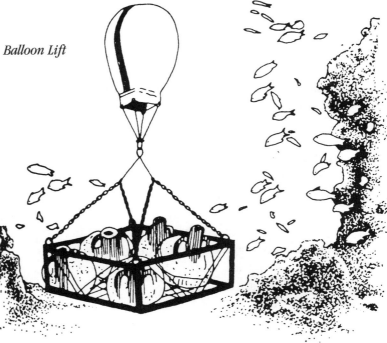

Balloon Lift

ANALYZING THE FINDS

Excavating and recording a find is just the beginning of an archaeologist's task. The artifacts must be analyzed and compared before the results can be announced. The following techniques will give you an idea of some of the numerous archaeological procedures used in the laboratory or workroom.

CARBON-14 DATING

In 1946, a method of dating objects such as wood, seeds, peat, hair, cloth, skin, and leather was discovered. Since carbon 14 is absorbed by all plants, this radioactive isotope (element) passes into all living matter. Once this matter dies, no new carbon is absorbed and the carbon begins to decay. Scientists have learned how to measure this decay and how to account for the effects of the Industrial Revolution and atomic weapons testing on carbon. By comparing the percentage of carbon in a dead item to that in a living one, the age of a discovered artifact can be determined fairly accurately.

THERMOLUMINESCENCE

Since almost all containers in the ancient world were made of clay, unbelievable quantities of pottery have been unearthed. After a ceramic piece has been fired in a kiln, the energy found in the pottery's particles is trapped within the object. Scientists reheat the piece of pottery so that this energy will be released. Thermoluminescence is the process of measuring the energy, thus dating the object.

Method of Recovering Lengths of Fragile Timbers From the Ocean's Floor (courtesy of Anne Vadeboncoeur)

The Druids and the Fall of Gaul

A play that details Vercingetorix's courageous stand against Caesar

CHARACTERS

Gauls

Celtillus—*most powerful chief in Gaul*
Vercingetorix—*son and popular heir of Celtillus*
Boduagnotus—*chief of a tribe of Gaul*
Bridiga—*daughter of Boduagnotus*
Carvillax—*young noble of Gaul*
Divitiacus—*noble of Gaul*

Druids

Cotuatus—*Chief Druid*
Segibo—*Druid*
Coprax—*Druid in charge of sacrificing*
Vertico—*Druid*

Romans

Caesar—*leader of the Romans*
Caius—*Roman general*
Titus—*Roman general*
Lucius—*Roman engineer*
Baculus—*Roman engineer*

Lurking in the sacred groves and wild places of Gaul were the ancient Druids, who were said to have originated in the primeval forests of Britain across the turbulent waters of the channel. The Druids dealt with all things sacred. They instructed the young in the secrets of religion, conducted the public and private sacrifices important to all the people of Gaul, explained the law, and sentenced offenders.

The other class of men in Gaul, other than the common people who were treated almost like slaves, were the nobles. They were a superstitious group who, when ill or in danger in battle, would resort to human sacrifice with the help of the Druids. Consequently, the nobles held the Druids in great respect, for they had sympathy with military ideals and encouraged bravery in war.

Caesar's armies conquered Gaul and its people, but the power of the Druids and their mysterious gods and rituals were not easily suppressed. The magic and wisdom of these "men of the oak tree" made a deep impression on the ancient world as far away as Egypt, and the Druids are said to have even predicted the fall of Rome.

ACT I

It is more than two thousand years ago in the territories of the Carnutes (KAR new teys) in the center of all Gaul (near the modern French town of Chartres). The Druids are assembling in their consecrated area for their annual meeting. They must elect a new chief

Druid, for the previous one recently died. They also must attend to the civil administration of the land. Many important decisions must be made, for Gaul is being threatened externally by the Romans from the south. Internally, the nation's unity is in danger because of discontent with the powerful chief Celtillus, who has tried to restore the monarchy and the divinity of kings in his own person. Celtillus is unpopular because of his selfish ambitions.

A strong opposition party of nobles who favor a republic ruled by an elected leader are also meeting not far from the sacred grove of the Druids. They seek the death of Celtillus.

The Druid priests support the tradition of "Divine Kingship" for religious reasons. They realize that a strong leader with the support of the gods as

*Gauls Scaling
Caesar's Fortification
Around Alesia*

well as the people is crucial. Vercingetorix, the young son and heir of Celtillus, is popular with both the Druids and the nobles. His ambition is to unite all the tribes of Gaul against the Romans. Unlike his father, he has the welfare of his nation at heart, not personal gain and glory.

A compromise must be found, for the future of Gaul is at stake.

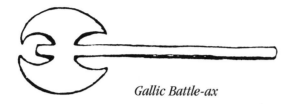

Gallic Battle-ax

Scene 1: *A gloomy forest in the center of Gaul. The undergrowth of shrubs is thick because the branches have been laced together, creating an impenetrable living wall. Somberly robed Druids pass through a hidden entrance to their sacred meeting place, an open space encircled by huge oaks. The limbs of the trees, covered with the parasitic mistletoe sacred to the Druids, form a dome that lets in only a few beams of sun. Dead leaves cover the ground, and the air is damp and cold in the dismal shade. Crudely carved, rotting images of ancient gods are propped up against the trunks of the trees. The doleful chanting of priests mourning their dead chief Druid is the only sound to be heard. This ceases when the eldest priest, Cotuatus, walks up to a wooden altar in the middle of the clearing. Cotuatus turns to face the many Druids who have gathered in the sacred grove.*

COTUATUS: We have gathered here for our annual meeting, possibly the most important one of our lives. The future of Gaul is at stake. There has been discord among our people, a dangerous situation, for we must be united against the invading Romans.

SEGIBO (SEG ee bo): But first we must choose a new leader. Our beloved chief Druid has been dead several weeks. I propose that you, Cotuatus, as our eldest and most respected priest, succeed him.

VERTICO: I agree with Segibo. No one else is as qualified to preside over us as you are, Cotuatus. We need a strong and wise leader during these trying times.

(A breeze stirs the treetops, and a sprig of mistletoe dislodges from a branch high above the priests and falls to the ground, landing at the feet of Cotuatus.)

SEGIBO: Truly a sign from the gods. Nothing is more sacred to us than the mistletoe. In the name of Dis, the god of the under earth, from whom all Gauls descend, I nominate Cotuatus to be our chief Druid and to possess supreme authority among us.

(The Druids all murmur their consent.)

COTUATUS: I am honored by your decision, and I will try to live up to your expectations and those of the gods. Let us now commence with our duties as judges. We are thought to be the most just men, and we must maintain the laws of our land. Bring forward the chief Celtillus, who has tried to restore the monarchy without our authority and assumes to possess Divine Kingship.

(Celtillus is brought into the clearing by two strong Druids. He is of large stature with an arrogant bearing. He is clad in tight-fitting red-and-blue-striped pants with a red cloak over his shoulders and wears a bronze helmet decorated with two horns on his head.)

COTUATUS: Celtillus, you have been accused of crowning yourself king of Gaul and have claimed divine rights. By whose authority did you give yourself this honor and power? Who proclaimed you the earthly representative of the gods?

CELTILLUS: I earned the title and the rights because of my courage, strength, and military skills. I command thousands of warriors, have won many battles, and have accumulated much wealth from the spoils of war. I felt that I deserved the honor I gave to myself.

COTUATUS: We Druids have always supported the divine right of kings for religious reasons. No one and no nation can succeed for long unless it is the will of the gods. What do you say, my brother priests?

SEGIBO: Druidism and kingship go together. One cannot survive without the other. We are the spokesmen for the gods, and Celtillus has acted without our consent.

VERTICO: Celtillus, you have committed a sacrilege. You assumed powers that are not yours to give, even to yourself. You have defied our laws and traditions.

SEGIBO: The nobles and your warriors have come to us demanding your death. They want a leader who will unite Gaul against the Romans, not someone who thinks only of his own personal gain and glory.

COTUATUS: We have heard enough! I command that you be sacrificed. We need to assure the gods of our loyalty and to give them your life. We need all the help of the gods to defend our borders and drive the dreaded Romans from our lands. Coprax, begin preparations to burn this arrogant chieftain as a sacrifice to Dis. Invite all who are worthy to witness the sacred event.

COPRAX: I will make a hollow wicker figure in his shape and collect wood for the fire.

COTUATUS: Celtillus, what do you have to say for yourself?

CELTILLUS: I accept my fate, for I know I will be reborn in another body. I do not fear death. I only ask that my son, Vercingetorix, be considered my successor.

COTUATUS: The nobles have already declared their loyalty to your son. Apparently he has the ability to organize a force against the Romans and desires to defend his homeland. Personal gain is not his objective. The welfare of Gaul is his only concern.

SEGIBO: Such a man deserves our support. Let us confer upon him the Divine Kingship.

COTUATUS: So be it. Inform Vercingetorix and the nobles of our decisions. Now let us go on with the sacrifice. The sooner we please the gods, the better it is for Gaul.

Scene 2: *The camp of the nobles a few miles from the sacred oak grove of the Druids. A messenger has just arrived at the hut of Vercingetorix with news from the priests. After receiving the message, the young noble turns to his fellow Gauls who have been meeting with him.*

VERCINGETORIX: I have just been told that the Druids are sacrificing my father to the gods and have proclaimed me king of the Gauls in his place. I expected their punishment of him, but I never imagined that they would give me their blessing and support. I mourn his death but rejoice that I am free to fight the Romans.

BODUAGNOTUS (bod u og NO tus)**:** You have been honored among all men to lead us. Your unselfish loyalty to our nation has earned you that privilege. Now you must unite the tribes of Gaul.

VERCINGETORIX: Thank you, my faithful friend. I will do the best I can.

BODUAGNOTUS: I would like to take this time to offer you the hand of my daughter, Bridiga (BRID ig uh), whom you have known since childhood. Marriage to her would bind our tribe to you.

VERCINGETORIX: I am so pleased at your offer. I hope she will share my feelings. Bring her to me.

(Bridiga is brought into the hut. Vercingetorix approaches her and takes her hands in his.)

VERCINGETORIX: Bridiga, will you be my bride and queen?

BRIDIGA: Oh, yes, if my father will consent.

BODUAGNOTUS: My child, you have my blessing.

BRIDIGA: *(turning to Vercingetorix)* I will gladly take my place at your side. I have loved you from the time we were children, and I could hope for no better and happier future.

Alesia From the South

118

VERCINGETORIX: Together we shall rule Gaul. After I have properly mourned my father's death, I will send messengers to all the tribes in Gaul to gather here for a celebration of our marriage. It will also be a good opportunity to discuss what actions we must take against the Romans.

BRIDIGA: I will leave to begin the preparations.

(After Bridiga exits, Vercingetorix turns to his friends.)

VERCINGETORIX: Carvillax (car VIL lax), bring sweet mead for us all to drink a toast to the memory of my father, to my beautiful bride, and to the future of Gaul.

CARVILLAX: Shall we use the skulls of our enemies that have been fashioned into drinking vessels?

VERCINGETORIX: Certainly, for this is a very special occasion.

(Carvillax brings the macabre vessels out of a chest and fills them with mead.)

VERCINGETORIX: May the gods look favorably upon the sacrifice of my father for the sake of our people and all of Gaul. *(Each man raises a gold-rimmed human skull to his lips and drinks.)* May we gain strength from these skulls of our slaughtered enemies.

ACT II

It is the year 52 B.C. in central Gaul. For an entire year Vercingetorix and Caesar have been engaged in a long and bitter series of battles. Despite Vercingetorix's efforts to unite the entire nation, many Gauls have refused to take any part in the war, and some tribes have even become allies of Caesar.

Although the Druids support his divine kingship, they can do little to aid Vercingetorix. They cannot take both sides and retain their power in Gaul. The priests themselves have become divided, and the chief Druid, Cotuatus, has begun to lose his authority. Sacrifices have been made, and the blessings of the gods have been sought, but to no avail. The time when the Druids, murmuring their incantations, could come between armies and stop a battle is over. Vercingetorix must make his last resistance against the Romans without the help of the gods and their priests.

Scene 1: *The strongly walled town of Alesia in Gaul. Vercingetorix has decided to camp here with more than eighty thousand men for his final resistance against the Romans. He is discussing his plans with his friends and officers in their headquarters.*

VERCINGETORIX: Caesar has finally caught up with us and is camped outside our walls. What have our scouts reported, Divitiacus?

DIVITIACUS (div ih TEE ah kus): The Romans are busy laying out camps on the hills surrounding us on three sides. Our scouts have seen legionnaires armed with picks and shovels digging trenches and making walls with the earth.

VERCINGETORIX: How many men do they have?

CARVILLAX: Only about fifty thousand. Not nearly as many as we expected.

VERCINGETORIX: That is true, but Caesar's skill in besieging cities makes up for his lack of troops. We need as many men as we can get for our final attempt at chasing the Romans from our land. Boduagnotus, I want you to leave with our cavalry to recruit help from the Gallic tribes that have not yet supported us. You, a revered elder chieftain, are respected among our people, and many will listen to you. I also want you to take your daughter, my wife Bridiga, with you to a distant town where she will be safe from the dangers of the inevitable battle.

BODUAGNOTUS: I will try to do as you say, Vercingetorix, but Bridiga will not willingly leave when you are faced with danger. It is not the way with the women of Gaul.

Alesia From the Northwest

VERCINGETORIX: Then I will send her on a mission to ask the Druids for their prayers to the gods for our victory. I will tell her to have the priests cut mistletoe from the holy oak trees with their golden daggers on the sixth day of the moon. We will decorate our shields with this sacred plant to give us strength and courage in battle. She cannot refuse to go on this important mission, for we need the assistance of our gods. The gods of the Romans are very powerful.

BODUAGNOTUS: I will have the cavalry prepare to depart late tonight.

VERCINGETORIX: Carvillax, deliver Bridiga to me so that I may tell her of my wishes and take my leave of her.

CARVILLAX: I will do so immediately. She will need what little time is left to prepare for her journey.

VERCINGETORIX: Divitiacus, have our scouts

Druid Worship in Ancient Gaul

continue watching the Romans and report to me at once if there is any change in their strategy.

DIVITIACUS: I will do as you command.

(The men leave at once to attend to their separate missions. Vercingetorix is left to ponder the fate of his people.)

Scene 2: *The tent of Caesar in the Roman camp. He is busy planning his strategies for the siege of Alesia. With Caesar are his generals and chief engineers.*

CAESAR: Lucius, I want camps built on the highest vantage points around Alesia. Join them to each other with long trenches and strong, thick walls of earth. We must circle the town as soon as possible.

LUCIUS: The men are working day and night. I am having three trenches dug in the more vulnerable areas, and the walls are being reinforced with trees and branches woven in.

CAESAR: Good. I also want rows of ditches and pits dug with sharpened, fire-hardened posts sunk in the bottom. Beyond these pits, lines of stakes topped with iron hooks and barbed points are to be driven into the ground. We must take no chances that any Gauls escape as did their cavalry last night. Caius (KAI us), have you discovered the purpose of that venture yet?

CAIUS: Our spies report that Vercingetorix has sent his trusted chieftain Boduagnotus to recruit more soldiers from the neighboring tribes. They also seek some sort of magic from their mysterious Druids.

CAESAR: That is what I expected. Then we shall build a line of fortification behind us as well, so that our camps are thoroughly protected. Lucius, proceed at once. We have no time to lose and must be ready when Boduagnotus returns with more Gauls.

TITUS: What are we to do about the magic of the Druids? I have heard that they can stop armies with their spells and chanting.

CAESAR: We must trust that our gods will protect us. Baculus, have your men construct towers on wheels that we can use to scale the stone walls enclosing the town. When they are completed, we will begin our siege.

BACULUS: I will have my men start cutting trees at once, for we will need much lumber to build several strong mobile structures.

TITUS: Caesar, when will we get reinforcements from Rome? We are already outnumbered. If Boduagnotus is successful, we will be in a real dilemma.

CAESAR: I expect more cohorts to arrive any day. But do not worry. The odds have been against us before, and we have been victorious. I will not accept defeat. Gaul will become a province of Rome before the year is over. This war has gone on long enough, and I am anxious to conquer more lands. You are all dismissed. We have work to do.

Siege Tower on Wheels

After six weeks of preparations, Caesar's army attacks Alesia. From their walls the Gauls throw javelins and stones and fire arrows at the Romans. The Romans hurl javelins, pointed stakes, leaden balls, and stones on the city from huge wooden towers. Many men are killed or wounded on both sides.

Just as the Romans begin to breach the walls of the city, Boduagnotus returns with two hundred fifty thousand Gauls and attacks the Romans from behind. The earthen walls, trenches, and deadly pits Caesar had constructed hinder the Gauls enough to give the Romans time to turn from their siege of Alesia and defend themselves.

At first Vercingetorix and his people are elated with the arrival of Boduagnotus and his recruits. But soon they receive word that Bridiga was unable to get the blessing of the Druids or the sacred mistletoe. The annual meeting of the priests in their holy oak grove was not held due to discord among the group. Both the Druids and the nobles are divided despite Vercingetorix's efforts. This news disheartens the Gauls because of their superstitious nature. They feel that the gods are no longer with them.

The Gauls continue to fight valiantly, but they are no match for the Romans and their engineering skills. Thousands of horses and men are impaled on the sharp stakes when they fall into the trenches and pits. Those who survive are speared by the expertly thrown javelins of the Romans. Anyone who manages to escape these obstacles is attacked from behind by several cohorts of legionnaires who have just arrived from Rome. Boduagnotus' remaining soldiers eventually flee into the surrounding forests.

From the crumbling walls of Alesia, Vercingetorix sees that all is lost for Gaul, and he reluctantly prepares to surrender to Caesar.

Scene 3: *The camp of Caesar the next morning. Vercingetorix, wearing an intricately made shirt of chain mail and trousers of many colors and armed with splendidly ornamented weapons, approaches on his war-horse decorated with rich trappings. After riding through the battlefield strewn with the fallen bodies of Romans and Gauls and circling the camp three times, he dismounts when he reaches Caesar's tent. The two leaders meet face to face. Vercingetorix then lays his sword at the feet of the Roman leader.*

VERCINGETORIX: With this sword I surrender myself so that you will be more lenient with my people. Your gods are more powerful than ours. I have lost the Divine Kingship.

CAESAR: Your bravery has made you worthy to be called king of the Gauls. I accept your surrender. Your nation will prosper as a province of Rome, and your people will be blessed by our gods. *(turning to a guard)* Lead this courageous and noble foe away and place him in chains.

Caesar sends Vercingetorix to Rome, where he is imprisoned for six years until his execution. The Druids lose their power and prestige in Gaul and retire to their sacred groves to practice magic and worship the gods. History will be the final judge of their role in the ancient world.

Project

BACKGROUND

In 52 B.C., within the walls of the hilltop town of Alesia, Vercingetorix, the Gallic chieftain, made his final stand against Julius Caesar, the Roman military leader in Gaul.

When Caesar learned that Vercingetorix had sent messengers to all the Gallic towns requesting support and relief troops, he acted quickly. He designed and built a double ring of siegeworks around Alesia. The inner ring, or the contravallation, was to keep Vercingetorix and those in Alesia from getting out, and the outer ring, or the circumvallation, was to keep the relieving Gauls from getting in.

SIEGEWORKS

MATERIALS NEEDED

- rectangular cardboard box approximately two by three feet or larger (sides of box should be ten to twelve inches high)
- dirt for box and "traps"
- water (to wet dirt)
- blue paper (to simulate rivers)
- toothpicks
- Popsicle sticks
- pointed dowels or toothpicks
- twigs (about three inches long) with little branches but no leaves
- string (to tie branches)
- spoons and knives (for digging)
- small twigs
- wood chips
- Christmas tree ornament hooks

NB *This model gives an idea of Caesar's strategies and is not an accurate scale model.*

Cross Section of Caesar's Siegeworks at Alesia

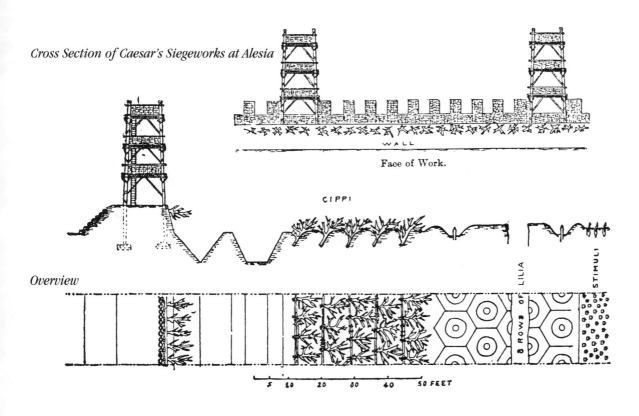

Face of Work.

CIPPI

Overview

LILIA   8 ROWS OF   STIMULI

5 10 20 30 40 50 FEET

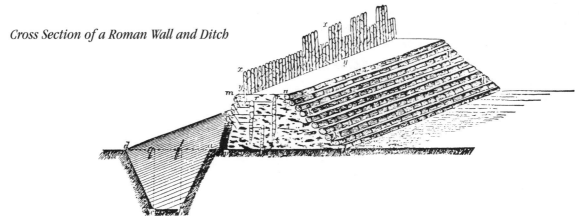

MODEL

1. Fill the box with dirt.

2. Carefully pat down the dirt so it is hard and level with the edge of the box. (Use water to make the dirt moist and easier to work with.)

3. The front of the box is one of the narrow sides.

4. Add more dirt near the back of the box to make the fortress of Alesia. Make it a triangular mound six inches high, six inches long, and four inches wide (see illustration).

5. Cut three-inch-wide strips of blue paper and run them along the sides of Alesia for the two rivers (see illustration).

6. With the spoon, dig out a trench eight inches long by six inches wide a little distance from the Alesia mound.

7. At the front end of the box, trace a line in the dirt from river to river, creating the cir-cumvallation, or outer line, of the siegeworks. *N.B. Caesar's circumvallation was thirteen to fourteen miles in circum-ference and circled Alesia. This model runs only from river to river. The plan of the circumvallation was similar to the contravallation, except that it had only one ditch and faced outward toward the troops coming to relieve Vercingetorix.*

8. About three inches from the circumvallation, trace a parallel line in the dirt from river to river, creating the contravallation, or inner line, of the siegeworks. *N.B. Caesar's contravallation was nine miles in cir-cumference.*

9. In front of the contravallation, dig two parallel ditches five inches wide by four inches deep with sloping sides. (Leave two inches of flat space between the ditches.)

10. Along the inner ditch, place a strip of blue paper to represent water. (Caesar diverted water from the river into this ditch.)

11. The inner ditch has a flat bottom; the outer ditch has a pointed bottom.

12. Use the dirt from the ditches to build a mound about three inches high atop and along the outside bank of the outer ditch.

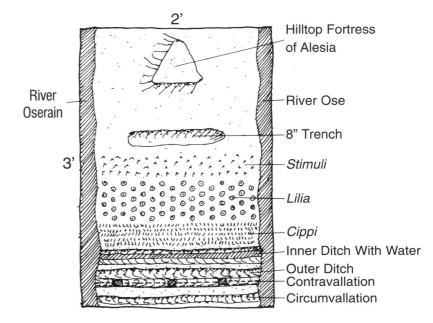

13. On top of the mound, line up Popsicle sticks for the palisade or fence. (At spaced intervals Caesar erected wooden towers with multiple stories, each story a platform surrounded by a fence. You can do this with Lincoln Logs or Popsicle sticks. Use ladders fashioned out of twigs or toothpicks to connect levels.)

Archer From Island of Crete

14. Stick twigs into the mound. (These stop any enemy from climbing up.)

15. Just beyond the inner ditch, dig five rows three inches deep from river to river and place twigs fastened together with string in the ditch. Pack dirt around the bottoms of the twigs. (These hamper the approaching enemy.) These are *cippi* ("tombstones")—Caesar's first trap.

16. To make the *lilia* ("lilies"), or Caesar's second trap, scoop out eight diagonal rows of pits two inches deep and two inches apart. Stick a pointed dowel or toothpick into the bottom of each pit. Pack lots of dirt around the dowel, allowing only the tip to stick out above the surface. Cover the pits with small twigs and wood chips. (These break the legs of the enemy's horses.)

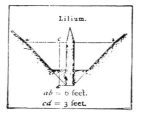

Lilium

17. For the *stimuli* ("goads"), Caesar's third trap, cut a pointed dowel or toothpick in half. Stick a small bent ornament hook into the flat end. Stick this into the dirt, metal point up. Scatter the goads thickly all in front of the lilia. (These cripple the legs and feet of anyone trying to cross the siegeworks.)

Stimulus

Puzzle Pages

CROSSWORD PUZZLE

Across

1. Strategy used at Alesia
2. Caesar held this office in Spain
4. One of Caesar's personal characteristics
7. Gauls to Caesar
9. Captured Caesar
10. Dug to prevent enemy escape
11. Caesar, Crassus, Pompey
12. Saved Rome
13. Stuck into ground at siegeworks
15. Vercingetorix stayed here in Rome
16. Type of water Gauls enjoyed
18. Caesar was this
19. What pirates wanted
21. What happened to pirates captured by Caesar
22. Marcas Petronius was one
25. Caesar was this for Jupiter
26. Unit of Roman money
27. Individual in an army
28. Part of Caesar's forces

Down

1. Caesar was a master at this
2. Title of Roman chief priest
3. Caesar in charge of public games when he held this office
5. Caesar appointed this for life
6. Marius made Caesar one
8. What happened to Caesar
14. What Caesar became in 58 B.C.
17. Part of Caesar's defenses
20. Excavation site
23. Number of talents pirates first asked for Caesar's ransom
24. What Crassus wanted

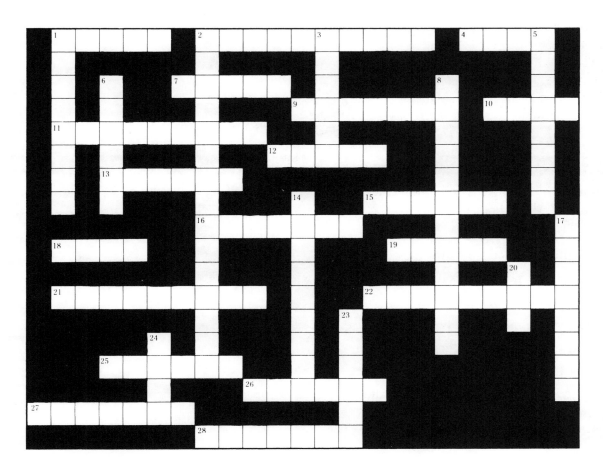

125

UNSCRAMBLE THE PEOPLE

Unscramble each of the six jumbled names below to determine the answers to the clues. Place the unscrambled names on the blank lines, then match each letter with its corresponding number to discover the name of a Gallic chieftain.

1. Gallic comic hero:

    raxesit __ __ __ __ __ __ __
     5 13

2. Gallic maiden who chose a Greek husband:

    tgsopy __ __ __ __ __ __
     7 9

3. Caesar's assistant:

    bunaesil __ __ __ __ __ __ __ __
     12 2

4. Petronius died here:

    vaeggior __ __ __ __ __ __ __ __
     3 1

5. Tribe in southern Gaul:

    vanirer __ __ __ __ __ __ __
     11 6

6. Discovered ancient sites of Alesia:

    nocello felsoft __ __ __ __ __ __ __ __ __ __ __ __ __ __
     4 10 8

Gallic chieftain: __ __ __ __ __ __ __ __ __ __ __ __ __
 1 2 3 4 5 6 7 8 9 10 11 12 13

WORD PUZZLE

Fill in the blanks by answering the clues. The letters in the squares will tell you the name of a seaport town in southern France.

1. Sea bordering Italy
2. Gyptos founded this town
3. Caesar lay siege to this town
4. Mountains in northern Italy
5. Caesar planned to study here
6. Caesar was proconsul here
7. "Farther" province of Gaul
8. The Rubicon divided these two lands
9. "Nearer" province of Gaul
10. Gaul today, and the last Gallic town to resist Caesar

ON ARCHAEOLOGY WORD FIND

Can you find the twenty-two words hidden in the maze below? They all can be found in the article "On Archaeology" on page 113. Clue: They are all archaeological terms and equipment.

archaeology	computer	grid	telephones
artifact	data	masks	thermoluminescence
balloon	dig	picks	trench
brushes	diver	shovel	trowels
bulldozer	excavate	sonar	
camera	find	spades	

```
D  B     L  M     F  M     P  P     S  S     H  F     T  O
A  B     C  N     R  C     K  I     E  H     T  L     R  C
T  R     A  D     A  O     E  C     D  O     B  B     O  N
A  U  T  O  N  R  H  C  N  E  R  T  I  K  W  C  A  V  M  A  D  C  B  M  W  T
T  S  P  I  D  O  E  T  O  L  A  K  S  S  D  M  P  E  L  I  O  M  P  A  E  Y
R  H  F  I  F  R  K  M  S  V  H  A  L  I  S  R  S  L  R  B  Y  U  F  S  L  L
C  E  R  G  E  A  X  W  A  R  C  H  A  E  O  L  O  G  Y  T  T  U  L  K  S  C
H  S  F  V  A  R  C  C  T  C  B  U  L  L  D  O  Z  E  R  E  S  K  T  S  F  G
N  P  I  C  H  O  X  T  E  L  E  P  H  O  N  E  S  M  R  R  W  H  X  O  I  Z
O  D  X  P  L  E  C  N  E  C  S  E  N  I  M  U  L  O  M  R  E  H  T  D  D  O
```

Match the correct word with the appropriate description.

1.	Bridiga	a. Roman conqueror of Gaul
2.	Celtillus	b. Ancient priests in Gaul
3.	Alesia	c. Became king of the Gauls
4.	Caesar	d. Went to fetch the sacred mistletoe as a charm for the defenders of Alesia
5.	Druids	e. Became a human sacrifice
6.	Vercingetorix	f. Gallic god of the under earth
7.	Baculus	g. Gauls drank this from their enemies' skulls
8.	Dis	h. Vercingetorix's last battleground
9.	mead	i. Vercingetorix's father-in-law
10.	Boduagnotus	j. Roman whose men were in charge of building towers to be wheeled up to Alesia

TRUE OR FALSE?

On the blank line write "True" or "False" about the corresponding statement.

1. Vercingetorix inherited the kingdom of Gaul from his father. _____

2. Vercingetorix planned to oppose his father's death sentence. _____

3. The Gauls were a very united race. _____

4. Gallic warriors preserved the skulls of their enemies to use as goblets. _____

5. The Gallic nobles could overrule the Druids' decisions. _____

6. Human sacrifice was commonly practiced by the Druids in times of danger and illness. _____

7. Caesar feared Vercingetorix and the power of the Druids. _____

8. Druidism originated in northern Gaul. _____

9. The Druids believed in reincarnation. _____

10. Caesar defeated Vercingetorix without any Roman reinforcements. _____

Topics for Comparison

1. Why did the Gauls lose to Rome? Would the results have been the same regardless of the generals? Compare and contrast the traits of the two peoples, the characteristics of their leaders, and the military strategies of each.

2. Caesar was a great military leader. His men loved and admired him. His popular support helped him attain his goals and brought him power. Throughout history many great generals have followed their military successes with leadership roles in government, e.g., George Washington, Dwight D. Eisenhower, Napoleon I. Compare and contrast the careers of these men with that of Caesar.

3. Compare and contrast the story of Gyptos and Euxenes with that of Odatis and Zariadres as recorded by the Greek scholar Athenaeus in his *Banquet of the Learned,* Book XIII, Chapter 35.

4. Do people still travel to healing springs today? Are there any in France? Do people leave models of their afflicted areas or any other mementos of thanksgiving? Include and compare the shrines at Lourdes in France and at Fátima in Portugal.

5. Crassus' plan was certainly crafty, but was it that easy? To succeed, did he not need good planning, constant readiness, worker cooperation, and a knowledge of carpentry, masonry, and restoration? Could anyone have done it? Is this comparable to the refurbishing and restoration of old buildings and mills today?

Suggestions for Essays and Written Reports

1. Each nation begins, rises, flourishes, and falls—some slowly, some gracefully, some tragically. Choose one nation and explain how it illustrates the previous sentence. Or choose three nations to illustrate the three possible demises of a nation.

2. Julius Caesar was ambitious. His goal was to rule Rome for a long period of time. Discuss his involvement in the Triumvirate, his choice of a province close to Rome, his five-year proconsulship, and his crossing of the Rubicon.

3. Considering the time in history, was Caesar's treatment of Vercingetorix justified? Was there an alternative? Did Vercingetorix's prison stay accomplish anything?

4. Why was Caesar able to control and dictate orders to the pirates when no other nation could? Take into account that nations often preferred to pay a tax to be left alone or to ransom captives and that each nation had many worries other than pirates. Discuss why the pirates were awed by Caesar's refined, fearless manner and by the fact that he dared to defy and laugh at them. What does this incident tell you about human nature?

5. Was the Roman policy of adopting and adapting foreign religious customs and gods a good political move? If so, why?

6. If the Druids had not been so disunited among themselves and had given the Gauls under Vercingetorix their blessing at Alesia, do you think it would have affected the outcome of the war? Why?

7. The Romans strongly condemned and attempted to annihilate the Druids and their beliefs (see page 112). After reading the play and learning more about the Druids, why do you think Roman leaders were so determined to eliminate the Druids?

Further Activities

1. Obtain a copy of the comic book *Astérix* at a library or bookstore and read about Astérix's battle against Julius Caesar.

2. Create your own cartoon about Alesia or some incident in Gaul that involved Caesar.

3. Caesar chose the area closest to Gaul as his province. If the Helvetii had not chosen to migrate, Caesar most likely would have found some reason to lead his legions into Gaul. Write what you think he might have done or what situation might have occurred.

4. Draw a picture, make a collage, or describe in vivid detail what sports, books, entertainment, or jobs Caesar would have enjoyed. Also show what he would have disliked. Use articles in this chapter, especially Suetonius' and Plutarch's descriptions, as your base.

5. Geese saved Rome with their cackling. Geese are still used today as guard animals, especially in Great Britain. Research where else geese are used and how effective they are. Also research other types of guard animals. Are animals more effective than alarms?

6. Reenact Gyptos' choosing a husband. The only prop you need is a goblet.

7. Research spas and mineral springs in France today. Are any built over ancient sites?

8. Read Caesar's complete description of when the Nervii attacked his men while they were fortifying the camp. See *Gallic Wars,* Book II, 18–27.

9. Read more about Napoleon III and Colonel Stoffel and their search for Alesia. Ask your librarian where you might find the information.

10. Excavate a small area in your schoolyard or backyard. Use a ladder or look out a window to get a better overview of the site. See if anything looks different from what you saw at ground level. This is a very simple method and is not designed for obtaining scientific results or information. It is merely geared to introducing a person to the science of archaeology.

a. Choose a suitable site that can be roped off for a few days.

b. Mark out an area two feet square with wooden stakes or sticks in each corner and in the middle of each side (eight stakes).

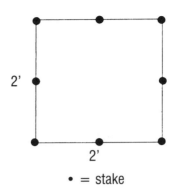

2'

2'

• = stake

c. Make a grid with string attached horizontally and vertically to parallel stakes on opposite sides. There should be six rows of string—three horizontal, three vertical.

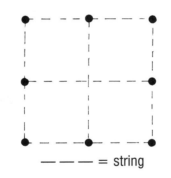

— — — = string

d. Make a corresponding grid on a large piece of graph paper.

e. Have a screen and pail ready to sift dirt.

f. Have a small shovel(s) or scoop(s) and ruler ready.

g. Use several boxes with covers to store "finds."

h. Carefully scoop out three inches of dirt. Make sides vertical or gently sloping toward bottom.

i. Check each scoopful. Place any finds in a box labeled "3-inch finds." (Each box must be labeled with a number representing the dirt level.) Also mark on the paper grid where each find was made.

j. Sift dirt through a screen for any tiny finds.

k. Place dirt in a large box to refill the hole later.

l. Carefully scoop out two more inches of dirt and do the same as above. Mark this box "5-inch finds."

m. Carefully scoop out two more inches of dirt and do the same as above. Mark this box "7-inch finds."

n. continue this procedure until you have a box marked "13-inch finds."

o. At the end of the excavation, refill the hole with dirt.

p. Take the boxes to your classroom or workroom and analyze your finds.

11. Act out the play. Use the descriptions in the play to make Gallic clothing. Research simple Roman soldiers' garb. Use a scarlet-colored cloak for Caesar. As a prop, use Caesar's siege-works around Alesia (made according to the directions on pages 122–124).

Topics for Debate

1. The Roman system of government with two consuls elected to rule for one year did not allow for a smoothly run government. Long-term projects were too difficult to implement.

2. Vercingetorix's leaders were wrong and unpatriotic when they surrendered him to Caesar.

3. Caesar was justified in executing the pirates. He also was merciful to hang them first.

Egypt versus Rome

Solem enim e mundo tollere videntur qui amicitiam e vita tollunt.

A world without friends is like a world without sunshine.

Cicero,
Roman orator and philosopher
(106–43 B.C.)

OVERVIEW

PEOPLES INVOLVED:
Egyptians, Romans

DECISIVE BATTLE:
Actium in Greece (31 B.C.)

GENERALS:
Cleopatra (Egyptian),
Julius Caesar, Mark Antony,
Octavius (Roman)

HISTORICAL SIGNIFICANCE:
Octavius' defeat of Antony and Cleopatra made Rome the controlling power of the Mediterranean world. Rome now became an empire.

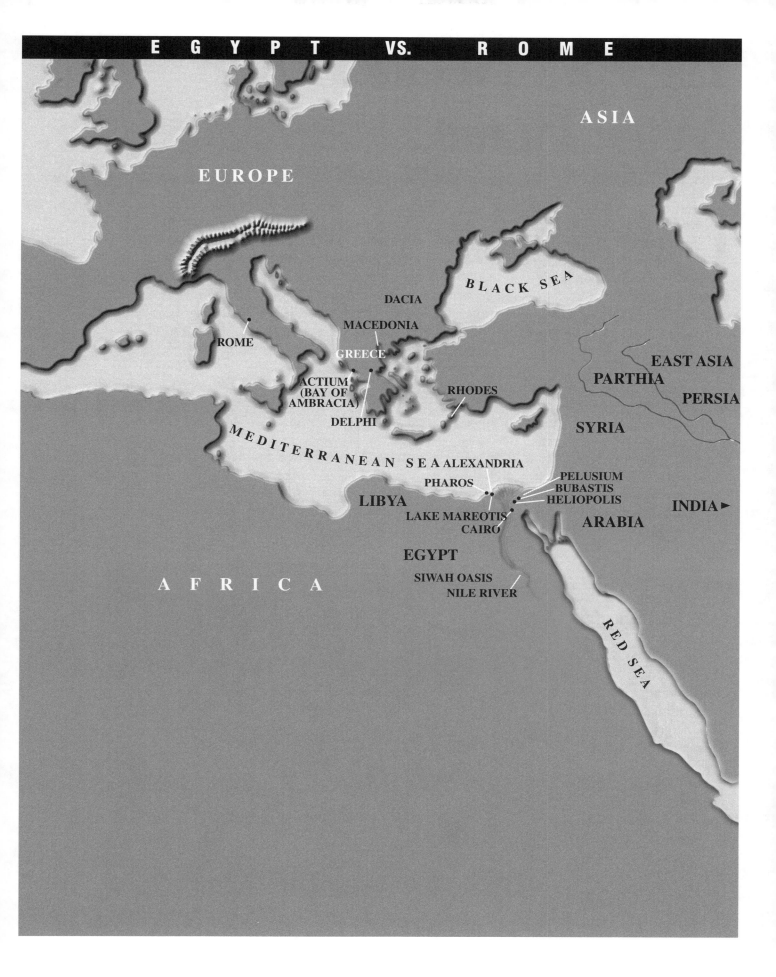

Egypt's Relationship With Rome

In ancient times Egypt's splendor and wealth were almost proverbial. The Nile River and its fertile banks produced an overabundance of crops. Egypt's location made it the gateway to East Asia and India. Under the mighty pharaohs, the earthly representatives of the gods, Egypt was a first-rate world power for centuries. Its name and commerce traveled the known world. Yet palace intrigue, feuding parties, and constant intermarriage within the royal family all contributed to the decline of the pharaohs.

Egypt's blessings also made it the target of greedy and power-hungry nations and rulers. In 525 B.C., Cambyses (cam BIH seas), king of Persia and son of Cyrus the Great, conquered Egypt. It remained under Persian control for generations. Then came Alexander the Great from Macedonia in northern Greece. Egypt welcomed him, for submission to Alexander meant liberation from oppressive Persian rule. When Alexander died in 323 B.C., no one individual was capable of succeeding him. As a result, numerous wars and conflicts broke out throughout his empire. Three of his officers eventually emerged, each taking a portion of the empire for himself.

Ptolemy (TOL eh me), a trusted friend of Alexander, assumed control of Egypt. Ptolemy I (as he became known) ruled wisely and justly. Egypt and its chief city of Alexandria prospered under him. But not a drop of Egyptian blood flowed through Ptolemy's veins. He was a Macedonian Greek who most likely spoke no Egyptian. But as was the ancient custom in Egypt and throughout much of the East, the emperor was considered divine and ruled by divine right. Ptolemy was accorded these honors. He became their pharaoh, and his descendants ruled for generations.

As Rome extended its control from west to east, it often came in contact with Egypt and Egyptian gods. Alliances and treaties between the two powers were signed and obeyed. Rome stood in awe of this magnificent and ancient power. The Egyptians, especially the rulers in Alexandria, knew and understood their wealth of resources, but they nervously watched as Rome extended its rule farther east.

Cleopatra on Her Barge (the first meeting of Antony and Cleopatra)

Ptolemy XII, Egypt's pharaoh at the time Julius Caesar began his conquests, realized his nation's declining status and knew that some form of allegiance or submission to Rome was inevitable. In his will he made Rome his heir, with the provision that his daughter Cleopatra and his son Ptolemy XIII be the co-rulers.

When Ptolemy XII died, his arrangement created great problems, for Cleopatra was eighteen and her brother was ten years old. Advisors of each sibling began to scheme and plot. Ptolemy XIII's supporters were quite ruthless and soon controlled the situation. They planned to rid themselves and Egypt of Cleopatra. When she learned of their plot, she fled to Syria and raised an army of mercenaries before returning to Egypt and civil war.

At this time the Roman general and statesman Pompey the Great sought refuge in Egypt. Pompey had just lost the Roman civil war to Julius Caesar and needed a place to rethink his plans, and perhaps even regroup his troops. Since Egypt had backed him in the civil war, Pompey felt that the Ptolemies were his allies. However, Ptolemy XIII's advisors saw Pompey's assassination as a means to win Caesar's favor. Without any hesitation, they killed Pompey and presented his head to Caesar when he arrived in Egypt.

Ptolemy XIII's supporters expected to receive Caesar's thanks, but they had miscalculated. Caesar saw Pompey as his former friend, the husband of his dead daughter, and a fellow Roman. He saw Ptolemy XIII's men as murderers and traitors. Caesar decided to act and settle the feud between Ptolemy XIII and Cleopatra himself.

Caesar sided with Cleopatra in the civil war. After some desperate street fighting on Caesar's part and the timely arrival of Roman reinforcements, Caesar defeated Ptolemy. But he did not claim Egypt as a Roman province.

Rather he made Cleopatra its queen.

Caesar remained in Egypt with Cleopatra for several months before returning to Rome and the business of governing his vast empire. In 46 B.C., Cleopatra journeyed to Rome at the request of Caesar. Her presence in Rome, combined with the intrigues and jealousies of many Roman senators, set the stage for the assassination of Julius Caesar on March 15, 44 B.C.

Cleopatra had no choice but to return to Egypt, since neither her safety nor her position in Rome was secure. She believed her dreams of Egypt aligning itself with Rome and controlling the world had died with Caesar. Three other men now ruled the Roman world, and each had his own domain: Lepidus, Africa; Octavius, the West; and Mark Antony, the East.

Cleopatra, however, remembered that the capable general Antony was a friend and supporter of Caesar. Perhaps she could rule the world with him. Cleopatra soon won Antony's admiration and heart, but on her terms. Yet her plans worked too well. Several Roman leaders began to fear that if Cleopatra won Antony's complete loyalty, the empire would be split or Antony would attempt to gain control of both the East and the West.

Antony did leave Egypt and Cleopatra for almost four years. During this time he waged several military campaigns and married Octavius' sister. But he later abandoned his Roman wife and returned to Cleopatra and their twins.

War between Octavius and Antony became inevitable. The days of treaties and talks had passed. Each leader sought to gain control of the entire Roman world and more. The report that Antony yielded to Cleopatra even in matters of state disgusted most Romans, including those who had always favored and backed him. Finally, Octavius declared war on Cleopatra.

Actium—The Final Clash

When Octavius and Antony pledged to rule the Roman world jointly, neither man favored the other. Each had a reason and a cause that he believed could be helped by such an agreement. Time, however, proved otherwise, for neither one had reckoned with the goals and ambitions of the young Cleopatra.

War was the result. Octavius declared it on Cleopatra, and an incensed but confident Antony responded by leading his navy and army to western Greece to guard the areas that remained loyal to him. Antony set up his camp and moored his fleet near Actium and the Bay of Ambracia (Arta).

Antony was a proven general, but Octavius had his good friend Marcus Vipsanius Agrippa, an exceptional general and strategist. Unfortunately, Antony allowed his personal feelings for Cleopatra and his overconfidence in his large fleet to distract him from organizing a well-planned strategy.

Sickness and famine were weakening Antony's forces. Octavius' galleys were successfully barring supply ships from reaching Antony's men. Many of Antony's trusted allies and commanders disliked Cleopatra intensely. Many resented her control, Egyptian control, over Antony, the representative of Rome. Several highly respected leaders had already deserted Antony for Octavius.

Agrippa

Antony and his followers began to sense the urgency of the situation when Octavius' forces lay to the north and south of his position and Octavius' fleet began advancing toward him. Antony knew that he could not successfully engage Octavius in battle without reinforcements. Therefore, he devised a clever plan. He ordered his oarsmen to dress as soldiers and to prepare the decks for battle. He then tied each oar in its rowing position. To Octavius, Antony's massive fleet seemed poised and ready to fight. Its size warned Octavius to wait until Agrippa and his troops arrived. Antony won the first round. Octavius was deceived.

But Antony could not stall for long. He had agreed to Cleopatra's wish that this be a naval rather than a land battle, even though he was a proven soldier. He burned the ships he could not use and fully manned the others. September 2, 31 B.C., was the fateful day.

It was a strange battle, without much success on either side. Many of the vessels in Octavius' fleet were long, fast, and easily maneuverable biremes. Antony's fleet resembled floating castles, with wooden towers housing men throwing all sorts of weapons. The rams of Octavius' fleet could not damage the thick sides of the enemy's vessels.

Suddenly a brisk wind began to blow. Cleopatra ordered her contingent of sixty ships to set their sails and head for Egypt. The wind quickly puffed out the purple silken sails of her flagships, which seemed to glisten in the sun, especially as the silver-tipped oars splashed in the water.

When Antony saw the Egyptian squadron departing, he completely forgot his training and position and abandoned his men and his ship for a faster one. With sail hoisted, he pursued his fleeing wife. Octavius immediately understood the situation—a sail in battle meant retreat. He ordered his fastest triremes to pursue them, but the two escaped to Egypt.

Unfortunately, few commanders to the left and rear of Antony's squadron saw this action, and the battle continued to rage on the seas. Even as the news spread, Antony's loyal troops thought the report a rumor and refused to stop fighting.

Octavius' men managed to break the enemy's oars, but they could not board the lofty vessels. Agrippa knew that he had to destroy the ships if he wished to win. Fire, the most destructive of weapons, was his answer. His men shot flaming arrows oiled with tar at Antony's fleet. This quickly destroyed the enemy's towers and defense machines.

Agrippa's strategy worked, and Octavius' fleet was victorious. Tens of thousands of men surrendered once they realized Antony had deserted them. Actium made Octavius master of the seas, but not of the Roman world, for Antony was still alive. When Antony committed suicide in 30 B.C., Octavius alone ruled the mighty Roman Empire. Also in 30 B.C., with the death of Cleopatra, Egypt became a Roman province.

Sea Fight at Actium

Julius Caesar

Julius Caesar was strong-willed and sometimes ruthless, but he was a proud Roman. He was fifty-two years old when he met Cleopatra. He saw in her all the qualities he admired: an undying loyalty to her country, a determined spirit, and a free will. He also saw that the young Cleopatra was a fearless, well-organized leader.

Caesar did stay for a time in Egypt, but from all accounts he never forgot that Rome, not Alexandria or Egypt, was the center of the world. Caesar did acknowledge, however, Alexandria's superiority in the arts and sciences and imported scholars and scientists to help him reform the calendar, improve the minting of coins, and review Rome's financial system.

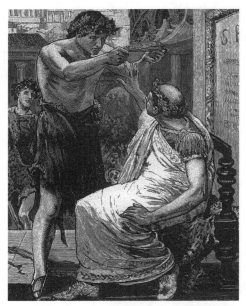

Antony Offering Crown to Caesar

Mark Antony

Mark Antony and Caesar were good friends, but their temperaments were quite different. Caesar set a goal and pursued it, changing his tactics and strategies whenever necessary. Antony was fickle. He was a great general, but he drank and played too much and too hard.

Cleopatra knew of Antony's reputation and acted in a manner she knew would win his praise and admiration.

Cleopatra did win Antony, but pressure from Rome made him rethink his motives, leave Egypt, and marry Octavius' sister. Later, when he realized how secure his position in the East really was, he abandoned his Roman wife and returned to Egypt and Cleopatra.

Antony was not ruthless or vindictive. He was just easily swayed. He let his emotions rule him. Antony's military qualities were eroded by the glamour and shining opulence of the East, where rulers were gods and royal life was a pageant. Antony even assumed the Eastern manner of dressing.

At Actium, his emotions totally overruled his reasoning powers when he pursued Cleopatra rather than remain with those fighting for his cause. After Actium, Antony lived alone in Egypt as a hermit, withdrawn from the world after defeat and disaster had crushed him. When he heard about Cleopatra's suicide plans, he immediately gave up all hope and fell on his sword.

Mark Antony

Octavius

Octavius was born in 63 B.C. to Julius Caesar's niece. When he was four years old, his father died and Caesar assumed an active role in his rearing. After Caesar died, his will made Octavius his heir and also revealed that Caesar had adopted his grandnephew.

Octavius' role in the Cleopatra story is minor yet significant. His total rejection of her pleas and entreaties brought an end to the rule of the Ptolemies. Cleopatra was the last of the line. Under Octavius, Egypt became an imperial province subject to him.

Octavius was not a seasoned general like Antony, nor did he have the experience of his uncle Julius Caesar. Octavius recognized capable individuals and sought to have them on his side (e.g., Agrippa, who masterminded the victory at Actium).

Octavius saw Rome as the center of the world and realized what would happen if Antony remained with Cleopatra. After his first solution of having Antony marry his sister did not work, Octavius felt he had no alternative except war.

With Antony's and Cleopatra's suicides, Octavius reigned supreme. His rule was one of Rome's longest, from 31 B.C. until his death in A.D. 14.

Octavius

Augustus On January 16, 27 B.C., the Roman senate honored Octavius by conferring on him the respected title of Augustus. Octavius had brought a welcome peace to Rome and a return to values and Roman ideals. Augustus was an appropriate title, for it meant "sacred" and "holy."

All succeeding emperors were given the title of Augustus automatically, but it was only with Octavius that it replaced the emperor's actual name. Consequently, history knows Octavius better as Augustus. The Romans did, too. When they voted to name a month of the year for him, they called it Augustus, our August.

Cleopatra

Cleopatra is perhaps the most famous woman the world has ever known. Every generation has studied her, countless authors have written about her, and historians have analyzed her every action.

Cleopatra was the last of the Ptolemies to rule Egypt. She is said to have been the first of the Ptolemies to learn and speak the Egyptian language.

As a child, Cleopatra was exposed to palace intrigue and murder. Yet her actions do not characterize her as overly cruel or vindictive. When she was eighteen, she and her younger brother inherited the kingdom of Egypt. Her brother, however, had friends and supporters who wanted him the sole ruler. Cleopatra recognized the maneuverings within the Egyptian court and realized that she would need help from Rome if she planned to rule Egypt. She also knew she had to be careful and could trust only a selected few.

When Julius Caesar summoned her and her brother to the palace in Alexandria, she formed an ingenious plan. She had her friend Apollodorus row her and a rug across the bay. Once they reached the other side, she had Apollodorus roll her up in the rug and carry the bundle into the palace. No one questioned Apollodorus, since it was a common custom to carry rugs over one's shoulder.

But can you imagine Julius Caesar's surprise when the rug was unrolled in from of him? Eventually, Cleopatra did win Caesar's support and with his support the rule of Egypt. Yet she wanted more—to be mistress of the Roman world.

Caesar's untimely death ruined whatever plans she had. Most Romans did not approve of an Egyptian queen influencing the ruler of Rome. Many historians believe that Cleopatra's presence in Rome from 46 to 44 B.C. was one of the factors that united conspirators against Caesar.

Cleopatra returned to Egypt saddened, but not defeated. She quietly waited until the Romans took sides for and against the assassins. Gradually Caesar's friend, Mark Antony, emerged as the Roman ruler in the East. Cleopatra had met him and knew much about him. When he sent a messenger requesting that she present herself to him, she dutifully obeyed. But she did not appear as an obedient servant. Rather, she came as the proud and regal queen of Egypt, one of the richest lands in the East.

When Antony learned her barge had arrived, he waited for her to come to him. Cleopatra, however, remained on the barge. Tired of waiting, Antony sent a messenger requesting that the queen of Egypt dine with him. Cleopatra replied by asking Antony to dine with her. Antony accepted. Cleopatra had won the first "contest."

At their first meeting, Cleopatra's galley was adorned with banks of silver-mounted oars and royal purple sails. The helmsman steered from beneath a golden structure made to resemble an elephant's head with the trunk raised high. Women dressed as sea nymphs and forest goddesses surrounded him. Musicians playing flutes, pipes, and harps accompanied the rowers. Cleopatra sat under

Egyptian Cooks Roasting a Goose and Cutting Up Meat

Egyptian Cooks Preparing to Boil Some Geese

an elaborate canopy, bespangled with gold. She was surrounded by young boys waving fans made of colored ostrich feathers and dressed as Cupid, the young god of love. She was dressed as Venus, the goddess of love, in loose, shiny robes. Sweet smells encircled the ship and reached out to the shore from bronze, incense-filled vases. The couches were covered with rich embroideries, the golden dishes were inlaid with precious stones, the dining room walls were decorated with tapestries intricately worked with silver and gold, and the floor was covered with flowers.

Death of Cleopatra (by Italian painter Dominiquin, 1581–1641)

Cleopatra repeated these ostentatious dinner parties to impress Antony with her wealth and power. Whenever she did consent to dine with Antony at his quarters, she somehow made him feel uneasy about the "simpleness" of his "rustic" banquets. On one occasion he asked Cleopatra what he could do to make his evenings more like hers. Cleopatra retorted that she spent much more on a meal than he did and quoted an outrageous sum. Antony laughed in disbelief. Cleopatra slowly turned and bid him dine with her the following evening.

The appointed hour arrived and so did Antony and Plancus, a man Cleopatra invited to estimate the value of the dinner. As the evening came to a close, Plancus announced that the amount spent was far short of the bet Cleopatra had made.

The queen then signaled a servant to bring her a goblet of vinegar. She plucked her two enormous pearl earrings from her ears and dropped one into the vinegar. As soon as it dissolved, she drank the goblet dry. She then started to do the same with the second earring, but Plancus stopped her and announced she had won the bet.

Even Antony's defeat at Actium did not destroy Cleopatra's fierce determination to succeed. Fate, however, decreed otherwise. Octavius saw Cleopatra as the cause of much bloodshed among the Romans. He also saw her as his greatest prize. To have her a captive in chains in his triumphal procession would be the ultimate victory. Octavius, however, did not know Cleopatra. She refused to consider such a possibility.

For years Cleopatra had conducted experiments with poisons, using condemned criminals as guinea pigs. She discovered that the asp was one of the swiftest and surest means of a quick, painless death.

As Octavius' forces closed in, Cleopatra prepared for the inevitable. When Antony's servants told the dejected general of Cleopatra's plans, he lost control and fell on his sword. Cleopatra, however, did not lose control of her emotions. When she learned that Antony was dying, she asked that he be brought to her. Antony died with the woman to whom he had yielded all, even his loyalty to Rome.

Cleopatra still did not yield to fate. She did meet Octavius. She was thirty-eight, tired, and battle weary, but still regal. Octavius admired her but was not won over as his predecessors had been. Cleopatra quickly realized the difference, and her self-reliance asserted itself. She sent a message to Octavius requesting that he allow her body to be buried in the same tomb as Antony's.

When Octavius read the letter, he knew what it meant and sent his men immediately. It was too late. Cleopatra was dead with two marks on her arm. Cleopatra died a queen in her own land by her own hand. For decades, she had kept Egypt free of Roman domination, and even after her death, Egypt entered the Roman world as a special imperial province subject to Octavius himself. Octavius granted her burial request, just as he granted her request to give Antony a proper and royal funeral.

Chronology of Cleopatra

69 B.C.   Cleopatra born

51 B.C.   Ptolemy XII, Cleopatra's father, dies

48 B.C.   Twenty-one-year-old Cleopatra meets fifty-two-year-old Julius Caesar (rug episode)

46 B.C.   Cleopatra joins Caesar in Rome

44 B.C.   Cleopatra returns to Egypt; Caesar assassinated

41 B.C.   Twenty-seven-year-old Cleopatra meets forty-two-year-old (approximately) Antony (dinner on barge)

40 B.C.   Antony leaves Cleopatra for Italy and marries Octavia

37 B.C.   Antony returns to Cleopatra in Egypt

32 B.C.   Octavius declares war on Cleopatra

31 B.C.   Battle of Actium in Greece; Antony and Cleopatra vs. Octavius

30 B.C.   Thirty-eight-year-old Cleopatra meets thirty-three-year-old Octavius

—   Cleopatra and Antony die, both by suicide

Beware the Ides of March

Soothsayers warned Caesar to "Beware the Ides of March." Priests had found no heart in an animal that was being sacrificed, and Caesar's wife, Calpurnia, had dreamed that she held her murdered husband in her arms.

On the morning of March 15, the Ides of March according to the Roman calendar, Caesar listened to these reports and weighed their merits. Only the previous evening at dinner he had said that a sudden death would be the best. He still agreed with that, but he wished he had added "not yet."

Gradually Caesar dismissed his anxieties about the ominous reports. He had much to do. The middle of the month signaled the start of all military campaigns, and he was leaving in three days for the East to defeat the Parthians, and perhaps even the Dacians.

Caesar did consider postponing his meeting with the senate and remaining quietly at home. However, one of the conspirators convinced him that such an action would be considered cowardly and that the senate was ready to proclaim him king of all the Roman provinces outside of Italy.

"Let us go then," replied Caesar. Minutes later Caesar lay dead, assassinated by men who had fought with him, men he trusted, men who days earlier had pledged allegiance to him.

The Ides of March was indeed a fateful day. The omens had been correct. For more than two thousand years now, the date March 15 has had an ominous ring, and the phrase "Beware the Ides of March" has come to mean "Take care not to be deceived by trusted friends and partners."

Death of Caesar (by 19th-century Italian painter Vincent Camuccini)

Alexandria

As Alexander the Great (356–323 B.C.) marched across the East conquering nation after nation, he chose eighteen especially well-situated locations as the settings for cities, each to be known as Alexandria. Alexander envisioned his new cities as cultural and commercial links along his trade route spanning Europe and Asia. After his death they continued to flourish and became centers of Greek life and thought.

The site Alexander chose in Egypt lay between the Mediterranean Sea and Lake Mareotis at the western end of the delta of the Nile River, on a tract of land a mile and a half wide. It was a perfect spot. The city would have two harbors and be a major port serving both the sea trade and the river trade.

Alexander asked the renowned architect Deinocrates of Rhodes to design a magnificent metropolis. Streets were laid out in an orderly manner with a splendid boulevard one hundred feet wide. The boulevard, which ran the length of the city, was to be lined with columns. Huge parks, magnificent palaces, a zoo, a museum, and a library for scholars from throughout the world were included in the plan.

Unfortunately, Alexander did not live to see the Egyptian city completed. However, Ptolemy I, Alexander's successor in Egypt, fulfilled his dreams. Ptolemy also commissioned his architects to design a mausoleum worthy of housing Alexander's remains.

Under Ptolemy I and his descendants (the last of whom was Cleopatra), Alexandria's fame grew throughout the ancient world. It became the center of learning, commerce, and industry, rivaling even Rome in importance. Scholars from around the world traveled to Alexandria to complete their education. The museum and the great library, containing hundreds of thousands of books, were celebrated everywhere.

Alexandria was also home to one of the seven wonders of the world: the Pharos of Alexandria (the Lighthouse of Alexandria). Construction began under Ptolemy I and was completed under Ptolemy II in 270 B.C. In A.D. 1375, the lighthouse was destroyed by an earthquake. Nothing remains today.

Even after Rome fell, Alexandria continued to flourish as a center of learning until its conquest by the Arabs in A.D. 638.

Alexander the Great Visits the Oracle in Egypt

Ammon

The Egyptians joyfully opened their gates to Alexander the Great, the conquering general from Macedonia. They would not be free under Alexander's rule, but life would be better than it had been under Persian domination.

Alexander won Egypt without a battle and rejoiced when he saw the warm welcome given him by the Egyptians. But his mind was preoccupied. He had often heard about the great oracle of the god Ammon in the desert of Libya to the southeast of Egypt. Like the famed oracle of Apollo at Delphi in Greece, the oracle of Ammon was respected throughout the Mediterranean world. The Egyptians associated him with their ram god, Amun, and the Greeks identified him with Zeus, the king of gods and men.

Alexander's personal goal was to consult with Ammon, and he carefully planned for the arduous trip that lay ahead. Ammon's temple was located in the beautiful Siwah oasis in the midst of the desert two hundred miles inland. Shifting sands, windstorms, and intense heat all made for an exciting but dangerous journey. One of Alexander's biographers mentioned several remarkable and mysterious incidents of the trip. He noted that when Alexander's group was going off course, two snakes appeared and guided the king to the temple. (Another author claimed it was crows, not snakes, that guided Alexander.) He also noted that the gods sent abundant rains, unusual for this sandy and waterless area.

What exactly happened at the temple is not clear. Historians agree that the oracles at Ammon's temple were given by nods and tokens or signs. Questions were written on clay or a similar material, asking whether it was better to follow one course of action or another. The pleas were made known to the priests, who carried the jeweled symbol of Ammon in a gilded boat from which dangled cups of silver. Tradition maintained that these holy representations of Ammon would then feel themselves swayed by the divine presence to answer yes or no or a confused jumble. Because the inner court-

Priestesses of Ammon

yard of the temple was quite small, it is believed that a priest acted as an intermediary, delivering the questions, watching for the response, and then reporting it. Only under certain circumstances could a person make his or her request in person.

What Alexander asked and what he heard or learned are mysteries that historians have debated for centuries. His only response to his men and advisors was that he had heard what he wanted to hear. Some believed that he had been told that he was invincible, others that he would conquer to the edge of the world, and still others that he was the true son of Ammon and also of the Greek god Zeus.

Sixteenth-Century Representation of the Phoenix

Egyptian Representation of the Phoenix

The Fabulous Phoenix The Egyptians have a sacred bird called a phoenix, which I myself have never seen except in pictures. It is a great rarity, even in Egypt. According to the accounts of the people of Heliopolis,[1] it only comes there once every five hundred years when the old phoenix dies. Its size and appearance, if it is like the pictures, are as follows: The feathers are partly red, partly golden, while its general shape and size are almost exactly those of the eagle. The story the Egyptians tell of what this bird does seems incredible to me. He comes all the way from Arabia to bring the parent bird, which is plastered over with myrrh,[2] to the temple of the sun, where the young bird buries the body. Tradition maintains that in order to bring him, the young phoenix forms a ball of the myrrh as big as he can carry, then hollows out the ball and puts the parent inside. He then covers over the opening with fresh myrrh so that the ball is exactly the same weight as it was originally. Such is the story they tell of the doings of this bird.

Herodotus, fifth century B.C. Greek writer and historian, Histories, *Book II, Chapter 73*

[1] Heliopolis, "the city of the sun," is the Greek name of one of ancient Egypt's more important cities. It was located in northern Egypt near present-day Cairo.

[2] Myrrh is a yellowish brown aromatic gum resin with a bitter, slightly pungent taste. It is commonly used in perfumes and incense.

Bastet: The Egyptian Cat Goddess

Why are all those people down on their knees? And why are they moaning so loudly?"

Any foreigner visiting ancient Egypt two to three thousand years ago had reason to ask such questions when he or she saw such a sight in public. Curious foreigners who moved closer to investigate might have added a third question: "Can they be crying about that dead cat?"

To a foreigner the scene was fascinating yet mysterious; to the Egyptians it was tragic, for the Egyptians considered cats sacred.

Bastet was the powerful cat goddess, and her worship lasted more than two thousand years, until the fall of Rome about the middle of the fifth century A.D. Bastet was closely identified with the sun, which the Egyptians believed was the source and sustainer of life and light. Hence, when a cat died, part of the life force on earth also died. Temples were erected to Bastet, and religious festivals were held in her honor.

According to some ancient sources, the Egyptians even opted to lose a battle rather than hurt a cat. In 525 B.C., the Persian king Cambyses used cats as armor. He ordered his men to seize as many cats as possible and proceed in attack formation against the city of Pelusium. The Egyptians, however, preferred

Bastet, the Egyptian Cat Goddess

to be conquered rather than fight off their attackers and hurt the cats.

Every Egyptian family had a statue of Bastet. Newlyweds bought amulets (charms) with reliefs of Bastet surrounded by kittens. The number of kittens supposedly revealed how many children the couple hoped to have. Amulets made of stone, glass, gold, and silver were sold by the thousands. Bastet's power against evil was believed to be so great that Egyptians wore little amulets around their necks, placed them in walls, and even buried them beneath the floors of houses and temples. Cats also were thought capable of curing a person who had been bitten by a snake.

As a religious offering to Bastet, Egyptians sacrificed cats specifically raised for this purpose. A special burial rite was performed: The Egyptians closed the dead cat's eyes, pressed its whiskers back against its lips, placed a turquoise collar around its neck, and bound it with thongs. These cats were mummified, because the Egyptians believed a cat had the power to ward off the evil demons of darkness.

Not everything about cats was considered religious or sacred. Cats were valued as unrivaled catchers of mice and rats. The ancient Egyptians also used cats to catch and retrieve birds. After attaching a lead to his cat, a hunter would maneuver his boat as close as possible to the papyrus marshes. He then allowed the cat to jump from the boat, still on the lead, and comb the thickets for ducks and other birds.

A Mummified Egyptian Cat

'Cat' Expressions Cats have lost the supernatural powers assigned to them by the ancient Egyptians, but they still command love and respect throughout the world. Our association with cats has even influenced the expressions we have developed to describe people and events:

- Cat's eyes
- Cat and mouse games
- I nearly had kittens!
- A person's cattiness
- A black cat crossed my path.

On Today's Ancients

During the past century, the Industrial Revolution, the Space Age, and computer technology have radically changed lifestyles throughout the world. Yet the past has not been forgotten. On the contrary, the past continues to stir our imagination. Its mysteries continue to intrigue us. Today's inventions are being used to analyze and even re-create the past. Surprisingly enough, with all our technological advances, we still have not been able to duplicate some of the superb techniques the ancients devised to build ships, monuments, and the like. Today's industrial and scientific companies continue to sponsor projects designed to duplicate, re-create, and test the theories and devices of the ancient Greeks and Romans.

THE *DAEDALUS* PROJECT

According to the ancient Greeks, Daedalus was a master craftsman who worked for Minos, king of Crete, an island in the Mediterranean Sea. Minos did not want to lose Daedalus, so he imprisoned the craftsman and his son Icarus in a tower. Since escape by land or sea was impossible, Daedalus planned to fly away. Using feathers, bits of thread, twine, and wax, he fashioned a set of wings for himself and his son. They escaped through the tower window by flying across the sea to the mainland.

Daedalus at Work Making Wings

For centuries, people have attempted to duplicate Daedalus' flight, but with no success until the 1980s. The *Daedalus* Project was initiated by several students and professors at the Massachusetts Institute of Technology in Cambridge, Massachusetts. Their goal was to design a human-powered aircraft that one person would pedal from Crete to mainland Greece. (The actual flight plan was from Heraklion, Crete, to the island of Santorini,

Daedalus Looking Down at His Son Icarus, Who Has Fallen Into the Sea

some seventy-four miles away.) The aircraft was made primarily of composite carbon, beaded Styrofoam, polystyrene foam, Kevlar (high-strength organic plastic fiber), steel piano wire, and Mylar (used as the skin of the aircraft).

Several companies sponsored the project and provided the needed funds. Greece also helped support and promote the project. Selfless dedication and team cooperation combined with modern technology produced the Space Age *Daedalus,* the name given to the human-powered pedal airplane. In October 1987, the *Daedalus* was unveiled. Several pilots, all of whom had undergone rigorous training programs, pedaled the *Daedalus* aircraft in trial runs. Adjustments were made in preparation for the target deadline. Pilot training and fitness schedules were rotated so that weather conditions would decide the day and the pilot for the first flight.

After an accident (probably due to atmospheric turbulence) damaged the right wing of *Daedalus* on February 7, 1988, a second backup aircraft, *Daedalus B* or *Daedalus 88,* was built.

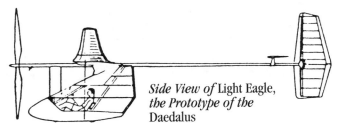

Side View of Light Eagle, *the Prototype of the* Daedalus

On the morning of April 23, 1988, conditions were judged right for the flight. The sea was calm, the temperature was below 70 degrees, the horizon was visible, and the wind blew from the south at a speed of less than three knots. Kanellos Kanellopoulos, a Greek cycling champion, was the pilot on duty. At 7:03 A.M., Kanellopoulos lifted off from Heraklion. Favorable tail winds made the historic, record-breaking flight faster than had been anticipated, with an average speed of 18.5 miles per hour. At 11:00 A.M., Kanellopoulos and *Daedalus 88* reached Santorini. Unfortunately, a strong gust of wind snapped the tail boom and forced the craft into the water just feet from the shore. But the flight was a success and a tribute to human ingenuity and perseverance.

The goal of the *Daedalus* Project was to advance the technology of low-speed and human-powered flight. But it will also benefit the studies of metallurgy, aerodynamics, nutrition, and human capabilities.

KYRENIA II

In 1967, an incredibly well-preserved Greek merchant ship dating to the end of the fourth century B.C. (about the time of Alexander the Great) was discovered about ninety feet below the surface of the Mediterranean Sea, about half a mile off the coast of Kyrenia, Cyprus. It was called the *Kyrenia* ship.

From studying the ship in detail, scholars have been able to learn much about the art of shipbuilding in ancient times and about Greece's maritime economy in the fourth century B.C.

Before anything could be moved, every inch of the site had to be accurately labeled, photographed, and marked. When the excavation began, the fragile pieces of the hull were placed on metal trays and lifted by balloon to the surface.

By 1969, the ship and its cargo were safely stored in Kyrenia's medieval castle, which today has become a museum. Since the ship's wooden sections would have dried to a quarter of their original size if exposed to air, a large freshwater tank was built in the castle to house the vessel. Polyethylene glycol was added to the water to penetrate and revive the wood.

In 1982, under the auspices of the Hellenic Institute for the Preservation of Nautical Tradition and the American Institute for Nautical Archaeology, a specially selected team began the construction of *Kyrenia II,* an exact duplicate of *Kyrenia I,* including even the mistakes made by the ancient shipbuilders. Hand-chiseled mortises and wooden pegs hold everything together on this pine-and-oak vessel, which is approximately forty-eight feet long.

As the only sailing replica of an ancient ship, *Kyrenia II* participated in the tall ships parade in New York harbor during the Statue of Liberty celebration in 1986. Later that summer, *Kyrenia II* made its first voyage along the ancient route from Greece to Cyprus. In the spring of 1987, it made the three-week return trip back to Greece. From April through October 1988, *Kyrenia II* was the Greek representative at the Silk Road Festival in Japan, which commemorates the waterways and vessels used in ancient times to carry the precious cargo of silk.

Kyrenia II was invited to be the Greek representative at the 1992 Summer Olympics in Barcelona, Spain.

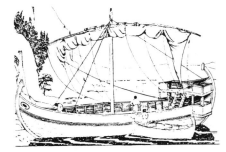

Greek Merchant Ship

OLYMPIAS

How did the ancients build their *triremes?* Where did the rowers sit? How did the oars fit? For centuries these questions have plagued historians, naval architects, and shipbuilders. No trireme has ever been found intact, and the descriptions found in the ancient texts are not precise. The *Kyrenia* ship did provide some valuable information, but it was a merchant ship.

Several theories and countless models of triremes have been proposed. In 1983, John Morrison, a classics professor at Cambridge University in England, and John Coates, Britain's former chief naval architect at the defense ministry, presented their design at an international conference.

With the backing of Britain's Trireme Trust and the Hellenic navy, *Olympias,* a full-scale reconstruction of a Greek trireme, became a reality. The vessel measures one hundred twenty feet long, and each of the one hundred seventy oars is thirteen feet long. Twenty thousand pinned mortise-and-tenon joints hold the hull together, just as they did more than two thousand years ago. This design allows for more interior space and makes for a very light, fast ship.

According to the ancients, their triremes achieved speeds of nine to ten knots per hour; on nonstop distance runs of at least one hundred twenty miles speeds reached seven to eight knots. After training and counterweighting the oars on the two top tiers, *Olympias'* crew managed to speed along at over nine knots per hour and to

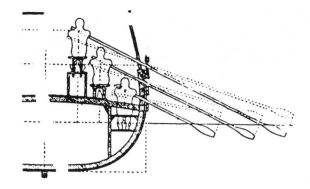

Cross Section of a Trireme

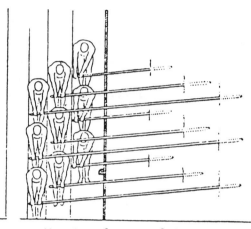

Top View of Rowers of a Trireme

turn 180 degrees in sixty seconds.

The Trireme Trust is considering constructing a second *Olympias* because they have learned so much from the original. Except for sea trials around Greece and the Aegean Sea, *Olympias* is generally on view in Piraeus, the port city of Athens, Greece.

The Children of Rome

A play about two brothers and their experiences in the classroom and at home

CHARACTERS

Tiro—*old Greek slave who is* paedagogus *(tutor) to Marcus and Gaius*
Marcus—*eldest son of a Roman family, age fourteen*
Gaius—*younger brother of Marcus, age nine*
Father—*father of Marcus and Gaius, a rich middle-class Roman citizen*

Mother—*mother of Marcus and Gaius*
Aesop—*freed Greek slave who runs an elementary school for students ages seven through twelve*
Orbilius—*widely known grammarian who has a school for children ages twelve through sixteen*
Quintus—*friend and classmate of Marcus*

It is 25 B.C., an important era in ancient Roman history. The civil strife of the preceding century is over. Six years have passed since the nephew of Julius Caesar, Octavius (now known as Augustus Caesar), defeated Mark Antony at the famous Battle of Actium. The Roman republic has ended, and the empire has begun. Augustus Caesar is laying the foundation of imperial power that will continue for more than four hundred years. This is a time of peace and prosperity for Rome, as well as the greatest period of Latin literature and art.

In the northwest area of the city, there lives a wealthy middle-class family that owns many vineyards in the country and has large interests in the wine trade here and abroad. The whitewashed house looks very simple from the outside. Shops on either side of the front door are rented out, and the rest of the wall area of the house has only a few small windows high up. The family of six and about twenty slaves live in the interior of the building with complete privacy from the business and noise of the street. They are not as rich as the extravagant, aristocratic patrician families in Rome, but they are happy and comfortable, and the lives of the children reflect their circumstances.

Scene 1: *The bedroom shared by the two sons of the Roman family. It is before dawn one day in May when their old paedagogus, who also was tutor to their father,*

awakens them. The entire household is up, for daylight hours are not wasted. Much of the day's activity takes place before midday.

Tiro: Wake up, boys. You must get ready for school. Your father was never late.

Marcus: *(yawning and jumping out of bed)* Oh, Tiro, I cannot believe father was always on time.

Tiro: Of course he was, just as you are, because I always get you up as early as I did him. You know how your schoolmaster dislikes tardiness.

Marcus: That I know, for more than one of my friends has been caned for being late.

Gaius: I certainly do not want to get caned for being tardy. I get enough of that when I make mistakes reading out loud.

Tiro: We will have to do something about that. Now both of you, clean your teeth with this powdered pumice stone and wash your hands and faces with this cold water. That will wake you up. I have your clothes all ready.

(After washing, the boys are given short-sleeved, belted tunics reaching to their knees and a clean toga praetexta. *The boys' togas are about twelve feet long and five feet wide, with one curved edge and one straight edge that is decorated with a purple band.)*

Marcus: In three years, when I am seventeen and old enough to serve in the army, I will be able to wear a *toga virilis,* which is plain white, not like this

Boy With Pet Monkey
(Pompeian wall painting)

one with a purple stripe, which is only for boys.

Gaius: I wish I did not have to wear a toga. I feel so clumsy in it.

Tiro: You must get used to wearing a toga. It is the distinctive attire of a Roman citizen, and when you are a gentleman, you will not think of appearing in public and on special occasions without one.

(Tiro helps Gaius drape the cloth around his body, under his right arm, and twice over his left shoulder. A fold, left in front, is used as a pocket, and a loose end hangs at the back. Marcus puts on his own.)

Marcus: Gaius, it took me a lot of practice before I could put on my toga correctly.

Tiro: Boys, do not forget to put your gold *bulla* around your neck. You need the good luck and powerful protection from the amulet found inside the locket—especially you, Gaius, when you are called upon to read aloud at school.

(A boy slave carries in a tray with the boys' light breakfast of bread, honey, cheese, fruit, and wine mixed with water.)

Tiro: We must leave soon. Drink your wine and bring the bread, fruit, and cheese to eat along the way, or you will be late. You will not have anything to eat until this afternoon. Now remember your manners and do not forget to kiss your mother good-bye.

(Their mother meets them near the doorway. She has been supervising the slaves, who are cleaning the house.)

Marcus: Good morning, mother.

Mother: Good morning, my son.

Marcus: Mother, may I bring my friend Quintus home this afternoon after school to stay for lunch?

Mother: Yes, you may, but you must not make too much noise and disturb Father, who will be working in his *tablinum* (office).

Marcus: All right. After we eat, Quintus can go with me for exercises at the Field of Mars before I go to the public baths.

Gaius: I wish I could bring a friend home. I have only my little sister Emilia to play with, and she is two years younger than I am.

Mother: When you are older, you may have a friend over. Just think how lucky you are to be going out. Poor little Emilia has to stay home and learn how to run a household, and so will baby Cornelia when she is older. *(kissing both boys)* Good-bye, my sons, and study hard. You know how important your education is to your father. He and Tiro have trained you since you were out of my care, and now you must learn from your schoolmasters. May the gods be with you.

Marcus: Good-bye, mother.

Gaius: Good-bye, mother.

The boys skip out the door, waving good-bye to the doorman, an old Gallic slave who lives in a little room, just inside the inner door. They are accompanied by Tiro and the boy slave, who carries their books in a round wooden satchel.

Scene 2: *Aesop's elementary school fifteen minutes later. It is on the ground floor of a building and occupies only one large room, which is near the street and quite noisy. The schoolmaster is a Greek freed slave named Aesop, and he has an assistant. Gaius finds an empty backless stool and joins his twenty-seven classmates, whose ages range from seven to twelve. Tiro joins the other paedagogi (plural of paedagogus) at the back of the room, where they gossip during the session.*

No one is late today, and all the students stop talking when Aesop enters the room and sits in a chair on a small platform. The

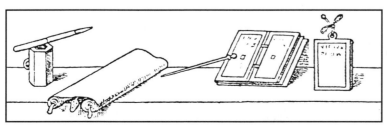

Ink Pot With Reed Pen; Roll With Cornua and Label; Stylus, Tablets, and Calculating Table

class is divided into two sections for reading. Aesop takes the younger boys today, including Gaius, and the assistant takes the older boys.

Aesop: Let us take these little wooden letters and spell out syllables of words.

Gaius: *(to himself)* I like working with these letters. Anything is better than reading out loud, especially with Tiro sitting in the back of the room today instead of my boy slave.

Aesop: Now let each of us read the words we have spelled to the rest of our section of the class. Gaius, you begin.

Gaius: *(again to himself)* I knew this was too good to be true. *(out loud)* B-u-l-l-a.

Aesop: Very good, Gaius, but why did you choose that word?

Gaius: I was hoping that if I chose *bulla,* the one I am wearing would bring me good luck and help me spell it correctly.

Aesop: An interesting thought, though I think that in the future you should rely more on your ability to learn and not on a good luck amulet.

(Other boys read their words out loud, and then Aesop calls in the special arithmetic teacher. Some boys take out an abacus, while others rely on their fingers to count. Gaius and the other younger boys multiply, divide, and do fractions and decimals.

Writing is the last subject taught. Every student has a pair of wax tablets and a pointed pen, called a stylus, with a smooth, flat end for erasing what has been written in the wax. The assistant takes the younger boys for this exercise and gives them simple words to copy in capital letters on the tablets resting on their knees. He gives Gaius abacus *to write, and Gaius copies it very neatly.)*

Gaius: *(to himself)* This is boring. I have three more

years of reading, arithmetic, and writing before I can go to the school of Orbilius. At least I have not received a caning today. Tiro will be pleased. I will not be happy until we are dismissed. It is almost time to go home.

Scene 3: *The school of the famous grammarian Orbilius. While Gaius and his classmates learn reading, arithmetic, and writing, Marcus and other boys ages twelve to sixteen learn rhetoric (the art of public speaking). This is the most important subject taught in Roman schools. To be able to speak clearly and well is often the key to public success for a citizen of Rome. The room where Marcus has his lessons is quiet, and the boys are busy studying Greek language and literature.*

Orbilius: Class, today we will read one of my favorite Greek poets, Homer. Marcus, would you recite some lines for us?

(Marcus stands and recites several lines of Homer in Greek, remembering all the words and pronouncing them perfectly.)

Orbilius: Marcus, where did you learn to speak Greek so well? It is not often that one so young recites with such good diction.

Marcus: Tiro, my paedagogus, was born and educated in Greece, and he has taught me to speak his native language. We often converse with each other in Greek.

Orbilius: That name sounds familiar. Was Tiro not tutor to your father as well?

Marcus: Yes, he was.

Orbilius: You are fortunate. Now let us study some Latin literature. I will read aloud a passage from a work of my former student, the Roman poet Horace, and then you, Quintus, will repeat it properly.

(Orbilius reads the passage, and Quintus stands and stammers through his recitation.)

Quintus: *(sitting down and turning to Marcus, whispering)* I hate poetry!

Orbilius: That was very poorly done, Quintus, and deserves a flogging. Come here so you can feel my strap. This will serve as an example to all of you to study and have more respect for our language. How well you use and speak Latin will determined the success you have in life.

(Quintus receives his flogging bravely, knowing he deserves it, then gingerly sits down.)

Orbilius: Now I will lecture on mythology for the rest of today's class.

Marcus: *(whispering)* Did that hurt? Old Orbilius has had a reputation for years for his floggings. Even my father remembers him for that.

Quintus: It certainly did hurt! I am ready for a day off. It is a good thing that tomorrow is the ninth day and a holiday. We have to wait two more months before we have our long summer holiday. I am glad the climate in Rome is so unhealthy in August and September that we cannot have classes. I am anxious to move to our country house this summer.

Marcus: I am, too. Can you come home with me today and have lunch with my family? We can go to the Field of Mars for exercises afterward.

Quintus: I would like that. When we are dismissed, I will send my boy slave home to tell my parents where I am. They will not mind, I am sure.

(An hour later, when Orbilius finishes his lecture on Greek mythology, the class is over and the boys go home together. Quintus sends his boy slave with his books to his parents' house, and the boy slave of Marcus accompanies them, carrying his master's books in his satchel. Soon they meet Tiro and Gaius on their way home.)

Marcus: Tiro, I did my Greek recitation perfectly this morning.

Tiro: I am proud of you. Even Gaius did well reading aloud. Your father and mother will be happy to hear of your achievements.

Scene 4: *The townhouse where Marcus and Gaius live. They are greeted at the door by the slave from Gaul, who lets them into the vestibule of the house. They continue on to the atrium, where the family spends much of its time. The boys' mother greets them there.*

Marcus: Good afternoon, mother. I would like you to meet my friend from school, Quintus.

Mother: Welcome to our home, Quintus. My husband and I know your parents.

Quintus: Thank you. I am happy to be here.

Mother: *(turning to the paedagogus)* Tiro, how did my sons do in school?

Greek Boys at Play (Design on a wine jug. One player rides on the back of another, whose eyes he covers. The object is for the team to knock over the specially placed stone.)

Tiro: They both did very well with their reading and recitation.

Mother: I will tell father. He will be especially pleased to hear of this, Marcus, for he has some special news for you at lunch. Now you boys go into the garden of the *peristylium* (courtyard) and play a game until the mid-day meal is ready. Emilia is playing with her dolls, and the baby is with her nurse. They will be glad to see you.

(Gaius leaves to get his army of men and animals, molded of clay by one of the slaves, to show Quintus. He has a mud fort in one corner of the garden, where he sets up his little soldiers. After showing off his toys to his brother's guest, Gaius proceeds to demolish the fort with stones from a small sling.)

Marcus: Quintus, let us play a game of odd-and-even before we have lunch.

Quintus: All right, that is one of my favorite games.

(The boys take turns guessing whether the other is holding an odd or even number of nuts in his hand. Gaius, bored with playing war, comes over to the older boys.)

Gaius: Quintus, would you like to play knucklebones with me?

Marcus: Gaius, that is a child's game. Besides lunch is almost ready.

(Soon a slave comes and gets the children for their midday meal, which the family has in the triclinium *(main dining room) at the opposite corner of the courtyard. The father of Marcus and Gaius enters the dining room at this time and greets his eldest son's guest.)*

Father: Welcome to our home, Quintus. I am glad that you have joined us.

Quintus: Thank you, sir.

Father: *(turning to his sons)* I have heard from your mother and Tiro that you have done well today. I am proud of you! Marcus, how is my old schoolmaster, Orbilius?

Marcus: He said that I was fortunate to have your paedagogus to teach me Greek.

Father: That is true. Tiro is an intelligent and loyal servant. He has served our family well. Does Orbilius still flog his pupils for the slightest offense?

Marcus: *(grinning)* He sure does.

(Quintus lowers his head, but Marcus does not embarrass his friend by telling the family of his flogging in class today.)

Father: Marcus, your education does not end in the schoolroom. I have taught you the necessary sports—javelin and discus throwing, riding, wrestling, boxing, and swimming. You have a strong, healthy body as well as a quick mind. You now need to learn of politics and social affairs. I have decided that you are old enough to begin accompanying me when I go to the Forum, the law courts, the senate, and the temples to learn more of our religious rites. It is time to put away childish things and assume the ways of manhood. You must be prepared to take our place as a citizen of Rome when you come of age.

Marcus: *(excited and happy to have his friend present to hear this momentous news)* Father, I am ready to accompany you and learn the ways of a man and a Roman citizen. Will I also be able to attend dinner parties with you?

Father: *(laughing and remembering his own youthful enthusiasm years ago)* Yes, my son. It is important that you hear the talk of men of affairs. Now let us have our lunch.

(The light meal of cold meat, vegetables, bread, and wine suddenly

becomes a festive occasion as the family and Quintus share the excitement of Marcus, who suddenly feels very important.)

Father: What are you boys doing this afternoon?

Marcus: We are going to the Field of Mars to play some sports and then to the public baths for our daily bath. We have been sitting in a stuffy classroom all morning, and it will feel good to get some fresh air and exercise.

Quintus: I would like to go for a swim in the Tiber River, too. It is more fun and challengng than the swimming bath.

Marcus: That is a great idea, but first I want to practice throwing the javelin. Some of our friends should be there, and we can have a contest.

Quintus: How about a wrestling match?

Marcus: If we have time.

Father: You boys certainly must have a great deal of energy. I will meet you at the baths at the ninth hour.*

Marcus: All right, father.

Mother: Do not be late for dinner. We are having guests, and you are to join us, Marcus.

Marcus: Thank you, mother. I will remember my manners and speak only when I am spoken to.

The boys excuse themselves, leave the dining room, and run out of the house and down the street to the athletic field, each one with his own thoughts. Marcus is happy with his new status in life and is just a little nervous thinking about the greater responsibilities he must soon assume. Quintus is determined to study harder and take school more seriously so that his father will consider him ready for the passage to adulthood.

*3 P.M. The Roman day was divided into two twelve-hour segments, 6 A.M. to 6 P.M. and 6 P.M. to 6 A.M.

Girls Playing Knucklebones (Using five bones from the ankle joint of a cloven-footed animal, the player would throw the bones into the air, one at a time. The object was to catch all five on the back of your hand without losing those already caught.)

156

Food, Fun, and a Werewolf

A play about preparations for a grand dinner party and a guest who once met a werewolf

CHARACTERS

Ummidia—*wife of Crassipes*
Master Cook—*slave skilled in gourmet cooking*
Chamberlain—*servant of Crassipes*
Slave—*slave who helps with cleaning and other menial work*
Crassipes—*wealthy Roman*
Manlius—*wealthy Roman*

Cytheris—*wife of Manlius*
Niceros—*Roman who is a frequent guest at banquets because of his clever stories*
Sarmentus & Gabba—*talented performers of wit and slapstick*
Clavus—*Roman senator*
Praecia—*wife of Clavus*

During the prosperous days of the Roman Empire, good eating and drinking were of great importance to wealthy Romans. Men who did not wish to spend their money on villas or fine bronzes could rid themselves of their wealth by gratifying their palates. Many Romans lost huge fortunes trying to surpass all rivals with the extravagance of excessive eating at their tables. Slaves who were good cooks were sold for the highest prices.

It was not merely the love of good living that inspired men, but deliberate gluttony became the pleasure of the table. Lucky was the man or woman who was invited to a grand banquet. Many Romans impatiently waited or begged for an invitation, even one that came at the last minute. A person felt unlucky if he or she had to dine alone at home.

There was a decline in the absurdities of gluttony by A.D. 150, but an evening of food and fun could still be had at the house of a rich Roman. One such banquet was held at the villa of the wealthy Crassipes and his wife, Ummidia. Seven lucky guests joined them on a late autumn afternoon. These guests spent the morning in anticipation of the coming meal, and they wondered if costly gifts would be distributed to everyone. Some were looking forward to the opportunity to discuss anything and everything. Others hoped there would be riddles and storytelling. All expected a lavish, well-cooked, and interesting dinner, for the banquets of Crassipes and his wife were renowned.

Scene 1: *The kitchen in the Roman villa of Crassipes one week before the banquet. Ummidia and her master cook, surrounded by copper pastry molds, dippers, ladles,* *spoons, and baking pans for small cakes, are going over the menu for the banquet. A charcoal fire in the brick hearth takes the chill from the cool autumn day.*

Ummidia: Your master and I want this meal to be a memorable one. I have read the description by the Roman writer Horace of a feast given for his wealthy patron, Maecenas, almost two hundred years ago. Let us try to reproduce that feast as closely as possible. The first course was Lucanian boar surrounded by turnips, lettuce, radishes, water parsnips, and anchovies. The boar was probably served cold.

Master Cook: My lady, I have all the fresh vegetables from the garden and plenty of anchovies, but the boar will have to be purchased from the local butcher, for I cannot get one from Lucania at such short notice.

Ummidia: That will do. The second course will be fowl, oysters, and fish all stuffed with a sauce made of the entrails of a flounder and a turbot.

Roman Banqueters

Master Cook: That is easy enough. I have ducks and chickens plucked and ready to cook. Of course, there is plenty of fresh fish this time of year.

Ummidia: The third course is more complicated. We must have a lamprey (eel) set on a bed of floating shrimp accompanied by a sauce made of olive oil, pickle from the juices of Iberian fish, five-year-old wine, white pepper and vinegar, herbs, and sea urchins.

Master Cook: I see that I will have to go to the market for many of these ingredients, although I doubt I will find pickles from the juices of Iberian fish.

Ummidia: The fourth course will be the most difficult to produce. Maecenas was served limbs of a crane sprinkled heavily with salt and some flour, the liver of a white goose fed with fattened figs, hares' wings, and blackbirds with scorched breasts.

Master Cook: They certainly were particular in those days. I am glad our meals are more simple today. The market does not provide such exotic produce very often. I will have to improvise. May I serve my special *dulcia domestica* (homemade sweets) for dessert?

Ummidia: Of course, we should have sweets. What do you suggest?

Master Cook: I will make stuffed dates. The seed is removed, and the date is stuffed with a nut or with nuts and ground pepper. Then it is sprinkled with salt and covered with honey. I also will slice fine white bread, with the crusts removed, into rather large pieces. These will be soaked in milk and

beaten eggs, fried in oil, and covered with honey.

Ummidia: They sound delicious and will be the perfect end to an elaborate meal. Begin preparations at once, and spare no cost. This banquet will be the talk of the city. I will send out the *vocator* (slave) with the invitations at once.

Scene 2: *It is early morning on the day of the banquet in the villa of Crassipes. While the master cook and his helpers are busily preparing the feast, the chamberlain, an upper slave, is giving orders to lower slaves to clean the entire house.*

Chamberlain: Hurry, we must clean the entire house, and we do not have much time.

Slave: I do not see why we cannot just clean the *triclinium* (dining room) where everyone will be eating.

Chamberlain: Silence, you lazy man! The whole villa has to be cleaned so our master and mistress will not be disgraced. Sweep and scrub the pavement. Polish the pillars and take down the spider webs.

(The chamberlain and slaves then move into the triclinium, the most important room to be made ready.)

Slave: I will clean the silverware.

Chamberlain: Do not forget the embossed dishes. Put out the best purple cushions embroidered with gold

Baker Selling Bread

Kitchen Stove

threads after you have dusted the three couches and arranged them around the citrus wood table. By the way, the table should be polished.

(Three elegant, broad inclined couches about three feet high and ten feet long are arranged on three sides of the small table, leaving the fourth side free so the slaves can move about with ease and serve the diners.)

Slave: Where do you want these small pillows?

Chamberlain: I will lay them on the cushions to mark the positions of the guests and our master and mistress. They will thrust them under their elbows as they recline and eat. There! Everything is ready. Let us leave, for it is nearly time for the guests to arrive.

Scene 3: *It is 4 P.M., and the street before the vestibule of the villa of Crassipes is crowded with the litters and servants of the seven guests. Crassipes and Ummidia greet each of the guests in the atrium, while most of the escorts leave to return later with torches when the banquet is over. A special servant remains with each guest and follows him or her into the triclinium, where he takes off the shoes of his master or mistress. These valets remain to help Crassipes' servants serve the meal.*

Crassipes, by custom, takes the host's place on the third couch with his wife, nearest the guest of honor, Manlius, and his wife, Cytheris. Slave boys pass around bowls of water and towels for everyone to wash his or her hands. The chamberlain then nods from the doorway that the cook is ready, and Ummidia nods back her approval that the dinner is to begin.

Crassipes: My friends, we have a special treat for you this evening. My wife has instructed our cook to prepare a feast similar to one described by Horace and given to his patron Maecenas almost two hundred years ago.

Manlius: I have read of that banquet. Surely you must have had difficulty obtaining the exotic dishes they served in those days.

Ummidia: Our cook is very skilled and has improvised where necessary.

Cytheris: I have heard of his skill, and I am sure we are all in for a treat.

(The first course is brought in and arranged carefully on a huge platter. The structor *[special slave] carves the boar.)*

Niceros: Ah, boar, my favorite meat. And what a delightful array of vegetables surrounds it.

Manlius: You may repay us later in the evening by telling one of your clever stories.

Niceros: That will be my pleasure.

(The diners eat the food with their fingers, and between the courses water and towels are passed around so the guests may wash their hands. Beautifully embossed silver cups filled with wine diluted with water are also passed to the guests. After the final course has been devoured and the delicate dulcia domestica enjoyed, the guests compliment their host on the fine meal.)

Crassipes: Let us rise now and take a turn around the colonnade in the *peristylium* (courtyard). Then we can return to the triclinium for some riddles and a story.

They all rise and leave the triclinium. The slaves hurriedly enter and change all the couch covers and pillows, sweep the floor, and bring in beautiful silver lamps to light the now dark room.

Scene 4: *The triclinium is now ready to receive the guests for the rest of the evening. Two great silver tankards have been placed on the tall inlaid sideboard, and they gleam in the warm light of the many lamps. One tankard is*

Bronze Utensils

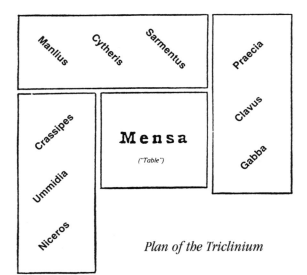

Plan of the Triclinium

filled with smoke; the other has a charcoal brazier beneath it and is steaming with hot water. As the guests return from their stroll, slaves pass out cups of wine, asking them whether they want it hot or cold. Other servants distribute garlands of flowers and little alabaster vials of expensive perfume. The guests sprinkle the perfume on their hands and hair. The conversation becomes merry as a flutist and a harpist provide background music from behind a curtain.

Cytheris: Ummidia, your gifts are delightful. What fragrant flowers and exquisite perfumes.

(The other guests all nod in agreement.)

Ummidia: Thank you. I chose them especially for tonight. Crassipes, let us have some riddles.

Crassipes: A good idea, my wife! Sarmentus and Gabba, can you provide us with a few of your famous riddles?

Sarmentus: We have three riddles from a book called *Deipnososphistae (Banquet of the Learned),* written by the Greek scholar Athenaeus.

Manlius: Great! I love Greek riddles.

Sarmentus: Can you name the two sisters: One produces the other and in turn becomes her daughter?

Clavus: They cannot be mortal creatures. Are they goddesses?

Sarmentus: They are night and day.

Crassipes: How clever! Gabba, let us hear one from you.

Gabba: Of everything produced by earth and sea, nothing—no man, no animal—has a growth that corresponds to this. When it is born, its size is the greatest. At middle age, it is scarcely visible. When it is old and hastens to its end, it again becomes greater than all the objects that surround it. What is it?

Praecia: That is much too difficult and confusing for me.

Gabba: The answer is very simple: shade.

Sarmentus: I will ask you one of my favorite riddles. What is the strongest of all things?

Niceros: Surely it must be the metal iron.

Sarmentus: Iron is the strongest element, but since a blacksmith can bend iron and love can bend a blacksmith, love is the strongest of all.

Cytheris: What a clever answer. I agree; love is the strongest of all.

Crassipes: Niceros, let us have one of your entertaining stories to end the evening.

Niceros: I will recount an adventure I have experienced.* Some time ago, when I was still a servant, I fell in love with the wife of the innkeeper. I believe you all know Melissa, a very beautiful woman and very good-natured. Whenever I asked her for anything, she never refused. If she made a penny, she gave me half. I did likewise.

One day her husband died while tending their lands. I desperately wanted to be with her in this time of sadness and need. Since my master had just left for the city on errands, I decided to go immediately to Melissa. I convinced one of our guests, a very brave soldier, to accompany me part of the way. We started off in the light of a very bright moon. When we approached a graveyard, my companion ran toward the tombstones. I, meanwhile, sat down and sang as I counted how many stones there were.

Numidia: I did not know you could sing.

160

Roman Banqueters

Niceros: Not really. It was a nervous reaction. To continue my story, all of a sudden I had an urge to look in the soldier's direction. My heart jumped to my throat. He had stripped off all his clothes and laid them on the side of the road. I stood still, unable to move. He circled around his clothes and then suddenly changed into a wolf.

Cytheris: You must be joking.

Niceros: No, I am not joking! Believe me, I would not joke about something as serious as this, even if you were to offer me a fortune.

Cytheris: That I do not intend to do.

Niceros: So to continue my story, he turned into a wolf and started howling. He then ran off into the woods. At first, I could not even remember where I was. Then, as I began to regain my thoughts, I went to pick up his clothes, but they had turned to stone. I was so terrified that I almost died of fright.

Praecia: I do not blame you. I would have died of fright.

Niceros: But my inner self-control and my strong family genes kept me sane. I pulled out my sword and killed every shadow until I arrived exhausted at Melissa's house.

Ummidia: How brave you were!

Niceros: I stopped at Melissa's threshold looking as pale as a ghost and breathing with great difficulty. Perspiration was pouring down my face and my body; I was drenched. My eyes were blank and staring. Melissa was surprised to see me at so late an hour and in such a state.

"If only you had come a little earlier," she said, "you could have helped me. A wolf crept into the farm area and attacked the livestock. What a mess he made. But we almost got him. One of the slaves pierced his neck with a spear."

Praecia: What happened to the soldier?

Niceros: I will tell you. I could not close my eyes that night after hearing her tale. Once the sun shone in the sky, I rushed back home. When I came to the spot where my friend's clothes had turned to stone, I found only bloodstains. I raced home.

There on the bed lay my soldier friend. A doctor was at his side tending a wound in his neck. Only then did I realize that my friendly companion was a werewolf. To this day I am not able to eat or do anything in his company, not even if death should be given me as an alternative.

Clavus: What an entertaining story. It is one of the best I have heard in a long time.

Manlius: Yes, an exciting ending to a perfect evening.

Cytheris: I wonder if the moon is out tonight.

Manlius: We shall soon find out. Crassipes and Ummidia, thank you for your hospitality. This banquet and evening have been a treat.

Clavus: Yes, they certainly have. But we must leave now, for it is nearly eight o'clock, and we must all be up by sunrise. Valet, bring our shoes.

The streets are dark and deserted, except for prowlers and the police. The goddess Diana is beginning her journey across the night sky in her silver chariot. The escorts arrive and assemble in the vestibule with their torches ready to accompany the tired and merry guests home. The seven guests leave after thanking Crassipes and Ummidia. The slaves clean the triclinium and put out the lamps. Soon everyone is asleep, dreaming of fun, food, and maybe even a few werewolves as the moon shines brightly over Rome.

Taken from Dinner of Trimalchio, by Petronius, the first century A.D. Roman novelist and close companion of the emperor Nero.

Acrobatic Dancer

Project

Roman eating customs did change with the centuries. Our plan is for a dinner party given around 30 B.C. (the time of Mark Antony, Octavius, and Cleopatra). A Roman host usually invited his guests personally, either on the day of the dinner or the day before. Sometimes he sent his servant or a worker on this errand. A dinner party began between three and four o'clock in the afternoon. The time varied with the season of the year and with the social position and occupation of the host. The party often lasted for hours.

PARTICULARS OF OUR PARTY

HOST—Marcus Julius Pollio

TIME—Ninth hour (*N.B. The ninth hour is equivalent to three o'clock in the afternoon. The Romans divided their day into two twelve-hour periods: 6 A.M. to 6 P.M. and 6 P.M. to 6 A.M.*)

DAY—*Hodie* ("today")

CLOTHES NEEDED

A garment called a *synthesis* was the most common dinner attire. However, since its shape is uncertain, use a *tunica* (a Roman garment that resembles a long T-shirt). Togas were not worn at dinner because they were too bulky. Servants also wore the tunica—very loosely, not floor length, and not belted. Everyone wore sandals.

PLACE AND GUESTS

LOCATION—Home, school, or any open area such as a barn, hall, gym, or backyard

GUESTS—Romans always worked with multiples of three guests. The minimum number of guests per table was three; the maximum number of guests per table was nine.

TABLES—One was the usual number for a regular dinner party. For a large group, the area available determined the number.

ITEMS NEEDED *(nine people per table)*
– three couches, cots, or athletic mats large enough to accommodate three people reclining sideways (A chaise lounge is ideal.)
– nine cushions, three on each couch, placed in a row alongside
– three coverlets or blankets, one to cover each couch
– one table (level with couch or mat)
– large serving dishes and trays
– saltcellars
– bowls filled with water
– perfume or cologne to sprinkle in water
– hand towels
– washcloth to clean table
– broom to sweep floor
– nine napkins
– nine garlands made of flowers, leaves, and ribbons

POSITION OF COUCHES AND TABLE

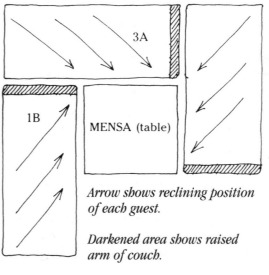

Arrow shows reclining position of each guest.

Darkened area shows raised arm of couch.

3A: Most distinguished guest. In this position he could get messages or leave without disturbing anyone.

1B: Host (N.B. His wife and family reclined with him on this couch. If they were not attending the dinner, the least important guests were accommodated here.)

THE DINNER

1. Guests arrive.
2. The host greets each guest, or a servant greets the guests and announces each by name.
3. Guests are ushered into the dining room.
4. Everyone pauses and calls upon the gods for their blessings. Morsels of food also are offered to the gods, especially to the host's ancestor gods.
5. The guests and host remove their sandals and place them underneath their couches. Wealthy

162

guests are accompanied by their own servants, who remove their masters' sandals. The guests' servants stay and help the host's servants with the meal.

6. Servants pass around bowls of water and towels for guests to wash their hands.

7. Servants bring in large serving dishes of precut, finger-size food and place them on the table.

8. Servants pass around water bowls and towels after each course. The diners do not use forks. Therefore, their hands get greasy and need washing. Often the water has been perfumed before being poured over the diners' hands.

9. Between courses slaves clear and wipe the table with a soft cloth or sponge.

10. Between the main course and dessert the diners get up and stretch. This allows time for servants to sweep the floor and freshen up the cushions. Often the table is removed and replaced by a new one.

11. Before dessert is served, servants distribute the garlands and crowns. Then an offering of wine, salt, and food bits is made to the host's ancestor gods.

Roman Banquet

12. The call for sandals signals the end of the party, and the guests leave immediately.

THE MENU

GUSTATIO (appetizer)
sliced tomatoes or cherry tomatoes
cut-up hard-boiled eggs
olives
sliced peppers
pasta
oysters
chestnuts
little sausages

CENA (main course)
roast beef
seafood stew
fish cakes
carrots
cabbage
bread

MENSAE SECUNDAE (dessert)
custard
apples
nuts

COMMISSATIO (wine supper or drinking bout)
wine

RECIPES

BOTELLUM (little sausages)
Combine hard-boiled egg yolks, chopped pine nuts, onion, leeks, raw ground pine (an herb), and fine pepper. Stuff the mixture into casings and cook in broth and wine.

ASSATURAM SIMPLICEM (simple roast)
Simply put meat in the oven, sprinkled generously with salt. Serve it glazed with honey.

EMBRACTUM BAIANUM (seafood stew)
Mince poached oysters, mussels (or scallops), and sea nettles. Place ingredients in a saucepan with toasted nuts, rue, celery, pepper, coriander, cumin, raisin wine, broth, reduced wine, and oil.

TYROPATINA (custard)

Use whatever amount of milk you choose and sweeten it with honey. To a pint of fluid, add five eggs; for half a pint, add three eggs. Beat well, then strain through a colander into an earthenware dish. Cook the mixture on a slow fire or in a hot-water bath in an oven. When thickened, sprinkle with pepper.

NB *The recipes included in ancient texts appear to be written for more experienced cooks. They do not include specific measurements.*

COMMISSATIO

Many Roman dinner parties continued after dessert. The commissatio was the wine supper or drinking bout.

MATERIALS NEEDED
– dice (to choose drinking master)
– grape juice (for wine)
– water, boiling and regular (to mix with juice)
– ice or snow
– large punch bowl and ladle
– goblets or cups

PROCEDURE

Each guest throws the dice. The person who throws the highest number becomes the drinking master. The drinking master decides the ratio of wine to water (usually one part wine to three parts water) and the size of the goblets or cups to be used. The servants then mix the wine with water in a large bowl. Diners have the choice of cold or hot wine. For cold, ser-

Wall Painting From Pompeii, Italy, of a Roman Banquet Attended by Cupids

vants add ice or snow. For hot, servants add boiling water. Rule of drinking bout: A guest must empty his goblet of wine in one gulp. At elaborate dinner parties, vials of perfume are given to each guest as a gift. The guests can then sprinkle themselves with the perfume.

ENTERTAINMENT

Guests tell stories or riddles. Each tries to outdo the other. Flutists and harpists provide background music. Jugglers, dancers, or acrobats perform.

Puzzle Pages

CROSSWORD PUZZLE

Across
2. Octavius' general
3. Apollo's oracle was located here
5. Egyptian cat goddess
7. Caesar's grandnephew
8. Cleopatra's father
9. This god had an oracle in Libya
11. Cleopatra, to entertain Antony, dressed boys as this god
12. King of Persia
14. Agrippa's first name
15. Architect who designed Alexandria
19. Caesar's first name
20. Alexandria was destroyed by them
21. Caesar's wife

Down
1. Greek historian
2. Concealed Cleopatra in a rug
3. Caesar hoped to conquer these people
4. Partner with Octavius and Antony
6. Cleopatra dressed as this goddess to meet Antony
9. Egyptian ram god
10. Cleopatra's nationality
13. Queen of Egypt
14. Antony's first name
16. Helped Cleopatra become queen
17. King of gods and men
18. Greeks consulted Apollo here

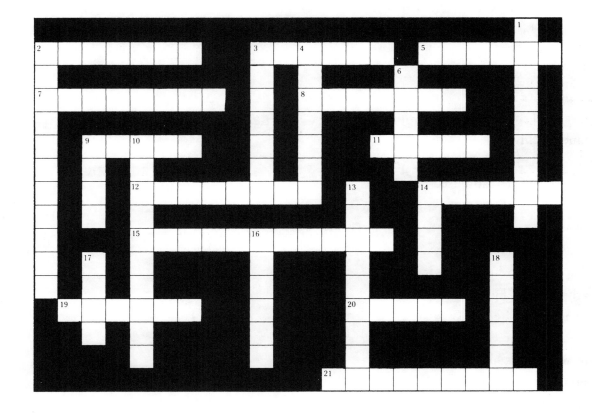

UNSCRAMBLE THE SITES

Unscramble each of the six jumbled sites below to determine the answers to the clues. Place the unscrambled words on the blank lines and then match each letter with its corresponding number to discover where Octavius and Antony fought.

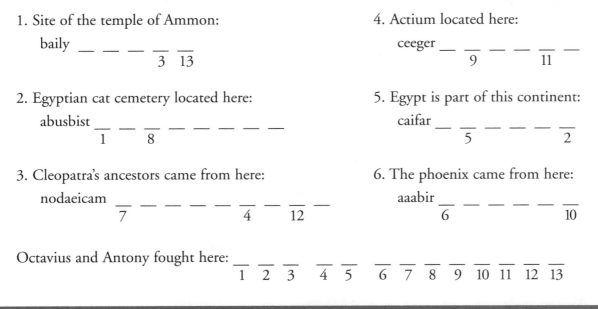

1. Site of the temple of Ammon:

   baily __ __ __ __ __
             3 13

2. Egyptian cat cemetery located here:

   abusbist __ __ __ __ __ __ __ __
          1   8

3. Cleopatra's ancestors came from here:

   nodaeicam __ __ __ __ __ __ __ __
         7   4 12

4. Actium located here:

   ceeger __ __ __ __ __ __
         9   11

5. Egypt is part of this continent:

   caifar __ __ __ __ __ __
        5   2

6. The phoenix came from here:

   aaabir __ __ __ __ __ __
        6   10

Octavius and Antony fought here: __ __ __ __ __ __ __ __ __ __ __ __ __
                  1 2 3   4 5   6 7 8 9 10 11 12 13

WORD PUZZLE

Fill in the blanks below, using the letters of the "famous warning" to help you.

1. Cleopatra was on this when she met Antony.   1.   B __ __ __ __

2. Agrippa used this to destroy Antony's ships.   2.   __ __ __ E

3. Antony used this to commit suicide.   3.   __ W __ __ __

4. Senate gave this name to Octavius.   4.   A __ __ __ __ __ __

5. Type of province Egypt became.   5.   __ __ __ __ R __ __ __

6. Cleopatra used this to dissolve earring.   6.   __ __ __ E __ __ __

7. *Pharos* means this.   7.   __ __ __ T __ __ __ __

8. Fabulous Arabian bird.   8.   __ H __ __ __ __ __

9. Type of earring Cleopatra used in bet.   9.   __ E __ __ __

10. Cleopatra's nationality.   10.   __ __ __ __ __ I __ __

11. Bastet was this.   11.   __ __ __ __ __ D __ __ __ __

12. There was one of these in Libya.   12.   __ __ __ __ E

13. What happened to Julius Caesar.   13.   __ __ __ S __ __ __ __ __ __ __

14. The early kings of Egypt.   14.   __ __ __ __ O __ __

15. Caesar's age when he met Cleopatra.   15.   F __ __ __ __ - __ __ __

16. What Amun was to the Egyptians.   16.   __ __ M __ __ __ __

17. Ancient war vessels had these on prows.   17.   __ A __ __ __

18. Cleopatra first met Caesar in one of these.   18.   R __ __ __

19. Type of war between Antony and Octavius.   19.   C __ __ __ __

20. Wonder of the world built on island.   20.   __ H __ __ __ __

Can you find the twenty-two words hidden in the maze below? They all can be found in the article "On Today's Ancients" on page 149.

Aegean	fly	oars	trireme
cargo	Greece	Olympias	vessel
Crete	grid	pilot	wax
Cyprus	hull	Piraeus	wing
Daedalus	Kyrenia	Santorini	
England	merchant	ship	

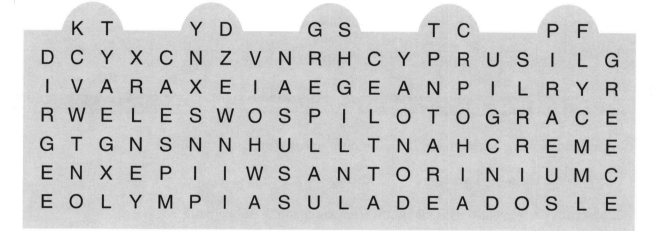

CAN YOU MATCH? (The Children of Rome)

Match the correct word with the appropriate description.

1. Octavius

2. *paedagogus*

3. toga

4. Orbilius

5. stylus

6. Quintus

7. rhetoric

8. Roman ninth hour

9. abacus

10. *bulla*

a. Amulet worn by young Roman boys

b. The art of public speaking—a required subject in ancient Roman upper schools

c. Marcus' school friend

d. Slave who was also a tutor and accompanied a young boy to school and to other lessons and activities

e. Roman emperor who was later known as Augustus Caesar

f. Three o'clock in the afternoon

g. The distinctive dress of a Roman citizen

h. Pointed pen Romans used for writing

i. Schoolmaster and Marcus' teacher

j. Counting board used by the ancient Romans

TRUE OR FALSE? (The Children of Rome)

On the blank line write "True" or "False" about the corresponding statement.

1. Boys wore the *toga praetexta* and men the *toga virilis*. _____

2. Marcus went regularly with his brother and sister to the public baths. _____

3. Roman students such as Gaius wrote on waxed tablets with the pointed end of the stylus. They erased errors with the flat end of the stylus. _____

4. Greek language and literature were two of the subjects taught in Marcus' school. _____

5. Homer was a Roman poet admired and read by all. _____

6. The Romans called their main dining room the *triclinium*. _____

7. Roman schoolchildren were on vacation in July and August. _____

8. The *peristylium* was an open courtyard in a Roman house. _____

9. Orbilius was known for flogging students who did not know their lessons well. _____

10. Marcus was going to the public baths in the Field of Mars. _____

CAN YOU MATCH? (Food, Fun, and a Werewolf)

Match the correct word with the appropriate description.

1. Niceros

    a. Told riddles at Ummidia's dinner party

2. werewolf

    b. Hostess who had her servants duplicate Horace's description of a great banquet

3. Crassipes

    c. Latin for "homemade sweets"

4. Petronius

    d. Guest of honor at Ummidia's dinner party

5. Gabba

    e. Host of a dinner party around A.D. 150

6. Ummidia

    f. Roman novelist who wrote the story of the werewolf

7. *dulcia domestica*

    g. Teller of the werewolf story

8. *vocator*

    h. A human who can turn into a wolf

9. Manlius

    i. Woman who had an encounter with a werewolf

10. Melissa

    j. A slave who distributed invitations

TRUE OR FALSE? (Food, Fun, and a Werewolf)

On the blank line write "True" or "False" about the corresponding statement.

1. By custom, the Romans reclined on couches at banquets and other meals in the *triclinium*. _____

2. The master cook preferred stuffed dates as his special treat for dessert. _____

3. Crassipes was planning to invite Horace to his dinner party. _____

4. While on his way to visit Melissa, Niceros changed into a werewolf. _____

5. Sarmentus and Gabba found their riddles in a book by a Greek scholar named Athenaeus. _____

6. Custom dictated that the fourth side of the dinner table be kept free of guests. This gave slaves room to serve the guests. _____

Topics for Comparison

1. Compare Egypt's geographical importance in ancient times with its importance in modern times. Discuss its role as the gateway between East and West, its fertile lands, and its fabled history.

2. Why was Cleopatra's suicide heroic? Was Antony's suicide also heroic? Compare and contrast the two.

3. Compare and contrast the actions of Cleopatra and Antony at the Battle of Actium. Was either one patriotic or heroic? Were both selfish and cowardly? Did either one act as a traitor? Remember that Cleopatra sailed away with the Egyptian squadron, not alone.

4. Cleopatra is never considered a military general. Yet her strategies won her a kingdom, Caesar, and Antony. Compare her actions and goals to a leader in battle.

5. Compare and contrast both Caesar's and Antony's relationships with Cleopatra. Would Antony ever have returned to Rome with Cleopatra? Were the two men's goals different? Who ruled in each relationship? Why or how did this happen?

6. Alexander the Great is a larger than life figure, almost godlike in his accomplishments. A few other individuals have the same image, e.g., Napoleon and Adolf Hitler. Can you name any others? List them and their deeds. Why do conquerors frequently become more famous than humanitarians? What does this show about human nature?

Suggestions for Essays and Written Reports

1. Why did Rome treat Egypt differently? Why did Octavius make it an imperial province? Was Rome that much in awe of this ancient land? Were its riches so great that it merited special treatment and should be subject to the Roman ruler himself?

2. Why do you think Cleopatra did not charm Octavius?

3. Why did Octavius declare war on Cleopatra and not Antony? Remember that war on Antony would have meant civil war.

4. What do you think Ammon said to Alexander the Great? Why do you think Alexander did not tell anyone? What does this tell you about his personality?

5. Julius Caesar dismissed the bad omens. Did the gods control the destiny of the Romans, or did these tales arise to explain disasters? Or was it some of each?

6. Make a list of the daily activities mentioned in the play "The Children of Rome" and then compare (or contrast) each activity on the list with one of your daily activities.

7. One line in the play "The Children of Rome" mentions that daylight hours were not wasted. Why do you think the author of the play made a point of including this line? Is the same true today? Why or why not?

8. Reread each of the riddles Sarmentus and Gabba tell. Then explain the answer to each.

9. Find out more about the Roman goddess Diana. Then explain why the author of the play "Food, Fun, and a Werewolf" ended the play with her journeying across the night sky in a silver chariot.

10. Read more about Maecenas and how he patronized the arts in ancient Rome. Think about what it means to patronize the arts. Then think of modern-day equivalents of Maecenas—these can be individuals, organizations, and foundations. Examples are: the National Endowment for the Arts, the Rockefeller Foundation, local community organizations that sponsor local theater groups, and the like.

Further Activities

1. Draw Cleopatra awaiting Antony on her barge. Get an art history book and see how artists have represented this meeting.

2. Read about the city of Alexandria today. Trace its history in a chronological outline.

3. Research the Pharos of Alexandria and the six other wonders of the ancient world: the Great Pyramid, the Hanging Gardens of Babylon, the Statue of Zeus at Olympia, the Mausoleum at Halicarnassus, the Temple of Artemis at Ephesus, and the Colossos of Rhodes.

4. Do a caricature of some episode in this chapter. For example, draw Antony on his high warships or Octavius and Agrippa in fast triremes.

5. Make a collage with scenes from Cleopatra's life. Include the rug episode, dinner on the barge, the earring in the goblet, and her suicide.

6. If Cleopatra had not existed, would the relationship between Antony and Octavius have survived? Imagine what history would have been like under these conditions.

7. Research the reasons for the formation of the Second Triumvirate. Research the history of each member and what happened to each.

8. Give examples of "cat expressions." Use each in a paragraph.

9. Research which cultures today worship a particular type of animal, e.g., the cow in India. Research the worship practices involved.

10. Are there any towns, newspapers, or the like near you that have the word "phoenix" in their name? Find out why each chose that name.

11. Read George Bernard Shaw's play *Caesar and Cleopatra.* Compare his treatment with historical facts.

12. Read William Shakespeare's play *Antony and Cleopatra.* Compare his treatment with historical facts.

13. Research the mythological tale of Daedalus and his son Icarus.

14. Do you have a "dream" project? If so, what is it, and what are your ideas about making it work?

15. Research how Roman schools were organized, who went to school, what subjects they studied, and who the teachers were. Compare and contrast Rome's schooling with that in the United States.

16. Research the typical design of a Roman house and then draw a diagram. Locate the rooms—the shops, too— mentioned in the play "The Children of Rome."

17. Carefully read the master cook's description of the dinner he will serve Crassipes and Ummidia's guests. Then make a poster that clearly depicts each course and the items served at each course. (You may draw the various foods or cut pictures from a food magazine or catalog.)

Topics for Debate

1. Caesar should not have invited Cleopatra to Rome. It showed a weakness in his nature and led to his assassination.

2. The money spent on projects such as *Daedalus*, *Kyrenia II*, and *Olympias* could be better utilized for humanitarian needs.

CROSSCOMPANION

Topics for Comparison

1. The Romans and Greeks consulted the oracles frequently. What made them so popular? Was it just superstition? Analyze and compare the answers given Croesus, Themistocles, and Alexander. What do the answers tell you about the priests and priestesses at the oracles? Compare these with the answers given to Oenomaus and Phalanthus. Did it make a difference that the last two men were mythical?

2. Pyrrhus of Greece and Hannibal of Carthage used mercenaries in their armies. They also both lost to the Romans. Was the fact that they used mercenaries one of the reasons? Are mercenaries as effective as native soldiers? Are there mercenaries today? If so, where and why do these soldiers of fortune fight?

3. The ancient world produced several families of leaders. There were Darius and Xerxes of Persia; Hamilcar Barca, Hannibal, and Hasdrubal of Carthage; and Decius Mus (I, II, III), the Scipios, and Caesar and Octavius of Rome. The modern world has done likewise. There were Napoleon I and III of France, the Churchills and the Mountbattens of England, and the Adamses and Kennedys of the United States. Compare and contrast one ancient and one modern family.

4. Dido of Carthage and Phalanthus of Sparta are both legendary people. Both were victims of wrongdoings, and both were told to seek a happier home in the West. Compare their tales, the consequences of their actions, the subsequent history of their cities, and their connection with Rome. Think of some modern-day people who were told the same thing, e.g., Brigham Young.

5. Compare Dido and Cleopatra. Keep in mind that they were both queens from the East and were strong-minded and fearless. They both fell in love with foreigners from the West and committed suicide as a result of these relationships. They both were foreigners in the lands they ruled and both had to struggle before becoming queen.

6. Themistocles used his navy to win. Rome used its navy to win. Is a navy essential to becoming a superpower? What great world powers have depended on navies? Do any today? Also note the reasons why some nations first formed a navy. Greece did it for protection; Rome did it to help an ally.

7. List and compare the various clever strategies devised by ancient leaders to defeat the enemy.

8. Compare and contrast Xerxes' and Hannibal's marches against the enemy. Xerxes headed straight for Athens. Hannibal seemed to avoid Rome. What were their reasons? Is one strategy better than the other, or does the outcome depend on who is the general?

9. According to legend, Hannibal vowed at the age of nine to defeat Rome and never stopped trying to destroy it. Think of other young people in history who have stayed with a goal from childhood, e.g., Annie Oakley, Luther Burbank, and Jacques Cousteau.

10. Compare Hannibal with Julius Caesar. Give clear examples. Keep in mind that they both were respected by and shared hardships with their soldiers, devised clever strategies, spent years on foreign soil, and introduced constitutional reforms at home.

11. Every country has its patriots. The number is especially high when the country is young. Their names are known and praised by all succeeding generations. Why? Compare and contrast some of our early patriots with those mentioned in these chapters.

Topics for Comparison

12. Compare Caesar's and Scipio's recognition of the arts produced by other culturally superior nations. Scipio looked to Greece, Caesar to Egypt. What were their reasons, motives, and goals? Were they correct? How did the Romans view their attitudes? Which Romans took note of the attitudes? Which Romans agreed with Caesar and Scipio? Have other statesmen and leaders in other countries done the same? Do these attitudes apply to the educated members of a society or to everyone? Compare the ancients with early Americans' regard for France and the French language.

13. Based on the articles in the preceding chapters, how do the East and West differ? Make a list of the differences and similarities.

Suggestions for Essays and Written Reports

1. Did Rome consciously or unconsciously send aid to foreign powers with the hope of possible conquest? Use the Mamertines in Sicily, Saguntum in Spain, the Aedui in Gaul, and Cleopatra in Egypt as examples.

2. Throughout history traitors have often played a decisive role in military campaigns. Use Ephialtes, Leonidas, Ptolemy XIII's supporters, and Pompey as examples. Have there been any comparable incidents in recent history? (Investigate spy trials here in the United States.)

3. Greece (Pyrrhus of Epirus) sent aid to Taras in Italy. Rome sent aid to the Mamertines in Sicily. Why was Rome an aggressor and not Greece?

Further Activities

1. The Greeks erected a monument on the plains of Marathon to their slain countrymen and to commemorate their victory. The French erected a monument to Vercingetorix. We do the same today. Visit a veterans' memorial near you. Learn about its history, the event it commemorates, the people it honors, and any ceremonies that take place involving it.

2. Re-create the first Boston Marathon. The distance does not have to be long, but wear clothes worn in 1897, e.g., toreador pants and heavy boots.

3. Research the awards and honors given heroes of battles in ancient times. Research the awards and honors given modern-day heroes. Compare the two.

4. Write a chronological outline of the city of Marseilles. Make sure to point out that it was an early Greek seaport in the western Mediterranean, that it aided Rome vs. Hannibal and Caesar vs. the Gauls, and that it is still a good seaport today.

5. Read why the Italian composer Ottorino Respighi (A.D. 1879–1936) composed the romantic tone poems "The Pines of Rome" and "Roman Festivals." Listen to each and picture what Respighi's music portrays.

Games

1. TRIVIA

a. Divide students into teams. The number on each team can vary.

b. Have each team make up a series of questions to ask the opposing team. Divide questions according to chapters. Then divide them into categories of people, places, and events.

c. The team with the greatest number of correct answers wins the game.

2. WHO AM I?

a. Have each student (or team with one spokesperson) research a personality mentioned in *The Classical Companion.*

b. Prepare a short speech for the "personality" to deliver to the opposing team.

c. The opposing team must guess who the personality is.

d. Time how long it takes each person or team to give the correct answer.

e. The person or team with the greatest number of correct answers and the fastest time is the winner.

3. WHERE AM I?

a. Copy or enlarge (use an overhead projector) the outline maps at the beginning of each main chapter.

b. Describe a particular area, city, or country.

c. The opposing person or team must name and locate the correct answer on the map.

d. Use a small marker to note the position on the map.

e. The person or team with the greatest number of correct marks wins.

Topic for Debate

A traitor is not worthy of respect. He deserves to be severely punished. Debate this issue and the type of punishment a traitor deserves. Use Ephialtes and Leonidas, Fabricius and Pyrrhus, Aaron Burr, and Alger Hiss as examples.

FURTHER READING

CHAPTER I:
Persia Versus Greece

Ancient Greeks, Creating the Classical Tradition, by Rosalie F. and Charles F. Baker III (New York: Oxford University Press, 1997), chronicles the lives and accomplishments of Greek figures, including Leonidas, Pheidippides, and Themistocles. (This book is also of use with Chapter II.)

Atlas of the Greek World, by Peter Levi (New York: Facts On File, 1980), complements its well-written text with well-chosen photos, illustrations, diagrams, and maps. (This book is also of use with Chapter II.)

Handbook to Life in Ancient Greece, by Lesley Adkins and Roy A. Adkins (New York: Facts On File, 1997), is an invaluable companion to anyone studying this period in history. (This book is also of use with Chapter II.)

The Persians is a play by the Greek playwright Aeschylus (525–456 B.C.), who took part in the Battle of Salamis.

Themistocles is a biography by the Greek biographer and philosopher Plutarch (c. A.D. 50–c. 120). Plutarch compares Themistocles to the Roman Camillus in the fourth set of his *Parallel Lives.*

The Persian Empire, by J.M. Cook (New York: Schocken Books, 1983), presents an informative history of early Persia and Iran.

CHAPTER II:
Greece Versus Rome

The Ancient City: Life in Classical Athens & Rome, by Peter Connolly and Hazel Dodge (New York: Oxford University Press, 1998), is an excellent reference book for ancient Greece and Rome.

Ancient Greece I and *Ancient Greece II* in the Teaching With Primary Sources Series (Peterborough, New Hampshire: Cobblestone Publishing, 1999) includes a great variety of images and activities on topics such as Law, Order, and Commerce; the Military; the Theater; and Greeks at Home. (This set is also of use with Chapter I.)

Atlas of the Roman World, by Tim Cornell and John Matthews (New York: Facts On File, 1982), complements its main text with wonderful photos, illustrations, diagrams, maps, and informative sidebars. (This book is also of use with Chapters III, IV, and V.)

The Greeks, by Roy Burrell, illustrated by Peter Connolly (New York: Oxford University Press, 1989), presents a wonderful overview of the history of the Greeks and their civilization.

Handbook to Life in Ancient Rome, by Lesley Adkins and Roy A. Adkins (New York: Facts On File, 1994), is an invaluable companion to anyone studying this period in history. (This book is also of use with Chapters III, IV, and V.)

History of Rome, by Michael Grant (New York: Charles Scribner's Sons, 1978), gives an extensive but concise history of Rome from its origins to its fall. (This book is also of use with Chapters III, IV, and V.)

CHAPTER III:
Carthage Versus Rome

Ancient Rome I and *Ancient Rome II* in the Teaching With Primary Sources Series (Peterborough, New Hampshire: Cobblestone Publishing, 1998) includes a great variety of images and activities on topics such as Government and Politics, the Military, and Daily Life. (This set is also of use with Chapters II, IV, and V.)

Hannibal, by Robert Green (Danbury, Connecticut: Franklin Watts, 1996), covers the details of Hannibal's career in a lively manner.

The Romans, by Roy Burrell, illustrated by Peter Connolly (New York: Oxford University Press, 1989), presents a wonderful overview of the history of the Romans and their civilization. (This book is also of use with Chapters II, IV, and V.)

CHAPTER IV:
Gaul Versus Rome

The Ancient Romans: Expanding the Classical Tradition, by Rosalie F. and Charles F. Baker III (New York: Oxford University Press, 1998), chronicles the lives and accomplishments of Roman figures, including Caesar and Crassus. (This book is also of use with Chapters II, III, and V.)

The Battle for Gaul, by Anne and Peter Wiseman (Boston: David R. Godine, Inc., 1985), is an easy-to-read translation of Julius Caesar's *Gallic Wars.* It includes excellent illustrations. Chapters 13, 14, and 16 of Book VI recount Caesar's description of the Druids.

Julius Caesar, by R. Burns (Broomall, Pennsylvania: Chelsea House, 1987), provides a comprehensive overview of the life and times of Caesar.

CHAPTER V:
Egypt Versus Rome

The Age of Augustus, by Don Nardo (San Diego, California: Lucent Books, 1997), focuses on the social, cultural, military, and political achievements of Rome's first emperor. Included are excerpts from primary and secondary sources.

Augustus Caesar, by Nancy Zinsser Walworth (New York: Chelsea House, 1989), is a well-researched and well-written biography of Rome's first emperor, accompanied by a great variety of black-and-white illustrations.

Caesar and Cleopatra, by George Bernard Shaw, is a wonderful and widely known play about Cleopatra's meeting and life with Caesar.

Antony and Cleopatra, by William Shakespeare, is a literary classic. It covers the period Cleopatra spent with Antony.

Apicius, Cookery, and Dining in Imperial Rome, translated by J.D. Vehling (New York: Dover Publications, Inc., 1977), includes many recipes from Apicius' cookbook.

INDEX

Chapter I

CROSSWORD PUZZLE

Across: 1. trireme, 2. ostracism, 4. ram, 6. democracy, 7. rivers, 9. fleet, 10. traitor, 11. evil, 14. soldiers, 15. Immortals, 16. good, 17. Ionian revolt, 19. Delphic, 21. twenty-two, 22. navy, 23. strategy, 24. city-states.
Down: 1. trieres, 3. marathon, 5. freedom, 8. spears, 12. Persian Wars, 13. victory, 16. golden, 18. died, 20. foot.

UNSCRAMBLE THE SITES

1. Lydia, 2. Peloponnesus, 3. Marathon, 4. Hellespont, 5. Eretria, 6. Persia. Where the Spartans bravely died: Thermopylae.

WORD PUZZLE

1. Hippias, 2. Ahuramazda, 3. Croesus, 4. Miltiades, 5. Herodotus, 6. Leonidas, 7. Ephialtes, 8. Thespians, 9. Themistocles, 10. Mardonius, 11. Xerxes, 12. Zoroaster.

WORD FIND

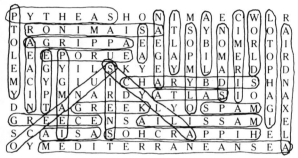

CAN YOU MATCH?

1. c, 2. d, 3. g, 4. i, 5. e, 6. h, 7. j, 8. f, 9. b, 10. a.

TRUE OR FALSE?

1. False. The play is a comedy.
2. True.
3. True.
4. False. Charisios and Pamphila are the baby's parents.
5. True.
6. True.
7. False. Chaerestratos is willing to help Charisios regardless of his faults or misdeeds.
8. True.

Chapter II

CROSSWORD PUZZLE

Across: 1. Salii, 3. Alexander, 5. Pythia, 7. Solon, 9. Dorus, 13. Ionians, 14. Pyrrhus, 15. Mars, 17. Dorians, 19. Solon, 22. Fabricius, 25. Achaeans, 26. Persians, 27. Aeolus, 28. Mus, 29. Hellenes. **Down:** 2. Aeolians, 3. Ammon, 4. Dodona, 6. Homer, 8. Graeci, 10. Romans, 11. Zeus, 12. Python, 16. Dorus, 18. Aryans, 20. Croesus, 21. Xuthus, 23. Hellas, 24. Cyrus.

UNSCRAMBLE THE CLUES

1. devotio, 2. dolphin, 3. phalanx, 4. mercenaries, 5. Pyrrhic, 6. tile. Ancients consulted: Delphic oracle.

WORD PUZZLE

1. Rome, 2. Aegean Sea, 3. Carthage, 4. Tarentum, 5. Sparta, 6. Greece, 7. Taras, 8. Crissa, 9. Epirus, 10. Sicily, 11. Delphi, 12. Argos.

WORD FIND

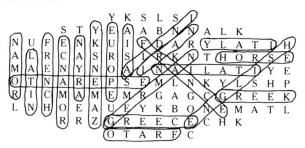

CAN YOU MATCH?

1. e, 2. d, 3. b, 4. h, 5. a, 6. c, 7. j, 8. i, 9. g, 10. f.

TRUE OR FALSE?

1. False. Archimedes did not like Hippocrates, but he helped him for the sake of his beloved Syracuse.
2. True.
3. True.
4. False. Marcellus ordered that Archimedes be left unharmed and brought to him. A Roman soldier, angered at Archimedes' refusal to come immediately, killed him.
5. True.
6. False. The Carthaginians and the Romans both wanted control of the island.
7. True. This ratio was 3:2. Marcellus had the ratio and a drawing of a cylinder circumscribing a sphere engraved on Archimedes' tombstone, just as the mathematician had always wanted.
8. True.
9. False. Because the Romans were unable to counteract Archimedes' war machines, Marcellus withdrew his troops from Syracuse to fight in other areas. He finally took Syracuse by scaling a wall that he noticed was poorly guarded.
10. True.

Chapter III

CROSSWORD PUZZLE

Across: 1. Rome, 3. Mediterranean, 5. Ebro, 8. Syracuse, 10. Egypt, 11. Spain, 12. Tyre, 13. Europe, 14. Etna, 17. Maillane, 18. Etruria, 20. Syracuse, 21. Gaul, 22. France, 25. Italy, 27. Metaurus, 28. Syria, 29. Cannae, 30. Sardinia, 31. Strait.
Down: 1. Rhône, 2. Messana, 4. Aegates, 6. Bithynia, 7. Olympus, 9. Carthage, 15. Troy, 16. Sicily, 19. Trasimenus, 21. Greece, 23. Corsica, 24. Africa, 26. Alps.

UNSCRAMBLE THE CLUES

1. human sacrifice, 2. Punic Wars, 3. refugees, 4. elephants, 5. soldiers, 6. javelin. Dido rested here: Wailing Fields.

WORD PUZZLE

1. Poeni, 2. Pyrrhus, 3. Regulus, 4. Pygmalion, 5. Aeneas, 6. Virgil, 7. Mamertines, 8. Romans, Poeni, 9. Publius, Gnaeus. Dido's brother: Pygmalion.

WORD FIND

CAN YOU MATCH?

1. f, 2. g, 3. e, 4. j, 5. i, 6. h, 7. c, 8. d, 9. a, 10. b.

TRUE OR FALSE?

1. False. Hannibal never left the elephants behind. Some died, but a few made it to Italy.
2. False. The Allobroges opposed Hannibal and attempted to stop him.
3. False. Cornelius traveled with his troops by sea rather than land.
4. True.
5. True. Hasdrubal believed that the elephants would scare any approaching enemy.
6. True. Hannibal's courage and determination, as well as the rapport he had with his men, won him the confidence and obedience of his troops.

Chapter IV

CROSSWORD PUZZLE

Across: 1. siege, 2. propraetor, 4. bald, 7. enemy, 9. pirates, 10. pits, 11. triumvirs, 12. geese, 13. spikes, 15. prison, 16. mineral, 18. bald, 19. money, 21. crucified, 22. centurion, 25. priest, 26. talent, 27. soldier, 28. cavalry. **Down:** 1. strategy, 2. Pontifex Maximus, 3. aedile, 5. dictator, 6. priest, 8. assassinated, 14. proconsul, 17. trenches, 20. dig, 23. twenty, 24. fire.

UNSCRAMBLE THE PEOPLE

1. Astérix, 2. Gyptos, 3. Labienus, 4. Gergovia, 5. Arverni, 6. Colonel Stoffel. Gallic chieftain: Vercingetorix.

WORD PUZZLE

1. Mediterranean, 2. Massilia, 3. Gergovia, 4. Alps, 5. Rhodes, 6. Illyricum, 7. Transalpine, 8. Gaul, Italy, 9. Cisalpine, 10. France, Alesia. French seaport: Marseilles.

WORD FIND

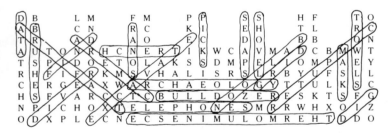

CAN YOU MATCH?

1. d, 2. e. 3. h, 4. a, 5. b, 6. c, 7. j, 8. f, 9. g, 10. i.

TRUE OR FALSE?

1. False. Vercingetorix's father was killed because he assumed the kingship. The Druids conferred the kingship on Vercingetorix.
2. False. Vercingetorix accepted the sentence as the proper decision of the Druids.
3. False. Many Gauls did unite under Vercingetorix's leadership, but many did not. Some allied themselves with Caesar.
4. True.
5. False. The Druids' rule was supreme. They could overrule the nobles.
6. True.
7. False. He believed his strategies and the power of the Roman gods were stronger.
8. False. Druidism is said to have originated in England.
9. True.
10. False. Caesar did defeat Vercingetorix, but he used both his own troops and reinforcements.

Chapter V

CROSSWORD PUZZLE

Across: 2. Agrippa, 3. Delphi, 5. Bastet, 7. Octavius, 8. Ptolemy, 9. Ammon, 11. Cupid, 12. Cambyses, 14. Marcus, 15. Deinocrates, 19. Julius, 20. Arabs, 21. Calpurnia. **Down:** 1. Herodotus, 2. Apollodorus, 3. Dacians, 4. Lepidus, 6. Venus, 9. Amun, 10. Macedonian, 13. Cleopatra, 14. Mark, 16. Caesar, 17. Zeus, 18. Delphi.

UNSCRAMBLE THE SITES

1. Libya, 2. Bubastis, 3. Macedonia, 4. Greece, 5. Africa, 6. Arabia. Where Octavius and Antony fought: Bay of Ambracia.

WORD PUZZLE

1. barge, 2. fire, 3. sword, 4. Augustus, 5. imperial, 6. vinegar, 7. lighthouse, 8. phoenix, 9. pearl, 10. Egyptian, 11. cat goddess, 12. oracle, 13. assassinated, 14. pharaohs, 15. fifty-two, 16. ram god, 17. rams, 18. rug, 19. civil, 20. Pharos.

WORD FIND

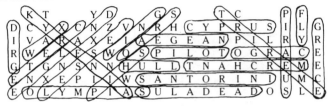

THE CHILDREN OF ROME
CAN YOU MATCH?

1. e, 2. d, 3. g, 4. i, 5. h, 6. c, 7. b, 8. f, 9. j, 10. a.

TRUE OR FALSE?

1. True. The *toga praetexta* had a purple stripe along the straight edge.
2. False. Marcus' brother was too young, and his sister, as was the custom for a young girl, spent most of her time at home.
3. True.
4. True.
5. False. Homer was a Greek poet. He wrote the *Iliad* and the *Odyssey.*
6. True.
7. False. Roman children were usually on vacation in August and September.
8. True.
9. True.
10. False. The Field of Mars was comparable to a present-day athletic field.

FOOD, FUN, AND A WEREWOLF
CAN YOU MATCH?

1. g, 2. h, 3. e, 4. f, 5. a, 6. b, 7. c, 8. j, 9. d, 10. i.

TRUE OR FALSE?

1. True.
2. True.
3. False. Horace lived about 150 years before Crassipes. Crassipes' menu was based on a description found in one of Horace's works.
4. False. Niceros' friend changed into a werewolf while the two were on their way to Melissa's house.
5. True.
6. True.